THE
EXECUTION
OF
CHARLES
HORMAN

THOMAS HAUSER

THE EXECUTION OF CHARLES HORMAN

An American Sacrifice

HARCOURT BRACE JOVANOVICH

NEW YORK AND LONDON

1978

Requests for permission to make copies of any part
of the work should be mailed to:
Permissions, Harcourt Brace Jovanovich, Inc.
757 Third Avenue, New York, N.Y. 10017

Printed in the United States of America

Library of Congress Cataloging in Publication Data

Hauser, Thomas.
The execution of Charles Horman.

1. Chile—History—Coup d'état, 1973.
2. Horman, Charles Edmund, 1942–1973.
3. Political prisoners—Chile. 4. Chile—
Relations (general) with the United States.
5. United States—Relations (general) with Chile.
6. Journalists—Chile—Biography. 7. Journalists
—United States—Biography. I. Title.
F3100.H387   983'.064'0924   [B]   78-53864

I S B N 0-15-129456-9

First edition

B C D E

For my mother and father,
who have always stood by me.

Walk light,
don't fight,
tiptoe through the barbed wire
days.

All the world's a place
to hide in.
I can't see the end
from where I am;
but when I get there
I will know.

—Charles Horman   1973

Charles Edmund Horman was born in New York City on May 15, 1942. He graduated from Harvard University, *magna cum laude,* Phi Beta Kappa, and was honorably discharged from the United States Air Force National Guard. In 1972, he settled temporarily in Chile with his wife Joyce to pursue a promising career in free-lance writing.

On September 17, 1973, six days after a military coup toppled the freely elected government of Salvador Allende, Charles Horman was arrested by the Chilean military. One month later, his fingerprints were matched with a body in the Santiago morgue. He was one of two American citizens to die in the coup in Chile.

Almost five years have passed since Charles Horman's death, yet the incident remains in public view. What has kept it there are rumors of the most disturbing nature. Specifically, it has been alleged with increasing credibility that Charles Horman was executed with the foreknowledge of American Embassy officials in Santiago because he stumbled upon evidence of United States involvement in the Chilean coup. An examination of this charge in its proper setting follows.

PART ONE

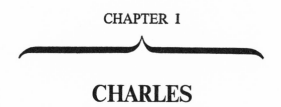

CHAPTER I

CHARLES

"Fifty-five thousand Americans died in Vietnam. With numbers like that, nobody cares about two who were killed in Chile." Elizabeth Horman leans forward in her chair. "I care. One of them was my son, and he was special." A half smile forms on her lips. "I suppose every mother says that about her son, but with Charles it was true. He was very special. Let me tell you about him.

"Charles was born with curly hair, pink cheeks, green eyes, and was very, very small. He was the kind of boy who almost obliterates himself because he's so shy. He learned too much too soon. At age three, he was afraid of being poisoned because he read the word 'poison' on a bottle of ammonia and the contents looked like water to him.

"He went to kindergarten a year early because we felt that, as an only child, he should be with other children. The other kids, who were bigger and older, took turns clobbering him. Finally, my husband Ed had to show him how to protect himself. 'If someone hits you,' Ed counseled, 'punch him in the mouth, and after that he'll leave you alone.' This was only partially satisfactory to Charles, who wanted to know what to do if he was set upon by two people. 'Give your full attention to whichever one is bigger,' Ed instructed. 'If you sock him good, the other one will run away.' "

A slightly self-conscious look crosses Elizabeth Horman's face. "You know, Charles abhorred violence all of his life. That's one of the things that make his death so intolerable.

"He loved books and always wanted to be read to. He had an

3

extraordinarily inquisitive mind and was perpetually exploring new things. Just after he turned four, I took him to the American Museum of Natural History, and he drew a complete picture of every dinosaur there. Then he got into first grade. I went to school on Parents' Day, and all the other children raised their hands to answer questions. Charles just sat there in the back of the room without moving a muscle. I asked him afterwards why he didn't raise his hand. 'Because I already know the answers,' he told me. That was all he needed for satisfaction. He didn't have to show off in front of other people. He was happy just knowing.

"That same Parents' Day, after the children began a written lesson, Charles's teacher came up to me and said, 'I want to show you something.' The children were working on a problem in which they were supposed to draw three rabbits plus two rabbits making five rabbits. Most of the kids were racing through the assignment, and had drawn all the rabbits in the wink of an eye. 'Look,' the teacher said to me, and I looked over Charles's shoulder. He had drawn one rabbit. He hadn't addressed himself to the problem at all, but you should have seen that rabbit. It had eyes, ears, a tail, even fingernails. It was the most perfect rabbit you ever saw. He couldn't have cared less about the assignment. I went home that night and told Ed, 'Wonderful. We have a genius on our hands, but he'll never get promoted out of the first grade.' "

She laughs at the memory.

Charles Horman's roots were embedded in New York City. He was born and raised there. His parents, Ed and Elizabeth, have lived in New York all of their lives. As a child, he learned from his father about shells and the sea, stars, and the tides—all part of what makes the world magical for little boys. He retained that knowledge in later years, taking great delight in pointing out constellations in the nighttime sky. Those who knew him have tried, on occasion, to parse out his talents. "He had Ed's sense of humor," they might say, "and definitely Ed's ability to collect and synthesize data. But he had Elizabeth's appreciation for the humanities and her artist's eye."

Whatever the source of his talents, Charles Horman was, first and foremost, the product of principled parents living principled lives. They gave him a strong sense of right and wrong, and the ability to appreciate a job well done. From their guidance and understanding sprang a remarkable record of youthful achievement.

At the Allen-Stevenson Grammar School in Manhattan, he was both first in his class and Student Body President. In autumn, 1957, he enrolled at the Phillips Exeter Academy in Rockingham County, New Hampshire. Renowned for its New England tradition and high academic standards, Exeter is set amid weather-beaten colonial houses by an old factory overlooking the Exeter River falls. Within this setting, seven hundred male students just past the age of puberty worked out their emotional problems on one another, twenty-four hours a day.

Always reticent in new social situations, Charles approached Exeter with great trepidation. His first months there were miserable. Once king of the hill at Allen-Stevenson, he was regarded as an odd, bookish sort by his older and tougher new classmates. They came into his room at night and plucked at the bow of his cello to keep him from studying. They hit him with sticks, pillows, and anything else they could lay their hands on. He was a fifteen-year-old boy whose voice had not yet matured, finding out that he hadn't grown up at all. To compound his misery, shortly after winter began, he broke his leg playing intramural ice hockey.

Slowly, Charles was accepted on his own terms. When he graduated from Exeter in 1960, he had been an honor student for each of his six terms and the first student elected President of both the school's literary magazine and historical debate society. Still, his individuality remained. Charles Donohue, a former classmate and now an attorney in New York recalls, "The big word at Exeter in those days was 'nego.' It was synonymous with a negative attitude towards life and, if you were cool, that was the attitude you adopted. You couldn't be cool if you showed too much enthusiasm for things. Charles Horman was different. Even then, he preferred to think of the world in positive terms."

Robert Kessler, Dean of Exeter, sums up Charles's years there in equally positive fashion: "He was an outstanding student, thoroughly responsible and reliable, respected by both his peers and his teachers. He had no arrogance with weaker students. He managed to accept the conventional requirements without giving up his own individual style. He was a leader."

One-third of Exeter's graduating class went to Harvard, and Charles was among them. Perhaps the most rewarding aspect of his college years was his involvement in the civil rights movement. Like many Northerners who intruded upon the deep South in an attempt to change basic institutions, he was badly treated. Fire hoses and police dogs were common fare. In Plaquemine, Louisiana, he was jailed for vagrancy despite having two hundred dollars in his wallet.

As his interest in the world around him grew, Charles began to seek out new means of expression. Following a series of summer jobs with CBS, the *New York Times,* and a New York construction company, he devoted the entire summer after his junior year at Harvard to creative writing. Returning to college in the fall, he wrote, "This last summer, I was able to find out that I do want to be a writer. Never before have I devoted myself with such singlemindedness or joy to any project or received such a sense of satisfaction from the work."

He graduated from Harvard in 1964, and was awarded a Fulbright Scholarship for further study. Harvard Professor Robert Kiely recalls, "I read his essays and short stories, and must have had hundreds of hours of conversations with him. He was the ideal student—not a mechanical grind nor someone who rested on his brains and floated through school on a cloud. He really wanted to learn."

In the summer of 1964, Charles's career plans were temporarily stalled by the burgeoning war in Vietnam. After enlisting in the Air Force National Guard, he served six months' active duty, followed by six years in the reserves. He began basic training fearful that his minimal physical gifts would embarrass him but learned that he was capable of doing all that was required. Greater confidence followed and, at the close of basic training, he stood in line with his fellow recruits as their commanding officer asked if any of them were experienced in communications. On raising his hand, Charles was immediately assigned the task of erecting telephone poles and stringing wires between them. Wearing a thick leather belt and spiked boots, he drove a spike into his ankle the first day on the job.

At the close of active duty (for which he was awarded the National Defense Service Medal), Charles Horman moved west. He had grown up in New York, been educated in the East, and seen the world only through the pages of the *New York Times.* His view of life was totally intellectual, and this troubled him. "I've never met anyone with an IQ of less than 130," he told a friend. "Somewhere, there must be different people."

After working briefly for KING-TV in Seattle, he was transferred to the station's Portland office, where he began making film documentaries. He lived in Oregon for two years, producing one film on the black community in Portland and another on the manufacture of napalm in Redwood City, California. Then, returning east, he took a job with WNET-TV—the New York–New Jersey educational television station. Jerry Cotts, a co-worker and, later, best man at Charles's wedding, recalls their television days together: "I was a staff cameraman and Charles was a writer-producer for the late-night news. For six months, we did little pieces—character studies of a typical New York cab driver; things like that. Finally, Charles talked the executive producer into letting us shoot a full segment with Herman Kahn at the Hudson Institute. We went up there and, for three or four days, were deluged with 1960s think-tank talk—kill ratios; if we nuke this, how many Americans and Chinese will die? Stuff like that. One afternoon, one of Kahn's lieutenants showed us a map of Brazil with a red wax line circumscribed across a portion

7

of the Amazon River. They were carrying out a feasibility study for flooding the entire surrounding area. Charles pointed to a city on the edge of the perimeter and asked, 'What will happen to the people who live here if the area is flooded?' The lieutenant shrugged his shoulders and answered, 'I don't know. I guess they'll get their feet wet.' "

As the war in Vietnam grew, Charles became increasingly wary of established institutions. In late 1967, he left WNET to work as a historian for the federal poverty program. The following June, he married Joyce Hamren, whom he described in apparently self-contradictory terms as "a free-spirited computer programmer." They moved into a small apartment on West 75th Street in Manhattan, and Charles once again turned his attention to writing. He was maced at the 1968 Democratic Convention in Chicago, which he covered for *The Nation* and the *Christian Science Monitor*. At the request of a Harvard classmate, he took a job with *Innovation,* a business magazine devoted to corporate management, and soon became the "staff liberal." Hardly an editorial meeting went by without Charles proclaiming, "I do not know how much longer I will wish to be associated with this organization." On the other side of the table, several staff members openly questioned the wisdom of the magazine's paying even lip service to a liberal point of view.

Meanwhile, the back room of the tiny West Side apartment was converted into a study. Each day at the close of work, Charles would come home, lodge himself behind the cluttered desk, and write. He wrote not for publication but because he enjoyed it; because he was fascinated by a myriad of things and wanted to preserve them on paper as best he could. He wrote for himself and his friends, on scraps of paper and in more elaborate personal journals. The journals grew throughout his years in New York and later in South America. Quite possibly, the data in them cost him his life.

Charles Horman was not a saint. He had faults, mostly those of youth and immaturity. He made mistakes and, like the rest of the world, was sometimes wrong in his judgments. But he was a warm, open, and compassionate person. He listened when other people talked. He cared about what they were doing and gained real pleasure from the accomplishments and joy of his friends.

He was a delight to be with. His conversation was sprinkled with anecdotes and stories which he made come alive. His sense of humor was sharp but never derogatory. He did not need a butt for his jokes to be appreciated. He accepted people for what they were and did not make judgments about them.

His curiosity was near-endless. He was never satisfied until he had experienced something for himself. He gave of himself as best he could and was never bitter when he failed.

He had a high sensitivity to moral values. He loved his wife, parents, and friends in a very special way. He was an idealist, with an optimism about people and human nature that led him to write, "Nothing attempted with love or kindness is bad." He was delighted with life and had much to give. Five years after his bullet-riddled body was found in the Santiago morgue, his murder remains intolerable.

CHAPTER II

CHILE-1970

The black car moved silently across the desert as its driver hummed softly to himself. To his right, a second man stared blankly out a side window at the seemingly endless stretches of parched dirt and sand. Behind them, in a corner of the back seat, Salvador Allende Gossens—Marxist candidate for the Presidency of Chile—slept. His schedule allotted four hours for sleep and, when the opportunity for more came, he seized upon it.

Three times before, Allende had sought the Presidency. Three times he had failed. In 1952, he had run a poor fourth in a field of four candidates while carrying the Socialist Party banner. On that occasion, he had expected little more. His intent in running had been to lay the foundation for a national party of the left which would grow in later years. The meager vote he received had been in line with his expectations.

Six years later, in 1958, Allende ran again. The results were electrifying. Supported by Chile's Socialist and Communist parties, he placed second among five candidates, losing the Presidency by 33,500 votes out of 1.2 million cast. In the six years since 1952, his support had increased fivefold. Only the splinter candidacy of Antonio Zamorano—a radical left-wing priest—had prevented his election.

Immediately after his narrow 1958 defeat, Allende began planning for the future. The Presidency was no longer hopelessly beyond his reach. To a reporter who queried, "Dr. Allende, what do you do when you are not running for President?" he jovially replied, "I sit and dream about being President." The dream was to be deferred. Running in 1964 against a moderate-conservative alliance headed by Eduardo Frei, Allende was badly beaten. Depressed by his inability to mount a successful challenge to unified opposition, at the close of the campaign he told a colleague, "I am tired of waiting for the future. They will mark upon my tombstone, 'Here lies Salvador Allende—future President of Chile.' " It was an uncharacteristic moment of despair for a man whose optimism had become legendary.

Salvador Allende Gossens was born in the Chilean port city of Valparaiso on July 26, 1908. The son of a well-to-do lawyer, he enrolled in medical school shortly after his father's death and, upon graduation, worked for eighteen months as an assistant coroner. In later years, he referred frequently to the experience. Through countless autopsies, he had learned firsthand the dramatic difference between the small number of Chileans who could afford proper nourishment and medical care and the vast majority who could not.

In 1933, Allende and a small group of compatriots founded Chile's Socialist Party. Four years later, at age twenty-nine, he was elected to the lower house of Congress. After two years in the Chamber of Deputies, he was named Minister of Health in the Cabinet of President Aguirre Cerda, where he gained national recognition for his humanitarian concerns.

Allende's formative political years were marked by strict adherence to the Constitution. He quarreled bitterly at times with Chile's Communist Party and went to great lengths to differentiate between world Communism and the Socialist banner he carried. The distinction was lost on some, who painted all Marxists with the same brush, but to Allende it was very real. "We are not going to imitate the Soviet Union," he declared. "We are going to look for our own way. Our aim is to tie Chile to all countries in the world, seeking only Chile's best interests. The only thing we want is our absolute independence . . . . I have read Marx, Engels, and Lenin, but I have also read Lincoln, Jefferson, and Washington. The United States fought against foreign forces that wanted to impede its development. This is why we read works by its founders. Americans cannot forget their own struggle and must realize what ours involves."

Elected to the Senate in 1945, Allende embarked upon twenty-five years of unbroken service in the upper house of Congress. During this time, he successfully sponsored over a hundred bills, most of them in the field of health care and women's rights. In 1968, he was elected President of the Senate. Now, in 1970, as he traversed Chile in yet another quest for the Presidency, he was a familiar figure to those who saw him. Short, stocky, with thick-rimmed glasses and a neatly trimmed mustache, he still looked more like the country doctor he had once been than a candidate for President. His graying hair and casual clothes reminded onlookers far more of themselves than the aloof figures who for so long had governed their country. The candidate was cranky at times but, generally, of good cheer. Clear, lively eyes shone out from behind his heavy glasses. With an arm draped on someone's shoulder or a warm embrace, Allende was never too high for fond physical gestures. And, when he spoke, it was of a nation whose promise was as yet unfulfilled.

Allende's Chile was a land of unsurpassed physical beauty; a geographic anomaly on the map of South America. Generally no more than 110 miles in width, it stretched for 2,650 miles along the continent's western coast. Its northern third was absolute desert—the driest region in the world, with an average rainfall of three one-hundredths of an inch per year. Yet this same desert contained the world's largest known copper reserves, estimated at 134 billion pounds.

Chile's eastern border runs along the Andes Mountains. The Pacific Ocean lies to the west. Four hundred miles into the Pacific, the Juan Fernández Islands wait. In the early 1700s, a Scottish sailor named Alexander Selkirk was marooned for four years on Mas a Tierra—the largest of the islands. His diary served as the basis for Daniel Defoe's *Robinson Crusoe*. Nineteen hundred miles west of Selkirk's domain stands Easter Island—Chile's most far-flung possession.

A fertile valley dominates Chile's central region, where most of its nine million people live. South of this valley, Chile again changes. For several hundred miles, the land resembles southwestern Canada in geography and climate. Then the mainland grows colder. Past Punta Arenas, the southernmost city in the world, lie the Straits of Magellan—the only interocean link in the Western Hemisphere other than the Panama Canal. Then Chile disintegrates into thousands of tiny islands leading to Antarctica.

Chile is less than half the size of Alaska, yet, if imprinted over North America, it would stretch from southern Mexico to the Yukon. It is a land of volcanos, gorges, and snow-capped mountains; a narrow ribbon so delicate and frail on a cartographer's map that one fears the pounding ocean waves will smash it to pieces.

Allende's Chile was a nation with remarkably stable political institutions. Following independence from Spain in 1818, the country was governed under a single Constitution until 1925, when a second Constitution became operational. By 1970, Chile enjoyed the longest period of continuous civilian rule on the South American continent and had manifested an uncommon capacity for the peaceful resolution of conflict.

Clearly, the Chilean people had much to be proud of, yet Allende knew that, within the structure of the constitutional government he was pledged to maintain, much inequality remained. Forty percent of all Chileans suffered from malnutrition. One-third of those who died each year were children. Women still gave birth without medical care. Epidemics ran rampant in towns with virtually no treatment of sewage or semblance of sanitation. Three percent of the population received over 40 percent of the nation's income. At the other end of the spectrum, 50 percent of the working population earned only slightly more than 10 percent of the wealth.

A country so rich should not have people so poor. A land so beautiful should not house its people in filth and decay. As Allende traveled country roads and touched "his people," their misery became unacceptable to him. His solution was "a uniquely Chilean road to Socialism"—one that would transfer power from one class of people to another; from the few who were rich to the many who were poor; from the foreign investors to the Chilean workers; a Chilean Revolution to be conducted by democratic electoral means. But first, the people must agree to follow.

In 1970, as Allende sought the Presidency for a fourth time, the opposition was again divided. Eduardo Frei was constitutionally ineligible to succeed himself for another six-year term, and the Christian Democrats had nominated Radomiro Tomic— Chile's fifty-six-year-old former Ambassador to Washington—as Frei's successor.

Tomic was unacceptable to the Chilean right. Frei had all but destroyed the fragile center-right coalition which had brought him to power. During his six years in office, the President had sought to fashion a "Revolution in Liberty," presiding over one of the most progressive administrations in Chile's history. Agrarian land reform and the partial state purchase of the Chilean copper industry had begun. Peasant unions had been legalized and educational spending increased. But the economic consequences had been disastrous. Inflation had risen to 35 percent annually, while the gross national product showed a sickly 2.3 percent climb.

Tomic was to the left of Frei, and the rightists wanted no part of him. Ten months before the election, they joined in support of Jorge Alessandri, the seventy-four-year-old former President, who had defeated Allende twelve years earlier.

With two viable opposition candidates committed to the campaign, an Allende victory was again possible. First, however, he had to win the support of his own party.

By 1970, the Allende platform had become familiar—too familiar, many of his former supporters argued. His three-pronged theme of agrarian reform, nationalization of the copper industry, and improved health care offered little more than Tomic. Indeed, Allende himself later conceded, "There were many respects in which Tomic's program had much in common with our own. Some would say that, on some points, it was even more advanced than ours."

Not until the second ballot did Allende capture the 1970 nomination of his own Socialist Party, and only then by a narrow 13-to-11 vote margin. Even this victory was short-lived. Five competing leftist parties, including the Communists, soon chose candidates of their own. Now it was the left that had fragmented.

Slowly, with all the skill he could muster, Allende began the process of reconciliation. Finally, in early summer 1970, the competing parties agreed to join a "Popular Unity" coalition with Allende as its nominee. The three-man field—Allende, Tomic, and Alessandri—was now complete. Salvador Allende was once again in active pursuit of the Presidency.

The black car continued its journey across the burning Atacama Desert. For months, the candidate had campaigned tirelessly. In Santiago, tens of thousands had turned out to hear him speak. In Valparaiso and Concepción, huge crowds had gathered. But far more representative of his crusade than the big city rallies was another scene that repeated itself up and down the spine of Chile.

"*Compañero.* They wait ahead."

Rubbing his eyes, the man in the back seat lifted his head and squinted at the colorful dot on the horizon. As his car drew nearer, he saw more clearly—a dozen peasants with their children and wives waiting under the broiling desert sun.

The driver slowed to a halt, and Allende stepped from his car. Almost deferentially, he asked his listeners to join him in singing their national anthem. When the last strains had subsided, he began to speak: "We are a rich country, but our riches are not in the people's hands. Half of our children under fifteen years of age suffer from malnutrition. Six hundred thousand of our children are mentally retarded because of insufficient protein supply. Only ten minutes from the Presidential Palace, Chileans live in tents in the mud."

Simply, but with compelling power, he talked to his followers: "Chile is rich in natural resources. We could be a rich country. Instead, we are poor. For more than four centuries, our most valuable natural resources have been owned by foreigners—first the Spanish, then the English, and now the North Americans. The profits taken from Chile by the American copper companies are equivalent to the entire present total of our wealth as a nation. These companies have wrested an entire Chile from our people—a whole Chile lost to Chileans forever. Chile today is only half the country it should be. We are a dependent, colonial nation."

With rising eloquence, he urged his listeners to break their colonial ties. In impassioned tones, he pleaded with them to take their own cause in their own hands and fight with him. "I do not promise wealth for all," he told them. "Only the hope of dignity and true freedom."

Then he was gone, the black car moving once again across the endless desert.

On September 4, 1970, the Chilean people voted. Tomic, who had hoped to capture the center against the two extremes, found instead that he had been crushed between them. He finished a poor third with 28 percent of the vote. Allende and Alessandri battled more closely. The latter won a plurality in Santiago but trailed in returns from outside the capital.

Ballots were counted late into the night. With the final tabulation, Allende had won by thirty-nine thousand votes—virtually the same narrow plurality by which he had been defeated twelve years earlier. Chile's Nobel Laureate, Pablo Neruda, wrote in celebration, "From the nitrate deserts, from the subterranean coal mines, from the terrible heights where copper lies buried and is extracted with inhuman labor by the hands of our people, a freedom movement of magnificent proportions has sprung."

Only one formality remained as a prerequisite to Allende's installation as President. Since no candidate had received a majority of the popular vote, the Constitution required that a

16

joint session of Congress be convened to formally name Frei's successor.

To most observers, Allende's election was now a foregone conclusion. Congress had, as a matter of course, always selected the plurality winner. The Congressional vote was considered as pro forma as that of the United States Electoral College in the wake of American elections. Allende himself had bowed gracefully to the same tradition in 1958, when he had lost to Alessandri by an even slimmer margin and then appeared before Congress to urge his rival's election.

On the morning of September 5, 1970, thousands of Allende supporters danced jubilantly in the streets. That afternoon, the victor was visited at his modest Santiago home by Tomic. The two men retired to Allende's study and talked beneath a portrait of Eleanor Roosevelt. At the close of their discussion, they walked to the front porch and embraced before the hundreds of onlookers who had gathered. Then, as the crowd surged forward, Tomic saluted his rival as "the winner and future President of Chile."

CHAPTER III

WASHINGTON, D.C.–
1970

"I don't see why we need to stand by and watch a country go Communist due to the irresponsibility of its own people."

The speaker was the Presidential Assistant for National Security Affairs, Henry Kissinger. With these words, he gave warning that the United States would not be bound by pieces of paper cast into a ballot box in a faraway land.

A Marxist regime in Chile was unacceptable to the administration of President Richard M. Nixon. Allende's repeated rejection of world Communism in favor of "Chilean Socialism" was irrelevant to those who viewed the world as a contest between "our team and theirs." Also discarded was the knowledge that both Communists and Socialists, Allende among them, had served previously in Chilean governments without incident.

The United States in 1970 was a nation that wielded power recklessly. Half a world away, American troops massed on the Vietnamese border for an "incursion" into Cambodia. At home, dissenters were monitored by the Federal Bureau of Investigation and Presidential "plumbers." This was the soil in which United States intervention in Chile flourished, but the seeds had been sown years earlier.

In March, 1961, John F. Kennedy announced a massive Inter-American "Alliance for Progress." Under his plan, the United States would provide a major portion of the estimated twenty billion dollars needed for economic development in Latin America by the year 1970. In return, it expected that the virtues of capitalism and "the American way of life" would be clearly demonstrated and the impact of a Soviet presence in Cuba blunted.

For ten years, Chile was the showcase nation for the Alliance. It received more American aid on a per capita basis than any other country in the Western Hemisphere, but this aid came at a price. In order to assure a climate which would enable the Chilean economy to flourish, the United States determined that it would also be necessary to control Chilean politics.

In 1964, the Central Intelligence Agency covertly spent over three million dollars in direct support of Eduardo Frei's Presidential campaign. An additional seventeen million dollars was invested in general anti-Marxist propaganda. Following Frei's election, the expenditures dwindled, but then increased as the 1970 campaign neared.

The primary source of available information concerning United States intervention in Chile is the Senate Select Committee to Study Governmental Operations with Respect to Intelligence Activities. Its published findings, popularly known as the Church Committee Report, outline White House and CIA conduct in chilling detail.

United States involvement in the Chilean election of 1970 was coordinated in the first instance by the 40 Committee—a subdivision of the National Security Council under the Chairmanship of Henry Kissinger. On March 25, 1970, the 40 Committee met and approved a plan for "propaganda and other activities" to be undertaken by the CIA "in an effort to prevent an election victory by Allende." On June 18, 1970, it met again and discussed a two-phase plan suggested by United States Ambassador to Chile, Edward Korry. The first phase of Korry's plan involved increased support for anti-Allende forces in Chile; the second called for the allotment of half a million dollars "to persuade certain shifts in voting" by the Chilean Congress in the event Allende emerged with a plurality in the September election.

Pursuant to directives from the 40 Committee, the CIA

19

mounted a massive preelection propaganda campaign in Chile. Widespread mailings, leafleting, and media advertising warned that an Allende victory would mean "the end of religion and family life." Predictions of a total economic collapse in the event of an Allende triumph were circulated throughout Santiago. Seeking to evoke images of Communist firing squads, CIA-financed sign teams painted the slogan "su paredón" ("your wall") on two thousand buildings. F.A.O. Schwarz, Jr., Chief Counsel to the Church Committee, later observed, "We looked at some of the general assets the CIA called upon. I remember, for example, how astonishing it was to us that they could, within twenty-four or forty-eight hours, get newsmen from some thirty countries around the world into Chile to write stories that were critical of Allende."

Despite it all, Allende won. On September 4, 1970, "the country doctor" achieved a plurality over Tomic and Alessandri to stand on the verge of the Presidency.

United States reaction to Allende's electoral triumph was swift. Judd Kessler, a high-ranking Agency for International Development (AID) official assigned to the American Embassy in Santiago recalls, "At the time Allende was elected, Ambassador Korry became semihysterical. His immediate reaction was stop everything, we can't deal with these people. The first cable that was sent from the United States Embassy in Chile after the election was originally entitled 'The End of Democracy in Chile.' That was scratched out, and the cable was retitled 'Allende Wins.'"

In Washington, reaction was the same. Korry was summoned home from Santiago for urgent talks and, with Kissinger, ushered into the White House Oval Office where the President sat waiting. The former Ambassador recalls: "The President started to bang his hand and said, 'That s.o.b.! That s.o.b.!' I must have looked astonished, because he said to me right away, 'Not you, Mr. Ambassador. It's that bastard Allende.' Then he led us over to his desk. I sat to his left and Henry sat to his right, and the President launched into a monologue of about seven minutes saying how he was going to smash Allende."

On September 7, 1970, the CIA circulated a formal assessment of Allende's victory. Its conclusions were far calmer than those of its Commander-in-Chief. In a brief memorandum, the Agency found, "The U.S. has no vital national interests within Chile . . . . The world military balance of power will not be significantly altered by an Allende government." The memorandum did, however, warn that an Allende victory would represent "a definite psychological setback to the U.S. and a definite psychological advance for the Marxist idea."

On September 8, 1970, the 40 Committee met for the first time subsequent to Allende's plurality victory. Minutes of the meeting reveal that Kissinger directed the United States Embassy in Santiago to prepare "a cold-blooded assessment of the pros and cons and problems and prospects involved should a Chilean military coup be organized now with U.S. assistance." Four days later, on behalf of the Embassy, Korry responded: "We believe it clear that the Chilean military will not move to prevent Allende's accession, barring the unlikely situation of national chaos and widespread violence." That same day, the CIA replied in kind: "Military action is impossible; the military is incapable and unwilling to seize power. We have no capability to motivate or instigate a coup."

On September 14, in the wake of these assessments, the 40 Committee met again. The prognosis for successful action was gloomy but, with the Chilean Congress scheduled to meet and formally name Frei's successor on October 24, there was little time to waste. With a military coup unlikely, the Committee chose instead to concentrate its efforts on a maneuver known as "the Frei gambit."

The Frei gambit, which later became known as "Track I," was designed to block Allende by reinstalling Chile's popular President, Eduardo Frei, in office. Initially, the proposal called for Frei to dissolve Congress, resign as President, and invite the military to take power. Then, the military would call for new elections in which Frei would be eligible to run again for the Presidency. However, the plan lacked an appropriate air of legitimacy. It required the questionable dissolution of Congress, a willingness on the part of the Chilean military to take and then relinquish power, and a risky second election in which Allende might again emerge victorious.

The Frei gambit was thus modified with the actual Congressional balloting as its new focus. The Senate and Chamber of Deputies had two hundred members between them. One hundred one votes were needed for election. Allende's coalition controlled only 83. The remaining 117 were in the hands of the Christian Democrats (78) and right-wing Nationalist Party (39). At the close of the September 14 meeting, Korry was instructed to approach Frei and determine whether the Chilean President would commit himself to a plan under which the Christian Democrats and Nationalists would defy tradition and vote for Alessandri—the second-place finisher. Alessandri, upon his installation as President, could then resign, paving the way for Frei to seek immediate reelection.

The Frei gambit might well have succeeded had it not been for one factor. It lacked the support of the man whose name it bore. Eduardo Frei was a political moderate. In many respects he disagreed virulently with Allende. But he would play no role in the subversion of the Chilean Constitution. On October 9, his Christian Democratic Party formally announced its support for Allende in the upcoming runoff, thus assuring the challenger of enough votes to become President. At the close of the party caucus, Christian Democratic Secretary, Benjamin Prado, declared, "To deny Allende the Presidency would be the same as telling thirty-six percent of the electorate, 'You have the right to participate in elections but not to win them. You can come in second or third, but never first.' "

Ten days later, Alessandri requested that his supporters in Congress also vote for Allende. Speaking in conciliatory terms, he described the next President of Chile as "a man whose long and proven democratic conviction, reflected in attitudes of constant respect for the constitution and the laws, is well known."

Track I was now at an end. It had led nowhere because, in the words of Ambassador Korry, "Frei wouldn't put his pants on." However, within the White House, plans for a last-ditch anti-Allende effort were under way. The Ambassador's September 12, 1970, assessment to the 40 Committee that a coup was unlikely had carried a qualifying proviso. It was unlikely *"barring national chaos and widespread violence."* Perhaps Korry was opposed to such measures, but others were not.

On September 15, 1970, at 3:25 P.M., Richard Nixon met in the White House Oval Office with three men. The President had been skeptical from the start that the Frei gambit would work. Now he suggested an alternative—one that would run without the knowledge of Korry, the 40 Committee, or the Departments of Defense and State. Henry Kissinger, one of the three men in attendance, was already familiar with the plan. So too, apparently, was John Mitchell—the President's Attorney General and chief political advisor. As the President spoke, the third man—Richard Helms, Director of the Central Intelligence Agency—jotted down notes on a lined sheet of paper:

> One in 10 chance perhaps, but save Chile!
> worth spending
> not concerned risks involved
> no involvement of Embassy
> $10,000,000 available, more if necessary
> full-time job—best men we have
> game plan
> make the economy scream

An Allende regime, the President told Helms, would be unacceptable. The CIA was to "play a direct role in organizing a military coup d'état in Chile to prevent Allende's accession to the Presidency." Helms was to report directly to Kissinger or CIA Deputy Director for Plans, Thomas Karamessines, who would act as a liaison with the White House. The effort, which was to be known as Track II, would be free from 40-Committee scrutiny. Kissinger later recalled, "Helms was to do whatever he could to prevent Allende from being seated . . . . The difference between the September 15 meeting and what was being done in general within the government was that *President Nixon was encouraging a more direct role for the CIA and actually organizing a coup.*" Helms later testified, "If I ever carried a marshall's baton in my knapsack out of the Oval Office, it was that day."

The following morning, Helms called a meeting of his staff to discuss the President's instructions. Two days later, he returned to the White House with Kissinger and Karamessines, and a three-fold program was set into motion. The CIA station in Santiago was instructed by cable to "(1) create a coup climate by propaganda, misinformation, and terrorist activities; (2) collect intelligence on coup-minded officers; and (3) inform those coup-minded officers that the U.S. Government will give them full support in a coup short of direct U.S. military intervention."

On September 21, 1970, Helms again cabled Santiago: "Purpose of exercise is to prevent Allende assumption of power. Paramilitary legerdemain has been discarded. Military solution is objective."

Twenty-four hours later, Kissinger and Karamessines attended a 40-Committee meeting at which the failing Frei gambit was discussed. Neither man made reference to Track II and, following the session, Kissinger assured Karamessines that his silence had been "perfect." "We're doing fine," Kissinger told him. "Keep it up." However, contrary to his assurance, they were not "doing fine." Like the Frei gambit, Track II was meeting with opposition from a Chilean who believed in his constitution.

United States efforts to collect intelligence on the Chilean military had accelerated with Helms's September 18, 1970, cable to Santiago. Almost immediately, attention had centered on General Rene Schneider—the fifty-seven-year-old Commander-in-Chief of the Chilean Army and the most powerful military man in Chile.

Schneider was a strict constitutionalist who believed strongly

24

in the tradition of military subordination to civilian rule. Several months earlier, he had attended a cocktail party at the United States Embassy in Santiago and been approached by two American military men who inquired about his political thinking. Schneider had excused himself and left the party immediately. Now, as rumors of an attempt to block Allende mounted in Santiago, Schneider went before the Army Polytechnic Academy to warn his fellow officers against military intervention:

We should not act stupidly in such a delicate moment in the Constitutional life of Chile. The armed forces cannot detain evolution and change. Our duty is to accept them . . . . A very significant group of Chileans is not disposed to allow to be snatched away from them an election victory that they believe will change the course of their lives. Our duty is to let these people make their experiment . . . . Senator Salvador Allende has given us assurances that he will remain within the bounds of the Constitution and the laws and that his program of change will not pose a threat to our western, Christian way of life.

Clearly, for Track II to succeed, it would be necessary to circumvent Schneider. A series of approaches to second-level Chilean military officers was thus begun. On October 5, 1970, an American military attaché informed selected generals in the Chilean Army and Air Force of Washington's pro-coup policy. Two days later, the same attaché approached members of the Chilean War Academy and promised to provide light weapons to would-be plotters. On October 8, 1970, the CIA Station Chief in Santiago informed a high-ranking Chilean police official that "the U.S. Government favors a military solution, and is willing to support it in any manner short of outright military intervention." All totaled, twenty-one separate recorded contacts were made with Chilean military and police officials. Those Chileans who indicated any inclination to stage a coup were given assurances of "strong support at the highest levels of the U.S. Government, both before and after a coup."

Still, the problem of Schneider remained. Any attempted coup would meet with his opposition, and the October 24 Congressional vote was fast approaching. In an act of desperation, CIA headquarters cabled the Santiago station and affirmatively urged the General's removal: "It [is] more important than ever to remove him. Anything we or station can do to effect removal of Schneider? Wish [to] inspire thoughts on both ends of this matter."

On October 13, 1970, the Santiago station responded. For several days, anti-Allende plotting had centered on two generals—Commander of the Santiago Garrison Camilo Valenzuela, and Roberto Viaux, a retired general who had been dismissed from the Army by Schneider the year before. Now, by cable from Santiago, Helms received the word he was waiting for: "Viaux intends to kidnap General Schneider within the next 48 hours in order to precipitate a coup."

The plot was all but operational. However, now Kissinger was having second thoughts. He had come to doubt that Viaux was strong enough to block Allende, even if Schneider was eliminated. Conferring with Karamessines and General Alexander Haig on the morning of October 15, Kissinger ordered that the CIA instruct Viaux as follows: "We have reviewed your plans and based on your information and ours, we come to the conclusion that your plans for a coup at this time cannot succeed. Failing, they may reduce your capabilities in the future. Preserve your assets. We will stay in touch. The time will come when you with all your other friends can do something. You will continue to have our support."

Four days later, the stronger Valenzuela informed his American contact that he was ready to proceed.

Shortly after 8:00 A.M. on the morning of October 22, 1970, the black military limousine that regularly drove General Rene Schneider to work met him at his Santiago home. The Congressional vote was two days off, and Schneider looked forward to it. Perhaps this final confirmation of Allende's victory would ease the pressures that had been building in Santiago.

The limousine moved west along Avenue Martin de Zamora.

As it turned down a narrow, one-way street towards the General's office, four vehicles blocked its route. One assailant smashed in the rear window with a sledge hammer, while another fired eight times into the car. Schneider was shot in the spleen, throat, and wrist. He died at the Santiago Military Hospital three days later—the first high Chilean official to be assassinated in one hundred forty years.

The assassination came to naught. President Frei, who had resisted previous American pressures, remained resolute. Hours after the shooting, he declared a state of martial law and placed all units of the armed forces and national police on twenty-four-hour alert. Two days later, the Chilean Congress confirmed Allende's election victory by a vote of 153 to 35.

On November 4, 1970, the world's first freely elected Marxist President was inaugurated. The following day, he addressed sixty thousand supporters in Santiago's vast National Stadium, and alluded to the turmoil that had so recently threatened: "The people of Chile are proud of having made the political road prevail over the violent one. This is a noble tradition, a lasting achievement. Throughout our battle for liberation, the slow and hard struggle for justice and equality, we have always preferred solving conflicts by means of persuasion and political action. From the bottom of our hearts, we Chileans reject fratricidal struggle. Respect for others, tolerance for others, is one of the most important sources of our cultural wealth."

Once again, there was jubilation in Santiago, but in Washington, D.C., new plans were already under way. "Track II never really ended," Thomas Karamessines later testified. "What we were told to do in effect was, well, Allende is now President . . . but continue our efforts. Stay alert and do what we can to contribute to the eventual achievement of the objectives and purposes of Track II . . . . The seeds that were laid in 1970 had their impact in 1973."

27

CHAPTER IV

ALLENDE'S CHILE – THE FIRST YEAR

Charles and Joyce Horman met in July, 1964. "I was traveling through France with a friend," Joyce recalls. "It was Bastille Day, and the hotels were jammed. Finally, someone suggested we go to a small town on the outskirts of Nice. When we got there, we couldn't find a hotel. I remember walking down a narrow street with confetti falling on my face, feeling very lost, when a young man in a blue-and-white-striped shirt stepped from a doorway and asked if I needed help. It was Charles. He was traveling in Europe with his parents and, after that, our paths seemed intertwined. We saw each other on the beach in Nice, at *A Hard Day's Night* in London, and in the Paris markets. Then Charles went back to New York, and I went on to Stockholm for a semester abroad."

Her fingers lock together and then release in a nervous gesture that repeats whenever she talks about Charles and Chile.

"That December, my father ordered me back to the University of Minnesota. He didn't think I could be studying seriously five thousand miles from home. I flew into New York, and there was a twelve-hour layover between planes, so I telephoned Charles. He invited me to his parents' home, and I helped trim the Christmas tree. We didn't see each other again for two years. Then, after I had graduated from college, Charles tracked me down in Connecticut where I was working as a computer programmer."

Charles and Joyce saw each other regularly from that point on

. . . weekends at Cape Cod . . . spring walks . . . drives through New England's autumn leaves. In June, 1968, they were married.

It was a union of different worlds. Charles Horman—educated at Exeter and Harvard; son of an industrial designer; grandson of a prominent attorney; great-grandson of a New York composer and orchestra conductor. Joyce Hamren—blonde with Scandinavian features; granddaughter of a Swedish immigrant who settled in Minnesota and found work as a lumberjack. Her father had run a small grocery store in Kiester, Minnesota, and was fighting with American troops in the jungles of New Guinea when Joyce was born. Not until the war ended eighteen months later did Duffy Hamren see his daughter for the first time.

Where Charles was shy, Joyce was outgoing. Where one was tentative, the other was bold. "You know," Charles confided to his mother days before the wedding, "Joyce doesn't read much, and she doesn't like theater or classical music."

"What does she like?" Elizabeth asked.

"Me."

That was enough. "If there was any problem in our marriage," Joyce recalls, "it was that we didn't have enough time alone with each other. We were exhausted each day after work. Add onto that time spent with friends and Charles's writing, and we didn't see each other enough before conking out at night. After a year, we decided to travel through South America so we'd have more time to spend with each other."

In preparation for the trip, they studied Spanish for several months and pooled their savings to buy a used camper. In late 1971, they left New York for Latin America, crossing into Mexico on December 3, Joyce's twenty-seventh birthday. Stopping where and when they wanted, they made their way south through Mexico and Guatemala. In El Salvador, the camper needed a new set of tubeless tires, but only tubed tires were available. Buying what was on the market, they sought to correct the deficiency with makeshift lining. Nine blowouts followed. The roads grew progressively worse in Nicaragua and Costa

Rica, and, when Charles and Joyce reached Panama, they decided to sell the camper. For the better part of a month, they sat by the Panama Canal with a large "For Sale" sign on the camper's front windshield, finally selling it for twenty-five hundred dollars.

Then the journey began anew . . . Colombia . . . Ecuador . . . . They traveled with peasants who sang their native songs in Spanish while Charles and Joyce sang American rock. On one level it was exciting, but on another they were in the midst of despair. For the first time in their lives, they were moving daily among people who were degradingly poor. They were learning what second- and third-class nationhood were all about.

In southern Ecuador the suffering verged on the unbearable. "We were traveling on a bus," Joyce remembers. "It was a long trip through the mountains, over very bumpy roads. In the back of the bus, an Indian family sat huddled together—a mother, father, and three children. They had a big tin can with jagged edges which they passed among them, and each person spat blood and phlegm into it. The whole family was dying of tuberculosis."

Day turned to night. The bus reeked of death. One of the children had dysentery, and the can served his purposes, too. The bus kept bouncing and Charles and Joyce gave up any thought of sleep. It was hard enough just to breathe in the stench. All night long, they heard coughing and people spitting up blood. "Finally," Joyce remembers, "Charles looked at me and asked, 'What kind of world is this?' Several weeks later, we crossed into Chile, where health care was free and every child received a half liter of milk a day. We reached Santiago, and Charles said, 'This is where I can write. This is where I want to be.' "

The Chile that Charles and Joyce Horman saw in July, 1972, was a land in the midst of change.

Taking office in November, 1970, Allende had told the Chilean people, "Chile now has in its government a new political force whose social function is to uphold not the traditional ruling class but the vast majority of the people."

Supported by a fifteen-man coalition Cabinet which included three Communists and four members of his own Socialist Party, the new President sought to make his Chilean Revolution a reality. The minimum wage was increased by 35 percent. A "people's health train" with free medical supplies and trained personnel was sent through rural provinces. In December, 1970, the government launched a program to provide every child and pregnant or nursing woman with free milk daily.

Land reform followed. Due to the inefficiency of its agricultural system, Chile in the 1960s had been forced to import 25 percent of its meat, one-third of its milk and 20 percent of all wheat consumed by its people. The Frei administration had presided over the enactment of remedial legislation which provided for the expropriation with compensation of excessively large, ill-managed estates. Thereafter, it had expropriated 8.5 million acres of land. During his first six months in office, Allende added 3.5 million acres to the total.

The new administration's efforts met with stunning success. By early 1971, food production had increased markedly, the rate of growth in the gross national product had tripled, and industrial production had risen 14.6 percent. Unemployment dropped from 8.3 to 3.9 percent, and inflation was reduced from 35 to 22 percent annually. Chile's infant mortality rate dropped by 11 percent. To Allende, the statistics were gratifying but hardly surprising. "I am a man who came to the Presidency after twenty-five years as a Senator," he reminded one listener. "I know what I am doing."

In the municipal elections of April, 1971, the people voted their thanks. Allende's Popular Unity coalition, which had received 36 percent of the vote only seven months earlier, gathered 49.7 percent of the total. Several months later, Fidel Castro visited Chile and paid tribute to its leader. Speaking in Santiago's National Stadium, the Cuban Premier told a crowd of eighty thousand, "A unique process is taking place in Chile. It is the process of change. It is a revolutionary process in which the revolutionaries are trying to carry out changes peacefully by legal and constitutional methods, using the very laws established by the society to maintain class domination. It is unique in the history of contemporary societies. It is unique in the history of humanity."

Allende responded in kind: "Chile is very different from Cuba . . . . We are not the Cuba of 1959. The right has not been crushed here by popular uprising. It has been only narrowly beaten in elections. Our only chance of success is legality, using all the weapons that the Constitution gives us . . . . Our road is much more difficult because it is within the limits of the law and the Constitution. We have to accept what Congress decides according to the precepts of the law. There is an autonomous judicial power that can make its own decisions. We don't expect to achieve socialism overnight."

Allende flowered in the first year and a half of his Presidency. The power to do good was in his hands and he held it dear. Yet he refused to place himself above the people. Shortly after his term began, he insisted that the practice of placing the Presidential portrait in all government offices be discontinued. It was, he scoffed, a wasteful and needless formality more suited to kingdoms than a democracy.

The President's private life remained largely unchanged. He continued to collect pre-Columbian ceramics, Impressionist art, and modern pastels. He still loved checkers, flowers, and good wine. More than ever, he sought to continue in the role of teacher. To student activists who supported his cause, Allende cautioned, "It is not important that a student, if he is a poor student, says to me that he is a left-winger. We need good students, good scholars. First they have to fulfill their responsibilities as students. Then they have the right to say they are political leaders."

His sense of humor remained sharp. Enrique Kirberg, former President of the Santiago Technical University and a close friend of Allende's, had the privilege of sitting next to the President at a banquet in honor of a visiting Chinese trade delegation. At the start of dinner, Allende made a brief toast:

It may well be that we will not reach a major commercial accor during the course of your visit. I do, however, ask one small favo: I would like each person in your great country to drink one bottl of Chilean wine each year. This is all I ask.

He then sat down and, as the visiting Chinese reflected o1 what seemed to be a modest enough request, Allende turned t(Kirberg and whispered, "That's eight hundred million bottle of wine."

Indeed, the only change in Allende's demeanor once he be came President was that his speeches became markedly longer One close friend who had studied American politics took note of the fact, and warned El Compañero that he was in danger o1 becoming "a Chilean Hubert Humphrey."

"But," Allende protested, "when I talk with the people I have so much to tell them."

Yet, even as the Allende Presidency flowered, the seeds of destruction were being sown. Allende had campaigned tirelessly on the theme that for Chile to be truly independent, control of basic industries must rest in Chilean hands. Toward this end, soon after his inauguration he had begun a process of nationalization. Chile's banking, communications, and automobile industries were all placed under partial government control. On the issue of copper, a crisis exploded.

For virtually the entire twentieth century, the Chilean economy had been characterized by dependence on the United States. One hundred ten American corporations had invested over one billion dollars in Chile. The largest American investors were the multinational copper companies. Kennecott Corporation owned and operated El Teniente—the largest underground copper mine in the world. From 1955 to 1970, it had realized an annual return of 34.8 percent on its Chilean investment compared with 10 percent on investments throughout the rest of the world. Anaconda Company controlled Chuquicamata—the world's largest open-pit copper mine. Its annual return in Chile for the same period was 20.2 percent compared with 3.5 percent elsewhere.

The profits reaped by both companies from their Chilean operations were incredible. Yet rather than refine copper locally, they shipped it to the United States for processing. American refineries gained twelve jobs for every one mining job in Chile.

Copper supplied 80 percent of Chile's export earnings. Whoever controlled the mines controlled Chile. In 1970, four-fifths of the nation's copper production was in American hands. The primary obligation of these multinational corporations was to their shareholders, not the Chilean people. To Allende, the need for a change was obvious.

On December 21, 1970, the President proposed a Constitutional Amendment authorizing the nationalization of Chile's copper industry. The idea was hardly novel. In 1969, the Frei administration had concluded separate pacts with Kennecott and Anaconda that called for partial Chilean ownership of the mines. Subsequently, Radomiro Tomic, Frei's successor as leader of the Christian Democratic Party and Allende's opponent in 1970, had called for full nationalization.

Allende's proposal was similar in most respects to Tomic's. It authorized the government to assume full state ownership of all minerals in the nation's subsoil and to take operational control of the mines owned by Anaconda, Kennecott, and a third American mining company, the Cerro Corporation. Compensation was to be paid to the companies based on the book value of their installations, with a deduction for previously earned "excessive profits." The proposal was founded on a Declaration of Principles adopted by the Seventeenth Session of the United Nations, which had held: "The right of peoples and nations to permanent sovereignty over their natural riches and resources is to be exercised by them in the interest of national development and the well-being of the people and the state."

Speaking in support of the Amendment, Allende declared, "The nationalization of our copper is not an act of vengeance or hatred directed towards any group, government or nation. We are exercising an inalienable right on behalf of a sovereign people—that of the full enjoyment of our national resources."

On July 11, 1971, the nationalization Amendment was unanimously passed by the Chilean Congress. Every Senator and Deputy present, representing every major Chilean party, voted in favor of the reform. Allende hailed the event as the "second independence" of the Chilean people and proclaimed July 11 as National Dignity Day. Three months later, his government announced that, because of "excessive profits" extracted from Chile, Kennecott and Anaconda would receive no compensation for their nationalized holdings. The Cerro Corporation was granted a claim of fourteen million dollars. Eduardo Novoa, Chief Legal Advisor to the President, defended the decision on compensation with an analogy to American history: "When Lincoln freed the slaves in the United States, there was no compensation paid to the planters." Allende himself appealed to the American people's sense of "historical purpose":

We know that our attempts to recover the basic natural resources of the country for the Chilean people will affect certain North American private interests. However, we are sure that these interests cannot be identified with the great historical purposes of the North American people. Relations between our two states have much vaster and more far-reaching objectives than the protection of private gain. When the people of Chile carry out the nationalization of their basic wealth, Chilean copper, they are not engaging in any action against the North American people, but placing at the service of Chile something which indisputably belongs to it.

Washington's official response was quick in coming. On October 13, 1971, Secretary of State William Rogers decried the Chilean government's ruling on compensation as "a serious departure from accepted standards of international law. The Chilean decision," the Secretary said, had "serious implications," and left the United States government "deeply disappointed and disturbed."

Just how disturbed was soon to become evident. One year earlier, Richard Nixon had failed in his attempt to keep Allende from the Presidency. Now he would wreak vengeance upon Chile with all the might he could muster.

CHAPTER V

CHARLES HORMAN
IN CHILE–1972

"When we got to Santiago in July, 1972," Joyce recalls, "it looked like paradise. After eight months of dusty roads and flea-infested beds, here was a place with flowers, sidewalk cafes, and warm, friendly people. We checked our luggage in a small hotel and began looking for a home as soon as possible."

Home became a six-bedroom house shared with three other Americans and two Europeans at 425 Paul Harris Avenue in the Los Condes section of Santiago. Located on a shady, tree-lined street, it had a terrace in front, balcony in back, and sprawling lawn surrounded by a white picket fence.

From Charles's point of view, the living arrangement was ideal—seven people with diverse interests and talents working together. Bob Brown was employed by the Chilean office of Alcoholics Anonymous. Janet Deucy worked for the Chilean Forestry Institute. Jim Ogden, a former Peace Corpsman, was a graphic designer. Two Europeans—Luis Mestris, a Spanish illustrator, and Yarda Plank, a Czech artist—completed the group. Together they had eleven cats, four rabbits, and a duck. Eventually, one of the cats had one litter too many, and Charles announced that enough was enough. By group vote, Bob Brown was assigned the task of disposal. He put the kittens in a box, took them down to the supermarket, and sat on the sidewalk for an entire day. Each child who asked for a kitten was interviewed to make certain that he or she would provide a proper home. Eventually, the neighborhood children, most of whom were young and quite shy, became the new household's biggest boosters.

"We introduced them to drawing," Joyce remembers. "Charles invited them to visit but they were too shy, so he put a stack of crayons and paper on the kitchen table and left the door open. One by one, the children wandered in. At first, they would only use a pencil or one crayon, and they made their drawings very, very small. Eventually, they grew bolder and more colorful. Before long, they were clamoring for larger and larger sheets of paper. They had come to realize that art was something they could be delighted with and very proud of."

That same realization was effecting Joyce as well. Arriving in Santiago, she had taken a job as a computer programmer with the Chilean Forestry Institute to supplement the money she and Charles had saved in New York. Several months later, she quit to devote full time to an artistic project of her own.

Working largely in his spare time, Charles had written the script for a children's animated cartoon called "The Sunshine Grabber." Now, Joyce resolved to bring the project to life. At her urging, Charles further refined the story and Bob Brown built a makeshift animation stand. Yarda and Luis assisted with the artwork, and Pablo de la Barra—a Chilean filmmaker who had worked with Costa Gavras in filming *State of Siege*—agreed to pay for materials while the project was being developed.

"Those first months in Chile," Joyce says, "were the most exciting of our lives. We were always learning. We were independent, full of energy, and free. If there was any cloud on our horizon, it was the growing political and economic turmoil. But Charles was more aware of that than I was."

Charles's growing expertise in Chilean politics was the product of hard work and concentration. From his arrival in Chile on, he had conscientiously read the Spanish-language press. Each day, like the journalist he was, he brought home three or four newspapers representing all points of view on the Chilean political spectrum and read them thoroughly. Underlining sentences, scribbling in column margins, he took note of who contradicted whom in an attempt to find out where the truth lay. In time, he had come to understand Chilean politics extremely well, and what he saw disturbed him.

The fabric of Chile's political system was being torn asunder by an economic crisis. By the end of 1972, all the exhilarating indices of the previous year had been reversed. For reasons that were not completely clear, the economy was coming undone. The price of copper on world markets, which had once exceeded eighty cents a pound, was half that amount. Mining production and industrial output were down, and Chile's rate of inflation had jumped to 160 percent—the highest in the industrial world.

An increasing shortage of food and consumer products had led to a burgeoning black market in Santiago. Black humor was the order of the day. One well-traveled story recounted a conversation allegedly carried on between Allende and a peasant who was being tutored in the administration's economic policies:

"If you have two houses," Allende explained, "the state takes one and you keep the other."

"I understand," said the peasant.

"If you have two cars, the state takes one and you keep the other."

"I understand," said the peasant.

"And," Allende continued, "if you have two chickens, the state takes one and you keep the other."

"Like hell," the peasant answered angrily.

"But," Allende protested, "I thought you understood our revolution."

"I do now," the peasant answered. "And I *have* two chickens."

The economic upheaval was upsetting to Charles. He was happy in Chile, moved by the vision of people voting for change, intent on molding their own future. Observing a social experiment that held out hope for a better way of life had fueled his creative energies. Now the social revolution seemed on the verge of failing.

As the turmoil grew, Charles joined a group of Americans in Santiago who were publishing a nonprofit magazine called FIN. A Spanish acronym for Source of North American Information,

FIN was devoted to reporting on United States activities in Chile and the American antiwar movement. It took articles that appeared in American newspapers and reprinted them on legal-size paper folded over into magazine format. Ten people worked on the publication, which generally sold several hundred copies per issue. In a sense, it was a mini-news service for the Chilean press. Its publishers suspected American involvement as a root cause of Chile's woes. Even they did not know its full extent. For what lay beneath the surface was an American effort later described by Senator Frank Church (Chairman of the Senate Select Committee) as "conflicting with all of our professed principles as a nation."

The goal of the Nixon administration in Chile was quite simple: Keep Salvador Allende from governing. Washington had tried in 1970 to subvert the Chilean electoral process by propaganda and bribes. When that failed, it sought to foment a military coup which led to the assassination of General Schneider. Once Allende was in power, the United States sought to undermine his capacity to govern by the systematic destruction of the Chilean economy.

As the Allende administration began to function, most observers within the American intelligence community had felt that the Chilean President posed little or no threat to the security of the United States. National intelligence estimates produced by the CIA reported that Allende was "careful not to subordinate Chilean interests to any Communist or Socialist power," and "was charting an independent, nationalistic course." Nonetheless, under the chairmanship of Henry Kissinger, a series of weekly interagency meetings attended by high-level officials from the Departments of the Treasury, Defense, and State soon began. "The whole purpose of these meetings," recalls one participant, "was to insure that the various aid agencies were rejiggered so [Allende] didn't get a penny." Even more ominous were twenty-two meetings of the 40 Committee at which "destabilization" of the Allende government was discussed.

Thus, long before compensation for American copper holdings had become an issue, the Nixon administration began to pursue a policy of economic strangulation towards Chile. Allende had inherited a foreign debt of three billion dollars from his predecessor—the second highest on a per capita basis in the world. Only Israel's was larger. The interest payments on this debt alone placed substantial burdens upon the Chilean economy, and much of the principal was scheduled to come due in the early 1970s. To use the analogy of Professors James Petras and Morris Morley, Chile had come to resemble a drug addict. "Daily injections of new foreign loans were necessary to nourish the habit cultivated by previous regimes. The economy had lost the capacity to sustain itself by its own efforts."

Using Allende's inherited national debt as a prime weapon, the Nixon administration began an "economic squeeze." Inter-American Development Bank aid to Chile was cut by 95 percent. The United States Export-Import Bank, which had loaned Chile six hundred million dollars prior to Allende's election, curtailed further credit. All totaled, nonmilitary American aid, which had averaged 159 million dollars annually during the Frei administration, dropped to less than one-tenth that amount.

The tools of production were also withheld. Chilean industry had been built upon American-made capital equipment. Ninety percent of the replacement parts for Chile's heavy industrial machinery were imported from the United States. Taking the automotive industry as an example, by late 1972, one-third of the diesel trucks at the Chuquicamata copper mine, one-fifth of all taxis, and one-third of all buses in Chile were not working because of a lack of spare parts.

Beset by American-spawned economic pressures, a growing number of Chileans took to the streets. The first mass demonstration in opposition to Allende came in December, 1971. Organized by the Christian Democratic and National parties, five thousand middle- and upper-class housewives marched through downtown Santiago protesting shortages in food. Outside the President's office, they shouted anti-Marxist slogans and crashed pots and pans together in what became known as the "March of the Empty Pots."

Allende's supporters quickly rallied to his defense. Whatever shortages did exist, they maintained, were due to the increased purchasing power of Chile's poor. By raising the wages paid to low-income workers, Allende had created a whole new class of consumers competing for goods on the open market. Furthermore, they argued, opposition rhetoric had encouraged Chileans to hoard goods and, in some instances, interfere with the production system.

In 1972, opposition to Allende escalated. A forty-eight-hour strike by eight thousand workers idled the Chuquicamata copper mine. In mid-May, a series of strikes by soft-drink bottlers, home-appliance manufacturers, and coal miners began. In August, a one-day anti-inflation strike by one hundred fifty thousand Santiago shopkeepers escalated into an unwieldy, rock-throwing demonstration. Then came Chile's first "national crisis."

Chile is a country reliant upon its trucking industry. Rail transportation is undeveloped, and the entire nation depends on trucks for the flow of goods. In mid-1972, Allende had proposed that the government establish a state trucking firm in the isolated southern city of Aysen. Fearing that this would lead to nationalization of the whole industry, on October 10, 1972, the Chilean Confederation of Truck Owners struck. Transportation of food and other essential goods was halted throughout Chile. Factories shut down for lack of raw materials, shopkeepers for lack of goods. Bankers, lawyers, and other professional workers joined the strike in large numbers.

Branding the strike as "seditious," Allende declared martial law in a four-hundred-mile strip surrounding Santiago. Military trucks were pressed into service for emergency deliveries to major cities and the union leaders arrested. By the time the strike was settled in return for numerous government concessions including a pledge that Chile's trucking industry would not be nationalized, the nation had undergone four weeks of chaos.

Polarization on the issue of economic management now threatened to destroy the stability of the Chilean government. In Santiago, the eighty-thousand-seat National Stadium had become a town hall for the nation. One week, Allende's forces gathered, charges of "economic imperialism" filling the air. The next week, opposition forces rallied to cries of "economic mismanagement." Of course, production has dropped, the opposition cried. How can Allende expect large farmers and businessmen facing expropriation to invest new sums of money in their businesses? Why has Allende increased the minimum wage by 35 percent when he knows that Chile's resources to support the raise are inadequate? And most important, how can Allende expect to receive American assistance while engaged in a program amounting to the confiscation of American property?

No one was immune from the crisis. For the poor, consumer goods were once again unavailable. For the middle class and the rich, there was often only one recourse. Joyce Horman recalls, "More and more, we found ourselves buying things like toothpaste and toilet paper on the black market. It was the only way we could get them."

Yet, through it all, Allende held firm. He believed in his vision and was pledged to fulfill it. To those who doubted his determination, the President resolved: "The course of history cannot be stopped; nations do not move backwards; social injustice cannot endure. No nation has so far succeeded in organizing a new society in the ways we have chosen to do it. And we are doing it in spite of the hardships that so often block our way."

In March, 1973, the Chilean people went to the polls to assess their progress as a nation. In a span of slightly more than two years, the Allende administration had nationalized 35 percent of Chile's industrial production and 40 percent of its cultivated land. It had put into effect far-reaching social reforms and sought to remake the Chilean way of life. But the cost of the President's crusade had been great. The economy was tottering and the polity was in turmoil. Now, the entire Chamber of

Deputies and half the Senate was standing for reelection, and Chile's rightist parties clamored for the two-thirds majority that would enable them to remove Allende constitutionally from office. Virtually all political pundits forecast heavy losses for the President. Confounding them all, his Popular Unity Party scored a stunning triumph. Official results from the March 4, 1973, balloting gave Allende's forces 43.4 percent of the total vote and a net increase of eight seats in Congress.

The Chilean people had spoken. By their vote, they had given notice that they would not be bullied by economic duress, whether applied by striking truckers or foreign powers. For two and a half years, the United States had sought to bring Allende to his knees by "peaceful means." It had secretly organized and financed the labor and trade groups whose strikes had paralyzed the Chilean economy. Hundreds of thousands of dollars had been funneled to the anti-Allende press. American agents had infiltrated the upper echelon of Chile's Socialist Party and paid government employees to make deliberate errors in their jobs, thereby adding to the economic chaos. Street demonstrations in opposition to government policies had been organized by the CIA. The cash outlay for these activities was 8.8 million dollars, exchanged on Chile's black market where American dollars were traded at five times the official rate of exchange. Keeping in mind that Chile's population was less than 5 percent that of the United States, a similar destabilization effort in this country would have involved the expenditure of eight hundred million dollars—over twenty times the amount spent by Richard Nixon in his 1968 election campaign. Yet, after all this, in the slums of Santiago and on rural farms throughout Chile, the people had stood by their President. If Allende was to be overthrown, it would need be by military means.

CHAPTER VI

NEW YORK–
AUGUST, 1973

In August, 1973, Charles Horman came home to New York and saw his parents for the last time.

"Prior to his final visit," Ed Horman recalls, "things had not been completely good between us. Charles had become somewhat intolerant of our life style, and I suppose at times I might have been unduly critical of him, too. While he was gone, things improved. We exchanged several soul-searching letters which brought us closer together. Still, we hadn't seen each other in eighteen months, and both Elizabeth and I were worried that he might not come back to New York for years. Finally, I telephoned Santiago and told him, 'Your mother and I have decided to visit Chile. We will be there in two weeks.' " The corners of Ed's mouth turn upwards in fond recollection. "There was a silence on the other end of the line that cost at least four dollars. Charles was in New York a week later."

He arrived on August 1, 1973, with Ed and Elizabeth at the airport to greet him. As the Lan Chile plane roared down the runway, Elizabeth hurried to the front gate and Ed rode an escalator to the upper-level lounge where he could watch the passengers disembark from the vantage point of a large plate-glass window. Finally, he saw the figure he was waiting for, dressed in maroon corduroy slacks with a brown leather jacket. Rushing to the gate, Ed realized how very much he had missed his son.

Charles was in New York for thirty days . . . going to

movies, eating hamburgers and chocolate ice cream . . . engaging in a myriad of distinctly American pleasures. He shopped for blue jeans, art supplies, and a dozen other items that were unavailable in Santiago. In between, he raised money for a film he was planning on the transition to socialism under Allende.

"He made me understand what the social revolution in Chile was all about," recalls a friend who contributed to the project. "He had a way of describing hunger and suffering that made you appreciate the enormity of Allende's task." Ed Horman agrees: "From the time Charles was a young boy, he had always been a very good writer. He could express himself beautifully and his originality of thought was superb. The one thing he had lacked was a solid frame of reference to work with. By August, 1973, he had one. He was able to convey exactly what was happening in Chile."

While in New York, Charles reestablished ties with many friends, among them an attractive twenty-eight-year-old writer named Terry Simon.

Born and raised in Waterloo, Iowa, Terry had a sense of independence and candor that could be vexatious as well as appealing. When a first-grade teacher complained to Mary Lou Simon that her daughter was an exemplary student save for the fact that she squirmed in her seat and talked incessantly, Terry responded, "Sure I talk and squirm. All the kids do. First grade is boring." Shortly afterwards, she went to sleep-away camp for the first time. "She was awfully young," her mother recalls, "and my husband and I were afraid she would be homesick. Then we got a letter that read, 'Dear Mom and Dad, Your letter came yesterday, but I haven't had time to read it. I only have time to write now because my counselor said I wouldn't get dinner tonight unless I wrote you, and I'm hungry.' "

From such beginnings, one might expect a monster to grow. What developed instead was an intelligent, sensitive woman. "She was a skinny little kid," Mary Lou Simon says, "a terrific tomboy, who loved to climb trees and get dirty. Then, about age thirteen, she started sitting on the front steps with boys and toned down some."

After graduating from the University of Iowa, Terry taught first and second grade for three years. Moving from Waterloo to New York in 1969, she began work as an editor for Scholastic Magazines and took an apartment across the hall from Charles and Joyce Horman.

"I met Charles under rather odd circumstances," she says. "I was a new tenant and didn't know any of the neighbors. One afternoon as I was walking upstairs, this fellow came down carrying a small bowl with a piece of tinfoil over it. When we reached each other, he stopped and asked:

" 'Hi! Did you just move in on the third floor?'

" 'Yes.'

" 'My wife and I live across the hall. My name is Charles Horman. Do you have cockroaches in your apartment?' "

Terry shakes her head in wonderment as she recounts the story. "I hadn't lived in New York too long and didn't know much about cockroaches, so I played straight man for him.

" 'No . . . at least I don't think so.'

" 'Well, I do,' Charles answered, 'and the landlord doesn't believe me, so I'm taking one down to show him.' "

"At that point," Terry continues, "Charles peeled the tinfoil off the bowl, and inside was the biggest, ugliest cockroach I'd ever seen. Then he asked where I was from, and told me to go upstairs to meet his wife. I went up, knocked on the door, introduced myself, and was handed a cup of coffee. Twenty minutes later, Charles came back with an empty bowl and joined us."

Terry and the Hormans became "family" to one another. Joyce was Middlewestern and reminded Terry of the people she had grown up with in Iowa. Charles was warm, open, and supportive. Later in the year, Terry met Ed and Elizabeth, and they became family, too. "There's a certain loving look that Elizabeth gets on her face," Terry explains, "which makes me feel as though I'm being hugged all over just by her looking at me."

Elizabeth responds in kind: "Terry has the kind of face that I as a painter dream of painting—good-looking but not flashy; willful but not overpowering, with an inner strength born of total integrity and lack of guile."

For two years, Terry and the Hormans remained neighbors and friends. Sunday mornings, Charles and Joyce would pick her up on the way to breakfast. Stopping at the corner to buy the *New York Times* and *Daily News,* they would walk into a restaurant and fight over who got the *News* comic section first. It was an intellectual game to see who could marshall the best arguments for his or her side and, invariably, Charles and Joyce wound up on the same side of the table reading the funnies together. Then, in due course, Charles would read both papers in their entirety. "He never read just one newspaper," recalls a friend. "He always had half the *New York Times* stuck inside part of the *Daily News* folded over two-thirds of the *New York Post*."

When Charles and Joyce settled in Chile, Ed and Elizabeth maintained their ties with Terry. Any news from Santiago was communicated from one home to the other. "I invited her for dinner often," Elizabeth recalls, "because seeing her helped me miss Charles less." When Charles returned to New York in August, 1973, Terry was among the first friends invited for dinner. Afterwards, he walked her home. "It was," she remembers, "the kind of warm, peaceful, quiet night that's beautiful anywhere. Charles felt like talking. He had been living in another world for over a year and the experience had changed him. Being back in New York was a sensory overload."

When they reached the building where they had been neighbors, Charles declined an invitation to come up for coffee. "I know I've lived here," he said, "but walking down this street, I have a sense that it was a different person. I'm not ready to go inside yet."

They talked on the sidewalk a while longer, and Terry decided to visit Chile. She was already planning a South American vacation and, at Charles's suggestion, decided to substitute Chile for Mexico on her itinerary. "I wasn't really aware of the danger in going," she says. "I knew there were problems, but I didn't think anything major would come of them in the ten days I planned to be there."

Simon Blattner, a close friend who spent a weekend with

47

Charles and Terry in August, recalls a later conversation with them: "I begged them to stay in New York," Blattner says, "but they were determined to go. All Charles had to do was pick up the phone and tell Joyce to come home, but he wanted to go back to Chile. It was as though he didn't want to miss the final act of the drama that was unfolding."

Ed and Elizabeth were equally apprehensive about Charles returning to Santiago. He had told them on several occasions during his stay in New York that a coup was inevitable, and more than a few hints of military restiveness were in the air. Both parents wanted him home, where he was safe. But Charles was convinced that any coup would be bloodless and, given his reportorial instincts, he wanted to be on the scene when it occurred.

On August 30, 1973, Ed and Elizabeth drove Charles and Terry to the airport to say good-bye. At the Lan Chile terminal, Charles wandered by a nearby newsstand, thumbing through several newspapers and magazines. Then he joined his parents for their last farewell.

Part of him wanted very much to stay in New York. He had experienced a wonderful time at home and had drawn considerably closer to his parents. "My folks are being absolutely lovely," he had written Joyce during the middle of his stay. "No pressure on any front. They think I look great. We have long talks. I really get the sense for the first time that there's some essential me they love, and jobs, politics, and religion fall outside that area. They just plain love me and are glad to see me."

Still, New York would always be there. He could come home again. "I'll see you in a year, if not sooner," he promised. Elizabeth and Ed hugged him good-bye, and then he was gone.

"He's grown up a lot these past two years," Ed said as he watched the Lan Chile plane taxi down the runway and lift off into the late afternoon sky.

"He sure has," Elizabeth replied. "He's a mature young man now. I can hardly wait to have him home again."

CHAPTER VII

SANTIAGO–
SEPTEMBER, 1973

When Charles and Terry arrived in Santiago, they discovered that spring had bloomed south of the equator. Joyce met them at the airport in a borrowed car and drove them home to 425 Paul Harris. There, Charles unpacked his suitcase and began parceling out his booty from New York—a gold medallion and scarf for Joyce . . . art supplies. . . . He particularly enjoyed the oohing and aahing that accompanied distribution of the toothpaste and deodorant.

Joyce broiled a chicken for dinner. "You don't know what I went through to get this," she said. Charles joked that their pet duck was getting fatter and might solve the next meal problem. "You don't understand," she told him. "Things here have gotten worse; much worse."

As Charles and Terry listened, Joyce outlined the deteriorating political situation to them. On July 26, just prior to Charles's departure for New York, the National Confederation of Truck Owners had struck again, charging the government with reneging on an earlier pledge to make new trucks and spare parts available to them. The strike spread quickly to Santiago and, by mid-August, the shortage of food and gas had become acute. Seeking to ease the crisis, ten thousand truck owners had left the Confederation and had begun operations in support of the government. In retaliation, the striking truckers had scattered six-pronged steel spikes on roads, dynamited bridges and tunnels, cut power lines, and sabotaged the operating truckers. Finally, the leader of the anti-union faction was assassinated.

49

The Chilean economy was rapidly becoming paralyzed. Fuel pumps were dry, unshipped food supplies were rotting, and factories were shutting down for lack of operating materials. Doctors, lawyers, and other professional workers had found themselves literally without food and had joined in the protest. Meanwhile, Rudolph Rauch—a *Time* magazine correspondent—visited a group of striking truckers enjoying a lavish dinner of steak, vegetables, and wine on the outskirts of Santiago. "Where does the money for that come from?" Rauch asked. "From the CIA," a trucker answered.

Even more ominous, though, were the rumblings of military discontent which Chile was experiencing for the first time. On June 29, 1973, one hundred troops from Santiago's Second Armored Regiment had surrounded Chile's Presidential office building, the Moneda. Taking control of the front plaza, they unleashed a barrage of small-arms fire in an effort to overpower the Presidential guards. After several hours of fierce fighting, the rebellion was crushed by troops loyal to the administration. However, twenty-two persons had been killed and thirty-four wounded in the first open attempt to overthrow an elected Chilean government in forty-two years.

In late August, the crisis further accelerated. For almost three years, the constitutional supremacy of Chile's President had been enforced by Commander-in-Chief of the Army General Carlos Prats. Named to his post by Eduardo Frei in the wake of General Schneider's assassination, Prats had been reappointed by Allende on the new President's first day in office.

Prats was not a Marxist, but, like Schneider, he was a strict Constitutionalist who felt that Allende had been legally elected and was entitled to a full term in office. For three tumultuous years, he had held firm to this belief. It was Prats's tactful pressure and skilled negotiation which had settled the first truckers' strike. It was Prats whom Allende singled out as "the man most responsible" for putting down the Army revolt in June, 1973. It was Prats more than any other military man who the President felt would struggle with him to uphold the constitutional order.

On August 22, 1973, the wives of three hundred Army officers serving under Prats's command marched on the General's home to protest his support of the Allende administration. The demonstration was unprecedented, and its meaning was clear. Prats's subordinates were informing him that they no longer recognized his authority and, in the ultimate rebuke to Latin *machismo,* were sending their wives to deliver the message. Prats resigned a day later. Shortly thereafter, his second in command—Augusto Pinochet—was named Commander-in-Chief of the Chilean Army.

Charles and Joyce spent the first night of their reunion together in Santiago on a mattress by the fireplace. The following morning, they took Terry on a tour of the city, and Charles mailed a letter to his parents:

The visit up there was really one of the nicest times of my life. I felt so warm and good staying with you. It's tough to imagine how it could have been better.

Then he and Joyce began the task of changing homes.

The move from Paul Harris was occasioned by necessity. Bob Brown and Janet Deucy had left the house, and the remaining residents lacked sufficient funds to maintain it on their own. Charles had come to New York leaving Joyce with the task of house hunting, and, in his absence, she had rented a small residence at 4126 Vicuña Mackenna for the two of them.

Unlike their previous home, the new quarters were located in the heart of a working-class neighborhood. The street was lined by wide, dusty paths instead of a sidewalk. In place of large private homes with flowers and well-kept lawns, most of Vicuña Mackenna was fronted by drab, gray apartments.

The house Joyce rented belonged to Renato Nuñez, a Chilean doctor. Nuñez and his wife lived in a large weather-worn structure set off from the rest of the neighborhood by a tall cast-iron fence. Behind the main house, past a lawn scarred by broad patches of dirt, was a small dwelling that had once served as servants' quarters. When Mrs. Nuñez became pregnant, the doctor decided to rent the smaller house as an additional source of income.

Terry's first few days in Santiago were spent helping Charles and Joyce pack. Once their belongings were crated, they rented a battered pickup truck and made several trips to Vicuña Mackenna, with Charles periodically hanging his head out the window to make certain nothing had fallen off the back of the truck.

When the furniture and crates were finally unloaded, Joyce and Terry announced that they were officially finished with moving. Joyce had spent the better part of a month apartment hunting, and Terry was anxious to see more of Chile than the inside of a truck. Charles, on the other hand, liked a certain degree of organization and wanted the new home settled. To satisfy everyone, Joyce and Terry decided to visit Chile's foremost ski resort at Portillo, while Charles stayed behind to straighten the house. When the women returned two nights later, everything was in order.

Before settling down to housework, Charles had written down his thoughts on returning to Chile after four weeks in New York. Then he had arranged the furniture, unpacked the crates, hung clothes in the closet, and put curtains on the bedroom windows. Kitchen utensils were in their drawers, and a heavy blanket with broad black-and-white stripes overlay the master bed. A blue-and-white tablecloth, candles upon it, covered the living-room table. It was a home.

Charles and Joyce were now settled, but the increasing polarization of Chile's political climate was making Terry uncomfortable. Opposition members of Congress had passed a resolution calling for Allende's resignation, and several political rallies had ended in violence. On the night of her return from Portillo, Terry decided that she should leave Chile. Charles and Joyce concurred, but suggested that first she visit Viña del Mar, seventy-five miles west of Santiago, to see Chile's Pacific coast.

In short order, it was agreed that Terry, Charles, and Joyce would visit Viña on Monday. Tuesday would be spent shopping, and Terry would leave Chile on Wednesday, September 12. On

Monday morning, Joyce realized that she had to renew her resident's visa and, at her suggestion, Charles and Terry went to Viña alone.

Transportation to the coast was erratic because of the strikes. No trains or buses were scheduled until late in the day, and private cars were prohibitively expensive. After an hour's search, Charles and Terry found a *collectivo* ("group cab") which brought them to Viña by midafternoon. Disembarking near the center of town, they began to explore with Charles acting as guide. After a walk of several hours and a Pacific sunset, they checked their watches. It was not yet 9:00 P.M., early for dinner by Chilean standards, but Charles was hungry and they planned to take a bus back to Santiago before midnight.

Finding a small restaurant in the center of Viña, they went inside. At one end of the room, a guitarist sat motionless, waiting for the more conventional dinner hour of 10:00 P.M. A group of waiters were clustered at a table talking to one another. Charles and Terry seated themselves and became the restaurant's first customers of the evening.

Because of the food shortage, the menu was sparse. They ordered chicken, which came chopped into little chunks stewed in a watery sauce. Just after ten, they walked to the bus station where a young clerk sat shuffling papers behind the counter. Charles asked in Spanish for two tickets on the late-night bus to Santiago.

"The bus will not run," the clerk answered. "The Army and truckers are fighting. The road is closed."

The train station was shut down for the night. No collectivos were in sight. Resigned to staying in Viña, they studied a bus schedule for the next day and decided to leave the following noon. Unresolved was the question of where to spend the night.

"Do you remember the Miramar Hotel," Charles asked, "the one we passed that looks like a castle?"

Terry nodded.

"I've always wanted to stay there," he said. "Let's see how expensive it is."

It was too late at night to call Joyce. The Hormans had never had their own telephone in Chile. At 425 Paul Harris, they relied on Mario and Isabella Carvajal, neighbors who lived two blocks away, for messages. The same understanding was in effect with Dr. Nuñez, but the doctor's wife was pregnant and Charles did not want to risk waking them.

"It's not unusual for the roads to be shut down," he assured Terry. "Joyce won't worry."

A town taxi took them to the Miramar Hotel. Looming above a rocky sea, it seemed more like the setting for a Gothic novel than a present-day reality. Inside, the hotel was less dramatic. The lobby was almost empty and its large chandelier sported several burned-out light bulbs. One clerk manned a long desk to the left of the main entrance.

Charles approached the desk and asked about room prices. Hearing they were modest, Terry reached for a registration card, but the clerk politely took it from her and handed it to Charles, who signed in for both of them. After writing down their separate names, he deliberated briefly, then used the 425 Paul Harris address that was listed on his Chilean identification card.

A bellhop appeared and led them upstairs to Room 315. Passing through a small entryway, they saw a bathroom to the left and a large square living area straight ahead. Two double beds were set apart on a side wall opposite a small dresser. Past the beds, a long curtain extended the full width of the room. Opening the curtain to reveal a huge plate-glass window and glass doors, the bellhop waved his arms and proclaimed, *"Valparaiso a noche!"* (Valparaiso at night).

Charles and Terry moved forward and peered out the window into the night. Across the bay, a huge black hill—one of forty-one that Valparaiso is built on—was visible, dotted thickly with lights at its base, more sparsely so towards the top. The movement of ships in the harbor was obscured. Ocean waves drummed loudly against the shore.

"I'm hungry," Charles announced. He ordered two beers and a Swiss cheese sandwich from room service and took them out on the balcony where Terry joined him. When he had finished eating, they went to sleep.

CHAPTER VIII

THE COUP

The disruption and turmoil had taken their toll on Chile and on Allende. As the nation foundered in crisis, the President's face became drawn. He slept fitfully and grew increasingly anguished for the plight of his country. Finally, after full deliberation, a plan to restore order was constructed.

For several months, Allende and Congress had been dead-locked over how best to handle the economic crisis. Under the Constitution, this deadlock empowered the President to call for a national referendum. If a majority of the people supported his rule, Congress would be dissolved and a new election held. This new vote would place in issue every seat in Congress and, in all probability, result in either a majority that Allende could work with or an opposition strong enough to impeach him. Either way, the crisis would be resolved by democratic means.

On September 7, 1973, Allende met with several high-ranking Generals, including the Commander-in-Chief of the Army, Augusto Pinochet, and took them into his confidence. Speaking frankly of the difficulties at hand, he told them that, four days hence, he would announce a national referendum. Following the meeting, the Generals caucused. They now knew that, on September 11, the people would be promised power of final decision. However, pressure from Washington dictated a military rather than a constitutional solution.

By 1973, American influence within the Chilean military was well established. Under a 1952 mutual-aid agreement, the United States had trained Chilean military officers for over twenty years. Much of this instruction took place in the Panama Canal Zone, which served as headquarters for United States military operations throughout Latin America.

There are fourteen American bases in the Canal Zone, each of them administered by the United States Southern Command. Most prominent among them is Fort Gulick where the Eighth Special Forces, more popularly known as Green Berets, are trained. Created to defend the Panama Canal, the Southern Command ultimately acquired a far broader range of responsibilities. As described by William Wipfler, for ten years head of the Latin American Division of the National Council of Churches, "The ideological content and motivation for the coup in Chile and right-wing repression elsewhere in Latin America comes directly from these training centers."

In the early 1970s, Chile's armed forces consisted of four branches: a thirty-thousand-man Army with its main strength in Santiago; a fifteen-thousand-man Navy headquartered in Valparaiso, where the American Naval Mission was also located; nine thousand Air Force corpsmen; and thirty thousand Carabiñeros—a national police force formed through the unification of Chile's local police authorities.

During the Allende years, while nonmilitary assistance to Chile was reduced by over 90 percent, American military aid increased dramatically. Tanks, heavy artillery, and other supplies were forwarded in growing quantity. The number of Chilean military personnel trained in Panama doubled. By increasing its support to the military, the Nixon administration built a power base of its own in Chile, independent from and hostile to Allende. Ultimately, this base became so strong that the United States was instrumental in determining which officers were promoted up the Chilean military ladder.

Inexorably, the United States worked its will on the selection of Chile's military command. General Cesar Ruiz had been named Commander-in-Chief of the Air Force by Allende in November, 1970. In 1973, in a vain effort to settle the truckers' strike, Ruiz reluctantly joined the President's cabinet as Minister of Public Works and Transportation. Unable to placate the

CIA-financed strikers, he resigned both his cabinet and Air Force positions in mid-1973. General Gustavo Leigh, a right-wing ideologue, was named as his successor.

General Carlos Prats was the next to fall. Appointed Commander-in-Chief of the Army in the wake of General Schneider's assassination, he had served for almost three years as military strong man and protector of the Allende government. On August 23, 1973, following the widely publicized demonstration by Army wives outside his home, Prats resigned. General Augusto Pinochet, Prats's second in command, was elevated to the role of Commander-in-Chief. Tall and powerfully built with tinted glasses to correct an eye defect, Pinochet had served in the armed forces since 1936. Particularly noteworthy on his record were a tour of duty in the United States as a military attaché assigned to the Chilean Embassy in Washington and visits to the United States Southern Command in the Panama Canal Zone in 1965, 1968, and 1972.

Following Prats's ouster, the position of José María Sepulveda as head of the Carabiñeros was seriously undermined, and he was ultimately succeeded by General Cesar Mendoza. By the end of August, 1973, the only Allende loyalist to retain his strength was the Commander-in-Chief of the Navy, Admiral Raul Montero.

The plotters were now on schedule. September was the ideal time for implementation of a coup. For fourteen years, the United States and Chilean navies had engaged in an annual training exercise known as Operation Unitas. In anticipation of the joint maneuver, the Chilean armed forces were at their peak.

On Sunday, September 9, 1973, an American guided-missile cruiser, two destroyers, and one submarine anchored just north of Chile. That night, General Augusto Pinochet of the Army, General Gustavo Leigh of the Air Force, and José Toribio Merino (Vice-Admiral in charge of the Chilean Naval Garrison at Valparaiso) exchanged a brief note. Signed first by Merino, the message read, "D-day is Tuesday. The hour is 0600." Pinochet and Leigh signed beneath Merino and wrote *"conforme"* (agreed) in the margin.

On Monday, September 10, at 4:00 P.M., a convoy of Chilean ships set sail from Valparaiso in the direction of four United States warships anchored off the coast of Chile. Under cover of night, they returned. Chilean troops dispersed throughout the city, cutting off all ties to the capital. Simultaneously, Admiral Montero, Allende's last supporter among the military high command, was placed under house arrest. Under the direction of Vice-Admiral Merino, the naval troops began rounding up known Allende sympathizers within the city and imprisoning them on ships docked in the harbor. By 3:00 A.M. on the morning of September 11, the plotters' hold on Valparaiso was complete.

As dawn approached, troops fanned out across Chile. Lists singling out Allende supporters for execution or arrest had been distributed to every region of the country. The Generals were pledged to "extirpate the Marxist cancer from Chile" and would carry out this pledge with ruthless efficiency. Resistance was light. Few troops opposed the coup, and the citizenry was largely unarmed. Only in Santiago was strong armed opposition encountered.

At 6:10 A.M., Salvador Allende was awakened by a telephone report that troops were advancing on the Moneda. He dressed quickly in a gray sweater, tweed jacket, and rust-colored pants and left his home by car. Shortly after 7:00 A.M., accompanied by a personal guard of twenty sharpshooters armed with automatic rifles, submachine guns, and a bazooka, he arrived at the Moneda. Then, after assigning defense positions to his followers, Allende telephoned his wife of thirty-four years with the somber warning that he might not see her again.

At 9:00 A.M., the President addressed his countrymen for the last time. The armed forces had moved swiftly, cutting off communications and travel centers throughout Chile, but two of Santiago's twenty-nine radio stations remained in government hands. As Allende reached the concluding portion of his remarks, two control center explosions cut him off the air, but not before the Chilean people heard his final words to them:

Surely this is the last opportunity I will have to address myself to you. My words do not come out of bitterness, but may they be the moral punishment for those who betrayed the oath they took as soldiers of Chile. They have the power, they can smash us, but the social processes are not detained. History is ours, and the People will make it.

People of my country, I want to thank you for the loyalty which you have always shown, the trust which you placed in a man who was only the interpreter of the great desires of justice, who gave his word that he would respect the Constitution and the law. I will always be beside you, or at least my memory will be.

I have faith in Chile and in her destiny. Other men will overcome this gray and bitter moment. May you continue to know that much sooner than later the great avenues through which free men will pass to build a better society will open.

Long live Chile!

Moments later, Vice-Admiral Patricio Carvajal telephoned the Moneda and informed the President that he and his family would be granted safe passage from Chile if he surrendered immediately. Allende refused, and the military command then broadcast a warning that the Moneda would be attacked by the national Air Force at 11:00 A.M. Shortly before the appointed hour, the President met with those who remained to defend him and told them that they were free to go. "All I ask," he said, "is that you give up your arms when you leave. Those of us who are going to oppose the military rebellion will need them."

Four minutes before noon, the air attack began. Streaking across the Santiago sky, two Hunter Hawk jets made the first of eight assaults on the two-hundred-year-old Moneda. Eighteen rockets struck the building's north wing, badly damaging the upper floor where the President's office was located. Minutes later, General Javier Palacios ordered the Second Tank Regiment to attack.

The battle raged for two hours, pitting the President and forty-two defenders against hundreds of troops backed by air power and tanks. By 1:00 P.M., large portions of the Moneda were engulfed by billowing smoke and flames. The loyalists continued to fight, threatened as much by smoke and exhaustion as by the assault from outside.

Their defense was futile. At 2:00 P.M., an infiltration team commanded by Captain Roberto Garrido broke through their lines and charged the state reception room on the second floor of the Moneda. Spotting a short, stocky figure across the room, Garrido loosed a burst of fire from his weapon and Salvador Allende fell. As the President collapsed, a group of his supporters charged the room and drove Garrido's troops from the floor. Dr. Enrique Paris, Allende's personal physician, bent over the body of his fallen comrade and felt his pulse. Blood streamed from six bullet wounds in the President's abdomen. Tearfully, Paris announced that Allende was dead.

Forty minutes later, the last defenders were overcome. Entering the banquet hall, General Palacios drew back a bloody Chilean flag which had been placed over the President's body, and threw it to one side. An aide to Palacios took a machine gun, and fired once into Allende's skull, splattering fragments of bone and blood around him.

CHAPTER IX

VIÑA DEL MAR

Tuesday, September 11, 1973

Charles Horman was an early riser. By the time Terry awoke, he was downstairs in the lobby. Rubbing her eyes, she crossed to the far end of the room, opened the glass doors, and stepped out onto the balcony. Scanning the horizon, she saw Viña, the harbor, the hills of Valparaiso, and the ocean beyond. A low-flying helicopter roared overhead and disappeared behind the hills. The sky was a deep blue.

The clerk from the previous night was still on duty when Terry entered the hotel lobby. Spotting Charles in a large cushioned chair across the room, she walked towards him and waved.

"Good morning," he said cheerfully. "Now that you're up, how would you like to spend the next few hours?"

"Let's get some coffee," she answered.

"I have a better idea. Why don't we hike into town and get something to eat? Then we can catch the noon bus back to Santiago."

They paid their bill and began walking towards Viña. On one side, the road was bordered by a stone wall and the sea. To the east, lavish mansions looked down upon them from atop a steep hill. Charles picked a small stone off the pavement and sent it hurtling towards the ocean. "Viña looks like the Scarsdale of Chile," he said.

Terry wasn't listening. She had begun to notice something different from the previous day. An unusual number of Chilean

61

flags were on display. "Is today a holiday?" she asked. "Those flags weren't here yesterday."

"I don't think so. We can check when we get to town."

The road was deserted. There were no cars, no other pedestrians. Past a bend, they came to a tiny stone building resembling a guardhouse. Out front, a solitary soldier not more than twenty years old approached, rifle in hand.

"Where are you going?" he demanded.

"For a walk."

"Where are you coming from?" His tone indicated that their first answer was unsatisfactory.

"We're tourists from Santiago," Charles explained. "Last night we stayed at the Miramar Hotel. We're going to Viña to get a bus home."

"I'm sorry," the soldier answered. "You must go back to your hotel now. The military has taken over Chile. A nationwide curfew is in effect."

Charles and Terry exchanged puzzled looks. They had woken up, checked out of the hotel, and walked for ten minutes with no indication that anything was amiss. Now a young man in a green uniform with baggy pants tucked into his boots was telling them that all of Chile was under military control.

"Has there really been a coup?" Charles asked.

"Yes."

Flags hanging from windows, helicopters roaring overhead, the road to Santiago shut down the previous night . . . in ten minutes of walking, they hadn't seen a soul. The pieces began to fit together. "How do you feel about it?" Charles asked.

The soldier shrugged his shoulders. "I voted for Allende, but I follow orders. Last night, officers came into our barracks. The men who were against the military becoming involved in government were shot."

Charles and Terry turned and began walking back towards the hotel. When they arrived, the lobby was still empty. Charles went to the main desk for a telephone token to call Joyce.

"The phones aren't working," the clerk told him. "You can't even make local calls. Listen!"

He reached beneath the counter and turned up the volume of a small transistor radio which was playing the "Washington Post March." "You see," he said. "Military music! The armed forces have taken over Chile. The phones have been turned off to prevent communication by the enemy."

As Charles and Terry listened, the music was interrupted by an announcer. "*Chilenas, Chilenos.* Be calm; all is well. Stay in your homes." The instruction was followed by a series of troop dispatches, and the music resumed.

"Talk about cultural dependence," Charles muttered. "At least they could have used Chilean martial music." He turned away from the desk, then started back to ask another question. "Is there any way to get in touch with someone in Santiago?"

"I'm afraid not," the clerk told him.

Charles shrugged his shoulders. The one saving grace was that the coup appeared to be bloodless. He was certain Joyce had awakened at home and found the same low-key situation that existed in Viña. "It looks like we're here for another day," he said at last. "We might as well get some breakfast."

The hotel dining room was manned by a skeleton crew. Workers from the night shift and employees who lived in the hotel were on duty, but the regular day staff had been trapped at home by the curfew. Charles and Terry ate without much enthusiasm and went back to the lobby for more news. American marches and troop dispatches were all the radio carried. After wandering onto the terrace, they lounged briefly on a pair of metal chairs, but the sun was too hot and they returned inside.

"There's no pool table here," Charles reported grumpily to Terry after inquiring at the desk. "I could have used the time to polish up my game for a rematch with Joyce. The last time we played, she beat the pants off me. She's the original Minnesota Fats."

Since they could not leave the hotel grounds, they went upstairs and spent the rest of the afternoon reading on their room balcony. At one point, Charles wandered down to the lobby to see if the television was working, but all programming had been cancelled. After dinner, they went back to their room.

63

and he started to write. For over an hour, he sat with a white pad and felt-tipped pen, writing several lines, then crossing them out. Again and again, he repeated the process.

"What's the matter?" Terry asked.

"I don't know. It's too quiet. I can't organize my thoughts. Things don't seem right."

Wednesday, September 12, 1973

The telephones were still shut off, but the curfew had been lifted for local daytime travel within Viña. At Charles's urging, Terry walked with him to town in search of a newspaper. Despite the coup, businesses appeared to be functioning normally. Shops were open and the benches by the main road were dotted with people. The only sign of change were the soldiers clustered on each street corner as a warning against crowds gathering.

Reaching the center of town, Charles spied a long line leading to a corner newsstand. Not knowing who controlled the new government or what had happened to Allende, he joined it. As the line moved forward, he saw people walking away with copies of *El Mercurio,* Chile's largest and most prominent right-wing newspaper. In big blue letters, its headline read, *"Allende Depuesto"* (Allende Deposed). Just as Charles reached the front of the line, the newsman sold his last paper, padlocked the stand, and walked away.

"Let's get some coffee," Terry suggested. "Maybe someone left a paper behind at a table."

"I have to get a paper first. Let's try down the block."

Every newsstand was closed. "Coffee now?" Terry asked.

"Not yet! Let's try the train station. I feel like we're the only people in Viña without a paper."

The newsstand at the station was shut tight. "I'm worried," Terry murmured as they walked back to the hotel empty-handed. "If we're trapped here for any length of time without a newspaper, you'll be impossible."

Back at the Miramar, an air of normality had returned. The day staff was once again at full strength, and the "Washington Post March" had been replaced by "You Are the Sunshine of My Life" as sung by Stevie Wonder. Shortly after noon, they ate a quick lunch in the dining room, then went out on the terrace to sit in the sun. Several yards away, a slightly overweight man with thinning reddish-brown hair sat talking with a short, red-haired woman. Folded up on the table next to them was a newspaper.

His eyes bulging, Charles walked over and asked in Spanish to borrow the paper. The man looked up and laughed. "You'd do better to ask in English."

"You're an American," Terry exclaimed.

"That's right."

"Are you a tourist?"

"Hardly."

"What are you doing down here?"

The man looked up from his chair and smiled. "I'm here with the United States Navy. *We came down to do a job and it's done.*"

Charles and Terry cast awkward glances at one another, and the man turned the conversation to small talk. His name was Arthur Creter, "a retired naval engineer on special assignment for the United States Navy." Wearing a short-sleeved shirt and casual slacks, he looked very much at home and far more attractive than his Chilean companion. The woman was dumpy and dark-skinned, wearing a light print dress. Beneath her red hair, Terry noticed, black roots were showing.

Creter was friendly and very chatty.

"Where are you from?" Charles asked.

"My home base is Panama."

"What's it like up there?"

"Very nice. It's easy to keep track of what's going on in Latin America."

"Do you travel down here a lot?"

"Yes. Always at military invitation, of course."

"Is this your first visit to Chile?"

"No," Creter answered. "It's my third time down."

"Have you been here long?"

"I got to the hotel yesterday. Before that, I was on a ship in the harbor for about a week."

The red-haired woman appeared edgy, and Terry shifted the conversation. "Do you have any idea how long we'll be stuck in Viña?"

"You'll be here until at least the end of the week," Creter answered. "I've been in situations like this before, and all you can do is wait it out. Don't worry, though, the coup went very smoothly. You're completely safe."

Charles was growing increasingly intense. "Was it planned far in advance?" he asked.

"It never goes this smoothly unless it's planned in advance."

"What happened?"

"About four-thirty on Tuesday morning, the military mobilized and placed soldiers across the country. Half an hour later, the whole country was under military control. I talked to the U.S. military in Panama within hours of the coup, and the news had already gotten there. It spread like wildfire."

"Do you think the United States will recognize the new government?"

"Well, it's up to the politicians now, but I don't think there's much doubt about it."

Again, Terry turned the conversation in another direction. "We'd like to get back to Santiago. Is there a United States Consulate in Valparaiso where we could get some help?"

"I really don't know," Creter told her.

"Do you want to come with us to find out?"

He laughed again. "A United States Consulate is the last place I'd go. They don't like to know too much about the military. Don't worry about me though. My friends in the Milgroup will take care of me."

"Milgroup?"

"The United States Military Group. Its naval headquarters are in Valparaiso."

Charles looked out towards the harbor. "Do you know what kind of ships those are out there?"

"Well," Creter answered, "there are two destroyers, a cruiser, and a submarine offshore. As for the harbor . . . "

The red-haired woman pointed to the sun and waved a hand in front of her face, motioning for Creter to come inside. Stopping in midsentence, he turned to go. "Enjoy the newspaper," he said. "There's not much news in it."

As Creter vanished, Charles turned to Terry. "That was incredible," he proclaimed. "I don't believe he said all that to us." Shaking his head, he picked up the paper and began to read. There was virtually no information about Allende other than the fact that he had been deposed. One story implied that he had left the country, another that he had "resisted to the death." All that was clear was that a four-man military junta was in control of Chile, and that Allende's Cabinet and supporters in Congress had been given until 4:00 P.M. that afternoon to surrender to the military or be declared fugitives from justice.

Upstairs in their room, Charles reflected further on the day's events. For some months, he had suspected United States involvement in a massive scheme to undermine the Allende government. American economic machinations were widely assumed, but he had probed more deeply beneath the surface. Relying largely on records available in the Santiago Library, he had come to believe that the United States had masterminded the 1970 assassination of General Rene Schneider. In December, 1972, long before the Church Committee had been convened, Charles had written his parents about the investigative study he was conducting:

About two years ago, when Allende was to take office, a fairly extraordinary attempted coup occurred in which a retired general tried to get the army to rise and keep Allende from taking office. He organized a plot involving army generals, the head of the national police, some very rich growers in the South, remnants of the Chilean Nazi party, and some armed groups associated with the right wing.

The groups killed Rene Schneider, head of the Chilean Army and the man most opposed to political intervention by the armed forces. An interesting thing is the enormous number of people who knew about it ahead of time, including Frei, his Ministers, the CIA, the American Ambassador, and several Senators. I got interested and started reading court records and police statements and talking to people. The whole thing is like a novel; like *Z*.

Now, his belief fueled by Arthur Creter's remarks, Charles felt that responsibility for the coup itself lay with the United States. "We've stumbled upon something very important," he told Terry that night. "I think we should keep a record of everything we see and hear while we're in Viña."

Terry reached for the green notebook she carried with her when she traveled, and began to write: "September 12, 1973— Conversation with American naval engineer in Viña del Mar . . . . "

Thursday, September 13, 1973

Lieutenant Colonel Patrick Ryan was an American military man in the classic mold. Graduating from Holy Cross College, he signed a contract to play football for the Green Bay Packers in 1953 but the cold-war military buildup intervened. Drafted by the Army, he enlisted instead in the United States Marines and began a career of unblemished service that spanned over twenty years.

A former Green Beret, Ryan trained in parachuting and scuba diving for the invasion of Cuba that never came. Three tours of duty in Vietnam followed. To one critic who worked for the American Embassy in Santiago, he was "a bloodthirsty anti-Communist," but Pat Ryan was just doing his job. "I've been taught that Communism is the enemy," he once said. His entire military career had been based on that premise.

On December 26, 1972, Pat Ryan arrived in Chile to become Deputy Chief of the United States Naval Mission in Valparaiso. Technically, the post made him the number-two American naval man in Chile but, in practice, he was regarded by many as number one. Ray Davis, Commander of the entire United States Military Group, was the titular head of its naval subdivision but his time was spent largely at United States Military Group headquarters in Santiago. This left Ryan as de facto chief of the Navy Section in Valparaiso, where the Chilean Navy also happened to be headquartered.

On September 13, 1973, martial law prevailed throughout Chile, but Ryan was free of its restrictions. Carrying a wallet-sized yellow-and-blue card which identified him as a member of the *Armada de Chile,* he was able to move freely through Valparaiso and Viña. For two days, he had been advising members of the United States Naval Mission on the military situation. Now he had decided to conduct a health and welfare check on the remaining American citizens he knew to be living in the area. His last stop was the Miramar Hotel to check on the welfare of a visiting naval engineer named Arthur Creter who, Ryan knew, had been sent to Chile by the United States Southern Command on "official Milgroup business."

The thirteenth started badly for Charles. The phones were still out of order, and he had become quite anxious to reach Joyce. Terry had just joined him in the hotel lobby, when they noticed a tall, heavy-set man dressed in olive trousers, dark tie, and fitted green jacket entering the room. Intrigued by the sight of an American military uniform, Charles walked over and said hello.

"Well, hello there," Pat Ryan answered. "What are you doing in this neck of the woods?"

Charles explained that he had come from Santiago and wanted to return home as soon as possible.

"You'll be here awhile," Ryan told him. "The roads are closed, and it will be a few days before they open again. Things have to be cleaned up in Santiago first."

Ryan's comment shook Charles. "What's happening in Santiago?" he asked.

"Allende's been killed, and buried right here in Viña, although I doubt you'll see that in the newspapers. Right now, the military is doing search and destroy missions, just like in Vietnam. The capital death toll is between fifteen hundred and three thousand."

Charles paled. "How soon will the roads be open?"

"Right now, I don't know. But I usually have information twenty-four to forty-eight hours in advance of the public. Give me your name and room number, and I'll keep you posted."

Charles dictated the information, which Ryan noted on a small pad. "I'll stop back later in the day if I learn anything," he promised. "But I'll be honest with you. For the time being, you're better off here than in Santiago."

Following Ryan's departure, Charles and Terry caucused. For the first time, Charles feared for Joyce's safety. She was alone in a new neighborhood with less than total command of the Spanish language, and conditions in Santiago were apparently dangerous and chaotic. "Why don't we check the phone book to see if there's a United States Consulate in Valparaiso?" Terry suggested. "Maybe they can help us." Taking her advice, Charles thumbed through a directory. Only a British Consulate was listed. "We can't phone because the lines are still dead," he said. "Let's go into town after lunch and see what we can learn."

Valparaiso was several miles further down the coast than Viña. After arriving by bus, they walked for several blocks, whereupon Charles fell victim to the urge for a newspaper. "Go find your paper," Terry told him, pointing to a nearby newsstand. "I'll meet you on that corner in an hour."

The Consulate looked highly unofficial. Located in a small building on the waterfront, it had an outer door marked by a plaque that read "Kendrick and Company." Walking into a reception room piled high with files on top of tables and shelves, Terry approached the lone clerk on duty. "Excuse me," she asked, "is this the British Consulate?"

"It is," he answered. "And it's also a private shipping company. Mr. Kendrick is in charge of both."

Terry explained that she was an American citizen stranded

in Viña and wanted to speak with someone about returning to Santiago. "Mr. Kendrick is at a meeting," the clerk told her. "Perhaps his secretary can help you."

Kendrick's secretary was a friendly, rather pleasant-looking Englishwoman with short, dark-brown hair. Like the reception area, her office was deluged with files. "Your best chance for assistance is the United States Naval Mission," she advised. "They know far more about what's going on down here than we do. I understand they knew about the coup well in advance." Pouring a cup of coffee for Terry, she looked down at the pile of papers on her desk. "You can wait for Mr. Kendrick if you'd like."

Terry seated herself on a bench and glanced around the room, making mental notes of the large ships pictured on the walls. As she waited, a balding, pot-bellied man in a brown suit came in from the street and asked the secretary if Kendrick was available. After learning that he was not, the man joined Terry on the bench. "I'm a security attaché assigned to the British Embassy in Santiago," he told her. "I've been trying to get back for three days."

"Great," she moaned to herself. "If embassy personnel can't travel, Charles and I will be stuck here for weeks."

Her thoughts were interrupted by the arrival of a very British-looking man in his mid-sixties with white hair, bright-pink cheeks, a pipe, and a tweed sports jacket. "That's Mr. Kendrick," the secretary announced. "I'll bring you in to see him."

Kendrick's office was shielded from his secretary's desk by an opaque glass wall. Inside, the furniture was arranged so that guests faced a large picture window overlooking the harbor while the Consul, sitting at his desk, had his back to the water.

"I really don't do much diplomatically," Kendrick confessed after Terry told him her story. "If you need money, I'll be glad to help you along but, as far as your getting back to Santiago, the Americans are the people to talk with. I'm told that they even had prior knowledge of the coup. The person for you to talk with is Patrick Ryan at the United States Naval Mission."

Terry thanked him for his concern. The money, she told him,

would not be necessary. As for Ryan, she had already met him. After locating Charles, she recounted her conversation with Kendrick, and they returned on foot to the Miramar.

Back at the hotel, they went upstairs to change what few clothes they had. Having expected to stay in Viña for less than a day, Terry had brought one extra shirt, a sweater, and a towel. Charles had carried a second shirt; nothing more. Filling the sink with water, Terry began to wash their front-line garb, only to be interrupted by a knock on the door. As she opened it, she saw Colonel Ryan.

"The phones still aren't working," he told her, "and nothing else is new. I just thought I'd let you know." Charles invited him in, but Ryan declined. "I have some other business to tend to," he explained, "but here's my card. It has my office and home phone numbers on it. Feel free to call if you need any help."

"Nice, but not too bright," Charles noted when Ryan had gone. "What good is a phone number if the phones aren't working?"

After Terry had hung their shirts up to dry, they went down to the hotel lobby. Passing Arthur Creter and his red-headed companion, they exchanged pleasantries and entered the dining room for dinner. Up in their room afterwards, Terry took out her green notebook and recorded the day's events. Ryan's mobility and apparent knowledge of the military situation stood out in her mind. When she had finished, she and Charles went out to sit on the balcony. As they talked, the sound of gunfire punctured the night. Frightened by the noise, they retreated inside, closed the glass doors, and turned off all the lights. Suddenly a huge fire erupted across the bay on a hill in Valparaiso. As it grew, the frequency of gunfire increased. Realizing that it was coming from far off in the distance, they crawled back out on the balcony, lying low to keep safe.

Across the bay, a group of ships was firing at a target on shore. Small cannons erupted and, every third round, a bright-red tracer arched through the night sky towards the hills, illuminating the vicinity where it landed. The sequence continued. Rifle shots on shore, then a red projectile from the ships followed by a barrage of cannons . . . all set against the flaming hillside. For over an hour, the battle raged, more like a Technicolor movie on a vast panoramic screen than reality. Then the shooting stopped, the fire died down, and Charles and Terry went to sleep.

Friday, September 14, 1973

The phones were still out of order, and Charles was growing increasingly anxious about Joyce. He and Terry had witnessed a battle on the bay with people shooting at each other. Ryan had reported three thousand dead in Santiago, and there were missions to search out and destroy the enemy. Four days after he had last seen his wife, Charles's face remained passive, but his hands revealed the strain. He had always had long, graceful fingers. Now, Terry noticed, he was fidgeting constantly with them.

Creter was sitting in the lobby with a carton of Kent cigarettes when they arrived downstairs for breakfast. It was the first time they had seen him without his ladyfriend, and Charles stopped to say hello. "How are you?" he asked.

"Okay," Creter answered. "Yourself?"

"Not bad."

Terry joined the conversation, and Creter turned his attention to her. "Where are you going when you leave Chile?" he asked.

"Peru and Bolivia."

"It's very pretty in Bolivia," he told her. "Of course, there are problems there now."

"Well," she said with a half smile, "if there are problems in Bolivia, maybe you'll be going there next."

"I *know* I'm going there next."

The remark struck Terry as odd. She wasn't quite sure what a "naval engineer" would be doing in Bolivia—one of two land-

73

locked countries in South America. Changing the subject, she asked, "Does your wife always travel with you?"

"Oh," Creter answered, "she's not my wife. She's my friend, banker, translator, and companion." As he finished the litany of her responsibilities, Patrick Ryan entered the lobby. Terry and Charles crossed the room to greet him and asked the familiar question of when they could go back to Santiago.

"If I were you," Ryan answered, "I wouldn't be so anxious to be there. It's a real battle zone." Charles sagged visibly, and Ryan sought to boost his spirits. "Look, I'll tell you what. I have some business here at the hotel. When that's finished, I'll drive you into Valparaiso. There are a few things I have to do at the Naval Mission, and then we can go to a place where you'll be able to radio your parents in the United States and tell them you're safe."

Charles and Terry expressed their gratitude and told Ryan that they would be in the dining room over coffee. After finishing his business, he picked them up and walked them to a white Chevrolet station wagon with diplomatic plates.

"Ladies first," he announced, opening the door as Terry climbed in. Charles followed, sitting in the front seat to her right. "Could you hold this for me?" Ryan asked, swinging a black attaché case onto Charles's lap.

"Sure."

Ryan walked around the front of the car and settled behind the wheel. When his key was in the ignition, he stopped. "Let me check one thing," he said, reaching for the case. Charles handed it to him, and Ryan snapped it open, revealing a .38 caliber pistol inside. After checking a file marked "Top Secret," he closed the case and handed it back to Charles.

"I will hold this for you," Charles announced solemnly, "but please don't go over any bumps."

During the drive to Valparaiso, they began to talk about the coup. Charles and Terry recounted the battle they had witnessed from their balcony the night before, and Ryan explained what had happened. "Some leftists came down out of the hills and set fire to a Carabiñeros station. Those were the flames you saw on the hillside. The Navy blasted the hell out of them from the water. The red tracers were so they'd be able to see what they were shooting at."

The car stopped at a blockade in the road and a young soldier approached, asking gruffly for identification. Ryan pulled the yellow-and-blue card from his wallet and thrust it forward. "Oh, Colonel Ryan. I'm sorry," the soldier responded. "Please, go ahead."

"How do you feel about the coup?" Charles asked as the car pulled away.

"Very good," Ryan told him. "I've been in a lot of frustrating situations before this. I was in Key West waiting to go in at the Bay of Pigs. I'd even taken advanced scuba courses in preparation for the invasion. If Kennedy had provided air cover and proper military support, we'd never have had these problems in Chile. After that, I served three tours of duty as a Green Beret in Vietnam. Our military strategy there was lousy too. We should have just gone in and wiped them up."

The United States Naval Mission was located on the seventh floor of an office building in Valparaiso. Two desks separated by large filing cabinets dominated the reception area with several private offices off to the side. "This is Roger Frauenfelder," Ryan said, introducing Charles and Terry to a young officer wearing a short-sleeved shirt and tie. "He's been down here for two years."

Frauenfelder said hello, then turned to Ryan. "We have a minor problem. The crane operator hasn't been able to get into the country. I think we should send him back to Panama until things calm down instead of paying a hundred and fifty dollars a day for him to sit around."

Ryan concurred. "Anything else?" he asked.

"One more thing. They want to talk with Creter again this afternoon. I've made arrangements for him to be picked up at the hotel."

"Fine."

On that note, Ryan went into an inner office, and Frauenfelder turned back to Charles and Terry. "Would you like some coffee?"

"Sure."

Putting a pot of water on a small burner, he walked to the window and pointed towards the harbor. "Do you see that ship there?"

They nodded.

"The former mayor and city officials of Valparaiso are being held prisoner on that ship."

"How do you feel about the coup?" Charles asked.

"Since I've been down here, I've become quite a supporter of that cause. The new government is expecting U.S. aid and I hope it's quick in coming. If it isn't, we'll be in an uncomfortable position here at the Naval Mission."

Charles joined Frauenfelder at the window. "Where are the American ships from Operation Unitas?"

"They're right out there," Frauenfelder answered, "chugging around just outside the harbor."

As the conversation waned, Charles and Terry went outside in search of a sandwich. By the time they returned, Ryan was ready. "Come on home with me while I get some lunch," he told them. "Then we'll radio your parents."

Reentering the white station wagon, Charles again raised the question of returning to Santiago. "The roads will be closed for another few days," Ryan said, "but there is one possibility. Captain Ray Davis, the head of the United States Military Group in Chile, is driving to Viña tonight with Herbert Thompson. Thompson is the number-two man in our Embassy in Santiago. I think you should stay put in Viña, but, if you want, I'll find out whether or not Davis has room in the car for you on the return trip."

Charles said he would appreciate the favor, and turned the conversation back to the Embassy. "How many military group people are assigned to our Embassy in Santiago?"

"Four or five," Ryan answered.

"What do they do?"

"Their job is to gather information."

"Are they spies?"

"They have a variety of functions," Ryan responded in a clipped voice indicating that this particular line of questioning had gone far enough.

"Are you friendly with many Chilean military officers?" Terry asked.

"Some," Ryan answered. "I took a Chilean Admiral named Huidobro to the United States to buy a million dollars' worth of arms this past July. The Chilean military is all right, but the truck drivers are the real heroes of this thing. They're the ones who brought the government down."

Ryan lived in a large two-story house on a quiet side street in Viña. Leading Charles and Terry into a room with highly polished, Spanish-looking furniture, he introduced them to his wife Audrey, then wandered into the kitchen for a beer.

Mrs. Ryan was a tall, slender woman with tightly drawn features that contrasted markedly with her husband's open, cheerful visage. "Disgruntled looking" was the phrase Charles later used to describe her. He had the distinct impression that she was tired of the pick-up-and-go of military life. She did not appear to be the sort of person who relished moving and making new friends every time her husband received a new assignment.

Ryan returned to the living room carrying a cold Schlitz beer for each of his guests. Just as he appeared, his son Marc, a light-haired boy of about four, came tearing into the room wearing a double cowboy holster, both guns drawn, shouting, "bang . . bang . . ," and vanished out the front door. Mrs. Ryan went to the kitchen and reappeared with a bowl of Campbell's vegetable soup and a Skippy peanut-butter sandwich—rare delicacies in Chile—for her husband.

As he demolished his sandwich, Ryan repeated his warning that the death toll in Santiago was nearing three thousand and that Vietnam-type search and destroy missions were under way. "You really should stay in Viña," his wife added. "It's much safer here. The shops and beauty parlor have already reopened."

Thanking them both for their concern, Charles and Terry promised to reconsider.

"Let's go," Ryan said when he had finished lunch. Leaving Mrs. Ryan inside, they stepped onto the porch, trying to avoid several hundred plastic toy soldiers scattered just outside the front door. "Marc was fighting World War III," Ryan observed, looking down with a laugh. "He must have gotten bored."

In a matter of minutes, they arrived at the home of Paul Eppley, where the Naval Mission radio was installed. There Ryan again recounted details of the coup, this time for Eppley: "There are three thousand dead in Santiago," he proclaimed. "And they're conducting search and destroy missions like in Vietnam." It was the third time in a matter of hours that Charles and Terry had heard the story, and they were beginning to think that their escort was sorry to be missing out on the action. "They bombed the Moneda with rockets," Ryan continued, adding a new piece of information. "You'd have to be a real hamburger to miss with a rocket."

When radio contact with the Southern Command in Panama was established, Eppley turned to Terry. "They'll pass any message you send on to the States, but this is unofficial traffic so I'd appreciate it if you were as brief as possible." Deciding that one message would be easier to transmit than two, she and Charles dictated a brief dispatch for Terry's mother in Waterloo, Iowa:

I'm safe and well. Delay leaving Chile. Tell Dad. Contact Charlie's parents at (212) RH 4-2339. Tell them all OK. Love, Terry.

Ryan then asked if he could send a message to relatives in New Jersey, and Eppley radioed, "Ryan family fine" with an additional reference to "the luck of the Irish." The Panama operator read both messages back for confirmation, and promised to notify Valparaiso when they had been transmitted to the United States. That done, Ryan drove Charles and Terry back to the hotel, promising to contact them the following morning

78

with more definite information on Ray Davis's plans for a return to Santiago.

"I don't know," Charles said shaking his head, when he and Terry were safely ensconced in their room. "Million-dollar shopping sprees for Chilean admirals . . . a naval engineer going to Bolivia . . . the list goes on and on. We seem to be stranded in the middle of a monumental victory celebration, and the winning team assumes we're wholeheartedly on its side."

"Do you think it's safe to keep taking notes?" Terry asked.

"Yes, but there's something else I want to get rid of. I have some political literature about United States involvement in Chilean politics. I brought it with me to read on the bus, and I'd feel safer without it."

Taking several pamphlets into the bathroom, he shredded the cover of one and dropped the pieces in the toilet. "It doesn't work," he called out a minute later. "It takes a dozen flushes for each page. At this rate, I'll be in the bathroom all night."

"Why don't we dump them in the ocean?" Terry suggested.

"Good idea. Let's go."

It was 5:30 P.M., half an hour before curfew. Terry gathered the pamphlets in a manila envelope and jammed it into her handbag, then walked with Charles through the hotel lobby and out toward the sea. Climbing down over several large rocks, they found an isolated spot on the edge of the ocean and readied to jettison the envelope. Just then, footsteps sounded behind them.

"Hello," said a tall Latin man looking down from above. "I see you're walking."

"That's right," Charles answered.

"So am I."

Terry pushed the envelope back into her purse. She recognized the man from the hotel lobby, where he had been very much in evidence the past few days. Yesterday, the desk clerk had identified him as one of the people Patrick Ryan had come to visit.

"I'm walking to town," the man continued.

79

"Not with curfew twenty minutes away," Terry thought to herself.

The man had no intention of leaving before they did. At five minutes to six, Charles and Terry turned and began walking back towards the hotel. The man, who had said he was walking to town, followed.

That night, almost six thousand miles away in Waterloo, Iowa, Mary Lou Simon mailed a letter to her daughter in South America. Not yet having received Terry's radio message, she wrote, "I pray you're okay. You're never out of my thoughts. And don't worry. I have myself under control and things in perspective. Faith in God and you will see me through."

Saturday, September 15, 1973

Pat Ryan appeared at the hotel shortly after breakfast. "I spoke with Ray Davis," he told Charles and Terry. "He'll drive you back to Santiago this afternoon. Pack up whatever you have, and meet me in the lobby around one o'clock. I'll treat you to lunch."

Greatly relieved, they went upstairs and gathered their belongings. "Let's try to get rid of the political literature one more time," Charles suggested. Terry put the manila envelope back in her handbag and accompanied him through the hotel past the terrace to the sea. With no one in sight, they dropped the envelope down among the rocks and watched as it was covered by the onrushing waves.

Arthur Creter was lounging in the lobby when they returned. "I hear you're going back to Santiago," he told them.

"That's right."

"Good luck." He looked at Terry. "If you ever come to Panama, let me know." Reaching for the notebook she carried, he turned to a blank page and began to write. "Here's my address," he told her. "I'd love to hear from you." Then he turned to Charles. "Did you fight in Vietnam?"

"No, I was in the Air Force Reserve."

"Well, I was in Vietnam. It was quite an experience." Creter paused as though on the verge of a great revelation. "Did you ever see pictures of the body piles in Saigon?"

"Not that I recall," Charles answered.

"Well, that's what it's like right now in Santiago . . . piles of bodies two- and three-hundred-people wide. It's an incredible sight."

As Creter spread his arms to provide a sense of proportion, Ryan entered the room. "All set," he asked.

"I have to check out," Charles told him. "Then we'll be ready."

Ryan accompanied him to the main desk and stood by as the bill was added. Noting that the clerk had undercharged him by eight dollars, Charles drew attention to the error. "I'm glad Ryan saw that," Terry commented later. "It showed the sort of person Charles was. He didn't want the hotel clerk to lose eight dollars out of his salary because of an error."

Rather than drive directly home where Ray Davis was to meet them, Ryan pulled his car to a halt outside a restaurant in Viña. "I've arranged a small going-away party," he told them. "Come on inside." Exchanging greetings with the maître d', he led Charles and Terry past a long bar to a corner table in the back of the room where two couples were already seated. "You've met Roger Frauenfelder," Ryan told them. "This is his wife, Gitla, and Ed and Corky Johnson. Ed has been with the Naval Mission for about three weeks."

Charles and Terry joined the group. The restaurant was relatively dark and well decorated, populated mostly by businessmen in suits. Charles, wearing maroon slacks and a print shirt with a brown sports jacket, felt slightly underdressed. Terry, who had on corduroy slacks and a T-shirt, felt more so. At the end of the meal, Ryan insisted on picking up the tab, then turned the conversation to Santiago.

"It's still not safe there," he warned. "You'd be much better off in Viña."

"My wife and I have an extra room in our house," Ed Johnson added. "You're welcome to stay as our guests if the Miramar Hotel is too expensive for you."

"We have a Ping-Pong table," Frauenfelder told them. "You're welcome at our home too."

"You're awfully nice . . . all of you," Charles answered. "I'd just feel more comfortable at home."

Ryan spread his hands flat across the table. "Then let's get you home."

As they got up to leave, the restaurant owner approached. "Could I ask a favor of your guests," he questioned Ryan.

"All right."

"My daughter lives in Santiago," the owner said, handing a slip of paper to Charles. "Here is her name and address. I would like very much to know that she is safe and well. Could you find out for me and send a message back through Colonel Ryan?"

"I'd be glad to," Charles assured him.

"Thank you. I will be very grateful."

Ryan was silent as they got in his car for the drive to meet Ray Davis. "Look," he said at last, "I really thought the people at lunch would talk you into staying but, since they didn't, there's something else you should know. Have you ever heard of MIR?"

Charles and Terry nodded, but Ryan continued as though he hadn't noticed their affirmation. "It's a very violent group of left-wing revolutionaries who operate in Chile. Ray Davis is the number-three American on their assassination list, right behind the United States Ambassador and the Deputy Chief of our diplomatic mission in Santiago. You run a genuine risk by riding in the same car with Ray Davis. I want you to know that while there's still time to change your minds about leaving with him."

Ryan's warning came close to tilting the balance of decision, but Charles was extremely worried about Joyce. The phones were still out of order, the roads might be closed for weeks, and he wanted a firsthand assurance that she was safe. Briefly, he considered asking Ryan to check on her welfare. Perhaps

Ray Davis could even bring her to Viña on his next trip from Santiago. However, the thought of involving Joyce with United States military personnel was disturbing. Charles felt that he had already witnessed "too much" in Viña and wanted as little contact with them as possible. Once again, he thanked Ryan for his concern but said that he was anxious to return to Santiago.

Ray Davis's blue Chevrolet was parked in front of Ryan's home when they arrived. Inside the living room, Audrey Ryan gave her husband a look that said, "It's about time; where were you?" Ryan introduced Charles and Terry to Davis and, the formalities completed, walked them to Davis's car. They thanked him again for his hospitality and shook hands good-bye.

In three days a strange affection had grown between them. The two stranded Americans represented an odd set of values to Ryan. As far as he was concerned, Charles was "a professional student, something I have little use for . . . but not a bad guy." Terry seemed "stronger and more worldly . . . a real nice gal." Basically, he liked them both.

For Charles and Terry, the breakdown of barriers had been even more compelling. They had come to Viña with a myriad of preconceptions about "career military, football-player types." Ryan had superseded those notions. He was a nice man, who had been extremely generous with them. "We left Viña with a good feeling about Pat Ryan," Terry says. "Of course, we didn't realize that what we had learned from him would probably contribute to Charles's murder."

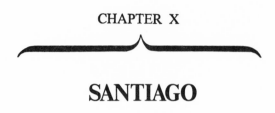

CHAPTER X

SANTIAGO

Saturday, September 15, 1973

Ray Davis did not particularly like his passengers. Terry was all right—"down to earth, obviously an intelligent girl," was how he described her—but Charles bothered him. When they got in the car, "the Harvard grad" "chose of his own volition to sit in back." That struck Davis as an unfriendly gesture, and he found himself conversing mostly with Terry, who was far more sociable.

"How long have you been in Chile?" she asked.

"One year as of today."

"What does your job entail?"

"I'm the senior United States Military Group officer in Chile."

"What does the Military Group do?"

"We help the Chilean Armed Forces improve their technical operating capacity."

"What else?"

"That's all."

Terry looked at Davis and winced. In more ways than one, he was the antithesis of Pat Ryan. Pale and slender with thinning brown hair, he was less than voluble and very much on his guard. The only apparent bond Ryan and Davis shared was their sense of what it meant to be an American.

"Do you see that building?" Davis asked as they passed a large compound on the outskirts of Valparaiso. "That's the Chilean Naval Academy. I'd been in Chile for two months when my Russian counterpart and I were invited to attend graduation ceremonies there as guests of honor. Allende was invited too," Davis continued. "When the Russian was introduced, the students booed. Then I was introduced as the delegate of the United

States and the students roared. There was a five-minute standing ovation, not for me, Ray Davis, but for the United States of America. It was the proudest moment of my life."

His story told, Davis fell momentarily silent, then began to point out sights along the road. "It's pretty country down here," he said to Terry. "Where are you from?"

"I grew up in Iowa, but I live in New York."

"I'm from Brooklyn," he told her. "I went to technical school there. Is the Brooklyn Naval Yard still open?"

"I don't know," she answered.

"I suppose it doesn't matter. I don't know many people in Brooklyn anymore."

There was virtually no traffic. At one point, the car slowed to a halt at a military roadblock, and Davis flashed his Armada de Chile card before resuming.

"Do you know how soon I'll be able to leave Chile?" Terry inquired.

"In about a week."

"How do you feel about the coup?"

"After what's gone on these past few months, no one should have been surprised. How do you feel about it?"

Davis had a way of deflecting questions without really answering them. He wasn't chatty except when it served to redirect the conversation.

"Did you go to college?" he asked her.

"Yes."

"Where?"

"The University of Iowa."

Terry was beginning to feel that Davis was asking questions not to be sociable but to gather information for some other motive.

"How about you?" he asked, turning his head halfway towards Charles in back.

"I went to Harvard."

"I read a book about Harvard once," Davis informed him. "It's called *Push Comes to Shove*. It's about the student rebellion. Did you read it?"

"I went to college before the days of rebellion," Charles answered. "There wasn't much pushing and shoving when I was at Harvard."

Terry offered Davis a piece of chocolate, and Charles returned to staring out the window. "Do you think the coup was well planned?" she asked. Davis gave a noncommittal answer and steered the conversation to another topic.

The car moved through the rolling hillside and entered a long, dark tunnel. Davis turned on his headlights, and, looking ahead, Terry saw a flatbed truck with half a dozen young men in back. The truck was old and rickety, its riders dressed in tattered work clothes. Davis moved his car up behind the truck and began to honk.

"Oh God," Terry thought to herself. "You can take the driver out of New York, but you can't take New York out of the driver." Then her "Oh God" became more urgent. Through the rear window, she saw a large pickup truck, also manned by young workmen, moving up behind them. Pat Ryan's warning about MIR flashed through her mind and, as Davis drew closer to the flatbed vehicle, she tried to laugh off her fantasies. Suddenly, the flatbed truck veered across the center line, completely blocking the tunnel, and stopped.

"This is it," Terry thought. "This is the MIR, and there's no way Charles and I will be able to explain why we're in a car with Ray Davis." Reaching around the side of her seat, she gripped Charles's ankle, sinking her nails deep into the skin. Davis screeched to a halt and began honking the horn more vigorously. The pickup truck pulled up alongside and several workmen jumped out, running towards the lead vehicle. Together with the riders from the flatbed truck, they moved the stalled vehicle to the side of the road.

"It's front wheel must have come off," Davis explained, resuming full speed and exiting from the tunnel.

The drive to Santiago took just over two hours. Unlike Viña, where the sky had been fresh and blue, the capital was gray overhead.

"It's after five and there's a 6:00 P.M. curfew," Davis told them when they reached the city. "I'm going to the Embassy, but I'll be glad to drive you home. I have twenty-four-hour road clearance."

"Thanks," Charles answered from the back seat, "but there's no need. We're staying at the Hotel Carerra for the night. It's right next door to the Embassy."

The announcement came as a surprise to Terry, who said nothing. Moments later, Davis pulled up in front of a large office building with an American flag out front. "This is the American Embassy," he announced.

"Is there any way I can find out about leaving the country?" Terry asked.

"Come on inside. There should be someone upstairs who can help you."

"I'll meet you in the lobby of the Carerra," Charles told her.

Taking the elevator to the Embassy reception room on the ninth floor, Davis unlocked a pair of big glass doors and ushered Terry inside. A large color portrait of Richard Nixon hung on the wall opposite the main desk.

"Normally, the Consul works in the Consulate building about a mile from here," Davis explained, "but they had some problems the day after the coup. A couple of windows were shot out, so he's working out of the Embassy for the time being. Let me see if he's still here." Disappearing inside, he returned several minutes later. "We don't know when the borders will open. All you can do is read the newspapers and listen to the radio." He reached into his wallet and handed her a slip of paper. "Here's my card. If you need anything, feel free to get in touch at the Embassy or my home."

Terry thanked him for his help and took the elevator back down to the ground floor. On the street, the last few pedestrians in sight were scurrying to get home before curfew. As she turned the corner walking towards the Carerra, her stomach sank. At the far end of the block stood the Moneda, its turrets gone, walls black from fire, and windows shattered. The iron gate which had once guarded the main entrance stood twisted and off to one side.

"This," she told herself, "is where it happened."

A large tank rumbled by, and she followed it down the street with her eyes. Every corner was lined with big, tough, hard-looking soldiers wearing riot helmets with bullet sashes across their chests. Suddenly, she was very frightened.

Charles was sitting in a large chair when Terry entered the hotel lobby.

"Why are we staying here instead of going home?" she asked.

"I didn't want Davis to know where we live. I don't trust him, and there wasn't time to get home on our own before curfew."

"Did you call Joyce?"

"I tried. The phones aren't working here either."

They registered at the main desk and went into the coffee shop for dinner. Afterwards, they retired to their room to record the day's "clues" in Terry's notebook and review her earlier notes on their stay in Viña. Then they went to bed.

Charles was unable to sleep. Santiago frightened him. The devastation was terrifying and, now that he was on the verge of making contact with Joyce, he was edging towards panic. Where was she? Had she survived the coup? Who was in the body piles Creter had talked about? Why had they come to Chile in the first place? For five days, he had blocked his fears with small talk and humor, but the underlying question preying on his mind throughout had been, "How is Joyce?" Now he was afraid to learn the answer.

"I can't sleep," he said at last, turning on the light. "God, I wish it were morning."

Sunday, September 16, 1973

Shortly after dawn, Charles was awakened from a fitful sleep by the ear-splitting noise of a jet roaring overhead. Dressing quickly, he went down to the hotel lobby, and did a swift double take. Several yards ahead stood a man talking on a pay telephone. For the first time since the coup, they were working.

Rushing to the main desk for a token, Charles checked his new landlord's telephone number in the pocket address book he carried and returned to the phone. The man was still talking. After a seemingly endless conversation, he hung up, then opened the coin slot to see if his token had been returned. After fishing around for what seemed an eternity, he finally moved on.

With Terry at his side, Charles deposited the token in the phone and began to dial. Halfway through the number, he was seized by a fit of violent trembling and dropped the receiver to his side. Sweating profusely, he began again, dialed several digits, and stopped.

"I can't remember the number," he cried.

Terry repeated it to him, and he started to dial a third time, then hung up. The token came back and he clutched it in his fist, bursting into tears. Reaching towards him, Terry peeled his fingers back, grasped the token, and dialed the number herself. On the fourth ring, the Hormans' landlord answered.

"*Está Joyce?*" Terry asked.

"*Ah, Joyce. Sí! Un momento.*"

Terry handed the receiver to Charles, who was leaning against her for support, and listened to his end of the conversation: "Thank God, you're there . . . . Are you safe? . . . We're fine; tired but fine . . . . Don't worry; we'll be home soon . . . I love you."

"She's okay, isn't she?" Terry asked when he hung up the phone.

Charles wiped the tears from his face and nodded.

Checking out of the Carerra, they walked past the blackened Moneda and hailed a collectivo. Their journey home was almost complete, but the streets of Santiago offered ample evidence that sanctuary would be hard to find. Bullet casings and broken glass littered the pavement. Soldiers lined each avenue, accosting cars and pedestrians at will. As the collectivo halted at a traffic light, four soldiers stepped off the curb and ordered its passengers out.

"Give us your *carnets* (Chilean identification cards)," the lead soldier demanded.

Charles and the driver held out their cards. Terry fumbled through her handbag and produced a passport. Immediately, the soldier to her left pressed the tip of his rifle behind her left ear.

"Get back in the car," the lead soldier instructed the driver. "You too," he ordered, pointing his rifle at Charles.

"Give me that," a third soldier demanded, snatching Terry's passport from her hand. Unable to move with the rifle pressed against her skull, she followed the third soldier with her eyes as he walked to a dry-cleaning store which had been appropriated for military use and checked the passport against a sheet of paper by the door. Then he returned, handed the passport back, and motioned her into the collectivo.

"You may go now," the lead soldier told them.

Minutes later, they arrived at 4126 Vicuña Mackenna. Leaping from the car, Charles unlocked the iron gate out front and rushed past the main house, stumbling over his pet duck on the way.

"Joyce, we're home," he shouted.

Joyce burst through the front door, and they embraced.

"I was worried sick," she told him. "I thought the two of you had been caught on the road the night of the coup."

"We were just as worried about you. We heard bad reports about Santiago. What happened here?"

As Charles and Terry listened, Joyce recounted what little she knew of the coup. Like most Chileans, she had learned of the insurrection by radio on the morning of the eleventh. Then, the bombing of the Moneda had begun, and explosions sounded for several hours. That afternoon, a twenty-four-hour curfew had been declared. Because she and Charles had just moved, there was little food in the house and she survived on beans and dried fruit set aside for camping for four days. On the afternoon of Saturday the fifteenth, the curfew was partially lifted, and she had gone across the street for groceries. With the exception of that one excursion, she had been confined indoors for five days.

"You two are real creeps," she told them, "living the good life in a resort hotel by the sea. Next time, I should be so lucky."

"Be quiet and listen," Charles answered. "We saw some very upsetting things in Viña."

Monday, September 17, 1973

On the morning of September 17, Charles, Joyce, and Terry decided to leave Chile as soon as possible. Charles felt that their knowledge from Viña marked them as potential liabilities to the new regime. Moreover, a wave of xenophobia was sweeping Santiago.

Under Allende, Chile had become a haven for political refugees from other Latin countries. Now, in seeking to root out and destroy all possible opposition, the Junta had begun to assail all but the most right-wing foreign influences. Armed forces radio was urging Chileans to report suspicious foreigners to the military. Santiago was leafleted with flyers reading, "There will be no mercy toward foreign extremists who have come to Chile to kill Chileans. Citizens, stay alert to discover and denounce them to the nearest authority."

The Viña revelations and antiforeign sentiment alone would have been adequate incentive to leave, but there was more. On their way home from the Carerra, Charles and Terry had witnessed scores of soldiers fueling street bonfires with confiscated books and papers. In her brief sojourn for groceries, Joyce had watched in horror as troops forcibly shaved the beards and cut the hair off innocent pedestrians. Women standing on milk lines were accosted by soldiers who slashed their pants with knives and warned, "Women in Chile wear skirts." Rumors of mass executions and torture carried on in Santiago's eighty-thousand-seat National Stadium were rampant.

Charles and Joyce had always planned on someday returning to New York. Events in the wake of Allende's fall made an immediate return advisable. After breakfast, it was agreed that Joyce would buy food for the next few days and visit several friends to make certain they had survived the coup. Meanwhile, Charles and Terry would arrange for air passage out of the country and rent a hotel room near the Embassy for Terry. That way they would have a place to stay if conditions worsened in Vicuña Mackenna or one of them was caught downtown just before curfew.

Late that morning, the trio walked to the bus station nearest their home. Joyce's transport came first, and she disappeared on board after kissing Charles good-bye. Twenty minutes later, the downtown Santiago bus arrived, and Charles and Terry climbed on, taking seats by the window. Crossing a small creek, they looked out and saw the body of a young man lying in the road. Off to the side, several soldiers stood clustered by a military truck, staring at the lifeless, blood-soaked form. The bus moved on without slowing, its passengers unwilling to give any sign of recognition that they had just seen a corpse.

In downtown Santiago, Charles bought a newspaper and walked with Terry to the Riviera Hotel. There, the bell captain took them to the top floor. "This is one of our nicest rooms," he promised, opening the door to a bright, pleasant room overlooking the Santa Lucia hill.

"Do you have an inside room off the street?" Charles inquired.

"Wait a minute," Terry protested. "I like this room."

"Look," Charles told her, "if there's gunfire on the street, I don't want you in a room with picture windows. It isn't safe."

The captain shook his head and led them down several floors to a dark alcove only slightly larger than the bed that was in it. One small window two feet square looked out over a kitchen airshaft, allowing the odor of food and banging of dishes to drift directly in.

"This is fine," Charles said. "We'll take it."

After leaving the hotel, they walked several blocks to a Braniff Airlines office. There Terry explained to the ticket agent on duty that she was a tourist and wanted to leave Chile with two American friends as soon as possible.

"The airports are closed to nonmilitary travel," he told her. "The only advice I can give you is to contact a Mrs. Tipton at the United States Embassy. She's compiling a list of two hundred Americans to be given priority on the first flight out. She should be able to help you."

After traveling on foot to the Embassy, they took an elevator to the ninth floor and walked past an empty reception desk to the switchboard operator on duty. "Could we speak with Mrs. Tipton?" Charles asked.

"No one by that name works here," the operator answered.

"Okay! Could we speak with whoever's in charge of helping United States citizens leave Chile?"

"That's not our job. You'll have to talk with someone at the Consulate."

As Charles began a slow burn, Terry interrupted. "We were told two days ago that the Consulate was closed because of gunfire and the Consul was working here. Is that still true?"

"I really don't know."

"Could you call and find out?"

"Look lady, if you want to know whether or not the Consulate is open, you'll have to go to the Consulate. It's lunch time, so nobody would be there now anyway."

"Do you know if a Mrs. Tipton works at the Consulate?"

The operator stared at the switchboard as if to ignore their existence. "No, I don't," he answered when it became clear they would stand over him until he replied.

Charles and Terry turned to leave, and a swarthy, dark-haired man approached. "I overheard your conversation," he said. "My name is Frank Manitzas. I'm with CBS News here in Santiago. If you want my advice, you'll stay in the Embassy and demand to see the Ambassador. The Consulate is a mile away, and the streets are pretty rough right now."

Charles thanked him, but said he didn't want to cause more of a fuss than necessary. If the Embassy was unwilling to help, he'd go to the Consulate. Down on the street, he and Terry stopped at a sidewalk cafe for juice and sandwiches, then walked to the Consulate. By the time they arrived, it was 4:00 P.M.

"It's getting pretty late," Charles said, looking at his watch. "I think I should head for home to beat the curfew. Can you handle this on your own?"

"Obviously," Terry answered.

"Okay. If you put our names on the flight list, I'll see that the tickets are paid for."

"When should we get in touch with each other?" she asked.

"Tomorrow is Chilean Independence Day. I don't know how easy it will be to travel around Santiago or whether or not the phones will be working. They're pretty erratic even in the best of times." He paused for a moment to think. "Why don't I meet you in your hotel room at 1:00 P. M. Wednesday; that's the day after tomorrow."

"Fine."

"Do you have enough money to get by until then?"

"I think so."

"Let me give you a little more just to make sure."

He handed her the equivalent of eight American dollars and said good-bye. Terry watched as he walked down the street towards the bus stop with a newspaper folded under his arm. She never saw him again.

Unlike the American Embassy, which occupied part of a larger office building, the United States Consulate was housed in a huge mansion. Terry entered the main lobby and approached a waist-high counter, catching the attention of a woman sitting at a cluttered desk by the wall.

"Could you help me?"

"Have you filled out a registration card?" the woman asked.

"No."

"You have to fill out a registration card first."

Terry completed the form and handed it back. "Now what was it you wanted?" the woman asked.

"Is there a Mrs. Tipton here?"

"I'm Mrs. Tipton."

Explaining that she was a tourist visiting two American friends, Terry recounted her experience at Braniff and asked that their names be put on the list of people seeking priority return to the United States.

"Well," Mrs. Tipton answered, "the gentleman at Braniff gave you incorrect information. As you can see, I work at the Consulate, not the Embassy. And, if you want to leave, you'll have to go back to the airline when the borders are open. We handled two emergency cases here at the Consulate, but everyone else is on their own. We're not responsible for people who want to leave, and I have no information about the necessary procedures."

"That's not much help," Terry noted.

"I'm sorry. There's nothing more I can do for you. You'll simply have to go back to your hotel room and wait."

Charles Horman arrived home shortly before 5:00 P.M. on the afternoon of Monday, September 17, 1973. Minutes later, a light-green truck carrying twelve to fifteen soldiers pulled up in front of 4126 Vicuña Mackenna. Leaping from the vehicle, the soldiers pushed through the front gate and poured across the lawn. As a small group of neighbors watched, the commanding officer ordered his men into the living quarters behind the main house. Twenty minutes later, they reappeared dragging Charles with them. Two soldiers followed, carrying a large box filled with books and papers. That night, the soldiers returned, seizing the bulk of Charles's remaining writings.

As the light-green truck pulled away, a young woman hailed a cab and followed. Turning right on Calle Nuble, the military vehicle picked up speed and proceeded directly to the National Stadium, where it disappeared from view behind the structure's cold gray walls. The final ordeal of Charles Horman had begun.

CHAPTER XI

THE REIGN OF TERROR

With Allende's death, Chile succumbed to military rule. Two days after the fall of the Moneda, Commander-in-Chief of the Army Augusto Pinochet assumed the role of President. Ruling with him were Cesar Mendoza and José Toribio Merino (newly appointed Commanders-in-Chief of the Carabiñeros and Navy) and Air Force head Gustavo Leigh. Together, these four men orchestrated a reign of terror unrivaled in modern-day Latin America.

The avowed goal of the ruling Junta was "the extermination of Marxism in Chile." Towards this end, arrest lists were distributed to military command posts across the country, and thousands of persons were imprisoned. Locked in their homes by a round-the-clock curfew, 75,000 Chileans were arrested. Fifteen thousand of these were executed. Bearing in mind the population of Chile, commensurate action in the United States would result in 1.8 million arrests and 360,000 deaths.

The military ruled like an occupying army in a foreign land. Throughout September, bodies were found on the streets of Santiago, bones crushed and fingernails removed. A group of peasants crossing the Nuble River in Central Chile found dozens of headless corpses, their arms tied, floating downstream. Fishermen in the port of Talcahuano halted work when their nets dragged in pieces of human flesh tossed into the sea by the Chilean Navy.

Detention centers sprang up across Chile. In the Atacama

96

Desert, six hundred prisoners were locked in an abandoned salt mine, where the temperature climbed to 110 degrees by day and plummeted below freezing at night. On Dawson Island, near the southernmost tip of Chile, prisoners were held with nothing more than the clothes on their back to guard against the Antarctic winds.

Torture became a tool of government policy. Mutilation was practiced for its own sake. Reliable reports confirm testicles smashed, eyes burned, and the forced ingestion of excrement. Insects were forced up the vaginas of pregnant women, who were then beaten with rifle butts until they aborted. On board the "tall ship" *Esmeralda,* off the coast of Valparaiso, prisoners were stripped naked, beaten, and left tied to ship masts to die.

Victor Jara was born to a poor peasant family in southern Chile. He grew up in the fields and learned his country's music by his father's side. At the time of the coup, he was perhaps the best known and most creative of Chile's "new left" performers. Singing at a student rally one day, outside a union mine the next, he was the foremost exponent of the protest-song movement that had been the lifeblood of the Allende revolution.

On September 12, 1973, Jara was arrested and taken to the eighty-five-hundred-seat indoor Chile Stadium in Santiago. His identity established, he was handed a guitar by guards and ordered to sing a protest song for his fellow captives. This done, the guards smashed both his wrists and ordered him to sing again. Six days later, Jara's wife Joan found her husband's body in a mound of anonymous corpses at the Santiago morgue, "battered, bloody, half-naked, and riddled with machine gun bullets, both hands hanging limp."

Jara's last gift to his countrymen was a poem written in the Chile Stadium just prior to his execution:

> There are six of us, lost in space
> among the stars,
> One dead

One beaten like I never believed a human could
be so beaten . . .
Slaughter is the badge of heroism.

Enrique Kirberg, Allende's personal confidant and President of the Santiago Technical University, was arrested with Jara. Recognized as a state official, he was taken to the basement of the Ministry of Defense, then to the Santiago Military Academy. Three days later, he was transferred with thirty former cabinet ministers and Allende aides to Dawson Island.

"In many respects," Kirberg said later, "the camp copied those of Nazi Germany to perfection. We were constantly watched by guards on top of machine-gun towers. Our barracks were surrounded by two barbed-wire fences separated by a barren strip of land. Each of us was told that the outer fence was electrified. Only the gas chambers were missing."

Kirberg survived. Other prisoners on Dawson Island were less fortunate. José Toha was the first Cabinet member appointed to office by Allende. Serving in succession as Minister of Interior, Defense, and Agriculture, he was one of the President's most loyal supporters. When he learned of the coup in the early morning hours of September 11, Toha rushed to the Moneda and fought furiously until Allende fell. Arrested and imprisoned on Dawson Island, he died a reported suicide in February, 1974. At death, Toha, who stood six feet four inches tall, had been reduced to a weight of one hundred fourteen pounds.

Dr. Enrique Paris, Allende's personal physician, met an equally gruesome fate. Seized at the Moneda on the afternoon of the coup, Paris was taken to the Ministry of Defense, interrogated, and tortured. Witnesses at a Santiago detention center reported seeing him four days later, his mind shattered. Repeating "I am Quinones the bull," again and again, Paris charged his guards and was clubbed to death.

In Concepción and Tejas Verdes, Valdivia and Chillan, the concentration camps grew. They flourished in the southernmost city of the world, Punta Arenas, and amidst the Incan ruins of

Arica. In Santiago, the eighty-five-hundred-seat Chile Stadium served as a way station for prisoners, many of whom, like Victor Jara, failed to survive. It, in turn, was overshadowed by the eighty-thousand-seat National Stadium in Santiago.

Built in 1935, the National Stadium suited the Junta's needs to perfection. Virtually escape-proof by virtue of surrounding fences and impregnable walls, equipped with locker rooms for prisoner interrogation and torture, it soon became the symbol of repression for a nation. Over half of the seven thousand prisoners held there in the weeks following the coup were maltreated. Water was forced up the nose of prisoners. Beatings and the application of electric shocks were common. American citizens were subjected to the same treatment as others.

Joseph Francis Doherty was a young Maryknoll priest, who had arrived in Santiago in July, 1973. Five days after the coup, he was seized by Chilean troops at the home of a fellow missionary, brought to the National Stadium, and placed in a cell with seventy other detainees. That night, in a corridor outside the cell, several dozen prisoners were forced to run a gantlet past soldiers who clubbed them as they ran. As Doherty watched in horror, one inmate fell and was shot in the chest when he failed to rise. He died minutes later. By noon the following day, 153 prisoners, sleeping in shifts of three hours each on the concrete floor, occupied the cell. Next to Doherty was an Argentinian who had been seized the day before. His glass eye had been ripped from his face during interrogation and salt poured in the open wound.

For three days, Doherty languished in his cell, shut off from the sun, fed nothing but bread and water. On Wednesday, September 19, his captors removed him to the Stadium's outdoor soccer field for an hour of fresh air, and he was transferred to a smaller cell with eight prisoners. The following morning, at 4:00 A.M., Doherty was awakened by a series of shots coming from the far end of the Stadium. "Machine-gun fire lasted ten to fifteen minutes," he recalls, "after which I heard the sound of pistols. Then the machine-gun fire began again followed by more pistol shots. The pattern continued until 5:00 A.M." Later that day, six new prisoners were added to the cell. One of them told of witnessing mass executions in the Stadium that morning.

"Where in the Stadium?" Doherty asked.

The prisoner pointed in the direction of the earlier gunfire.

"How many people were executed?"

"Four hundred . . . five hundred . . . . What the hell do numbers mean? I don't think we'll be allowed to leave here alive after what we've seen."

That afternoon, Doherty was brought to a dimly lit room and seated at a plain wood table opposite a single interrogator.

"Your name?"

"Joseph Francis Doherty."

"Age?"

"Twenty-nine."

"Date of arrival in Chile?"

"July 28, 1973."

"Have you ever read or brought Marxist literature into Chile?"

"No, sir."

"Have you ever read or brought literature dealing with Che Guevara?"

"No, sir."

The interrogator stared hard at Doherty for a period of thirty seconds. "You are a priest," he said at last. "You are a leftist, and you are obviously lying."

Two days later, Doherty was recalled for a second interrogation. "I want you to tell me," his inquisitor asked, "if there is any compatibility between Marxism, Communism, and Christianity."

"I don't think I can answer that," Doherty told him. "I've studied theology and philosophy, not political science."

"You must have touched on Marxism in your studies. I will repeat the question, and I want you to answer it. Is there any compatibility between Marxism, Communism, and Christianity?"

His life hanging in the balance, Doherty responded: "One

must reject Marxism and Communism because their fundamental principle is class struggle. Christianity teaches love of neighbor, which is incompatible with class struggle."

The answer was satisfactory. Doherty was released four days later. In ten days of detention, he had lost twenty-six pounds.

Adam and Patricia Garrett-Schesch, students at the University of Wisconsin, arrived in Chile on November 2, 1970, to fulfill research requirements for their respective Ph.D. degrees. Three days after the coup, twenty Carabiñeros broke into their home and carried them to the National Stadium. Adam was severely beaten; both he and his wife were threatened with death. The threats assumed new urgency on Saturday, September 15, as Patricia sat on a low wall underneath the stands awaiting interrogation. Looking up a ramp, she saw a young man being led onto the soccer field by a military guard, who handed him a cigarette and left him standing alone near the end zone. Then a second prisoner was led out, followed by a third. The pattern continued until thirty-seven people stood on the field. Spontaneously, the group began to sing. Then, heavy fire from automatic weapons imposed a deadly silence.

That afternoon, Patricia was reunited with her husband. Adam recounts what followed as they stared at the interrogation rooms by their cell:

We saw several different kinds of lines we can find no words for but the "life" and "death" lines. Each time they were organized, the same sequence of events took place. One by one, prisoners would be brought to a registration booth. After a little paper work, they were put into one of two lines. One line was composed of people who had been given back their personal documents and possessions. They were usually allowed to leave their arms at their sides and were unguarded. The second line was formed by prisoners under heavy guard. This line would be led out and, within a few minutes, we would hear a heavy sustained outburst of automatic weapon fire from the stadium. None of the people in this line ever returned. From late Saturday afternoon through Tuesday evening, more than four hundred people were led out in this fashion.

101

On September 21, 1973, the Garrett-Schesches were released from custody without explanation. Still, the reign of terror continued.

Jim Ritter was a twenty-nine-year-old physicist educated at Princeton University, who moved to Chile in 1972 to accept a Professorship at Catholic University in Santiago. On September 23, 1973, he was arrested at his apartment in the presence of his four-year-old son.

"Ten soldiers came in with their submachine guns and started searching," Ritter recalls. "All my records . . . private correspondence . . . books . . . clothes. The officer in charge of the group wrote a number on my forearm in the style done to Jews in Nazi Germany. I was given two minutes to say good-bye to my son and marched out at gunpoint."

Ritter was taken to the Tacna Regiment headquarters and interrogated for three hours. Then he was loaded onto the back of a truck with a dozen other prisoners and the beating began:

We were told to lie down on our stomachs, hands clasped behind our necks, and to spread our legs. I assumed this was to prevent escape or something. Then they started beating us. First they would kick the Chilean on my left in the stomach five or six times, and his whole body would jump with each kick. Then you knew it was going to be your turn. They were going to kick you in the stomach and there was nothing you could do. Then they took the butts of the submachine guns and started hitting us on the back of the head and kidneys. Finally, one guy stomped very hard on my ankles, about ten times on each. Then he kicked me in the crotch.

Half an hour later, the beating ceased and Ritter was driven to the National Stadium. There, he realized how badly he was hurt: "They prodded us into the stadium with machine guns and stood us up against the wall. I couldn't stand up as well as I thought I could. I was really worried that if I slipped they might kill me."

Ritter was interrogated for three days. The savage beating of his first night was not repeated, but the work of his Chilean captors was evident on others: "I remember a worker being brought into our section. He had been beaten with a rubber hose filled with cement until his back was completely black. He couldn't move. We got a mattress for him and turned him over every couple of hours to prevent him from getting bedsores. We had to sit him up and feed him."

Like Joseph Doherty and the Garrett-Schesches, Ritter survived. Charles Horman would not.

Rafael Gonzalez was tired. A twenty-year veteran of the Chilean Intelligence Service, he had worked endlessly since the coup. On September 11, he had accompanied rebel troops inside the Moneda to collect papers from the office of Salvador Allende. He had seen the President dead, "his head wide open, some of his scalp on the back of the wall." Eventually, the days blurred, and Gonzalez all but lost track of time. "I didn't know when was Monday, Tuesday, Wednesday, or Saturday," he later recalled. "I worked like a dog, night and day. I didn't have time even for eating." For ten days, he had scarcely slept.

Gonzalez was politically unaffiliated. He had fulfilled his duties under a succession of governments and, when the Junta seized power, he obeyed its commands. Now he had been summoned to the office of General Augusto Lutz, Director of Army Intelligence, on the ninth floor of the Ministry of Defense.

"They called me because I was to act as interpreter," Gonzalez remembers. "An American was in the next room sitting. I heard that his name was Charles Horman, and I heard that he knew a lot."

Looking around the room, Gonzalez sensed that the meeting was important. With Lutz was Colonel Victor Hugo Barria, second in command of Chilean Army Intelligence. A third man, whom Gonzalez presumed to be an American because of his clothes, stood by but said nothing.

Lutz was brief and to the point. Charles Horman was a "special case." He had come recently from Valparaiso and "knew too much."

"He has to disappear," Lutz ordered.

PART TWO

CHAPTER XII

ED AND ELIZABETH HORMAN– SEPTEMBER, 1973

Elizabeth Horman rises from her chair and begins to walk through the modest New York apartment she and her husband have shared for thirty-eight years . . . one bedroom, a tiny kitchen, a small study that Charles once lived in, a living room with a table for dining lodged against the back wall. Outside, a small terrace is dotted with plants.

"Ed and I have been married for almost forty years, but I'll never forget those four weeks in autumn, 1973. I've tried, and I can't. What saw us through were our religious convictions and the trust and love we'd built up over a lifetime. I want to tell you a little about us so you'll understand.

"First, let me tell you about Ed. He's very tender and very tough. All through our marriage, I've been able to lean on him, but he's never kept me from standing on my own. He's extra-ordinarily knowledgeable, like an encyclopedia. He knows a lot about nature, animals, plants, things like that, but he never preaches or throws unwanted facts at you." She stops and smiles. "I could talk about Ed for days."

The object of Elizabeth's affection is a balding man of medium height with the word "decent" stamped all over him. His voice has a remarkably clear timbre that carries a ring of sturdy assurance. A thick fringe of gray hair and modest side-burns frame a face that is unusually round.

"Ed was thirty-one when we met," Elizabeth says. "I was slightly younger—how much so, I won't tell you. Both of us grew up in New York, but there were plenty of dissimilarities between us. I was an artist at heart and moved in slightly Bohemian circles. Long before we met, I had graduated from Barnard and begun teaching high school. I was a good teacher, but it was too much like sitting by the side of a river and watching the water flow. I wanted to flow with it, so I began taking courses at the Art Students League. It was the most wonderful experience of my life, just sitting there and drawing for hours, surrounded by people who loved to draw as much as I did." She pauses to reflect on what was certainly a difficult decision for a young woman in less liberated times. "Then I had a decision to make. I wanted to draw, but the question was could I do it and eat at the same time?"

After five years of teaching, Elizabeth began a career in art, which led ultimately to critical acclaim and her election as President of the National Association of Women Artists. "The best part of my early years professionally," she recalls, "were the murals I painted. One of them was a panoramic view of the New York skyline that was commissioned by the bar at India House in Manhattan, where no women were allowed. Needless to say, there was a problem when I showed up. Finally, they agreed to let me paint. I worked for three days, and they never offered me lunch. I felt like asking if they knew how badly I could mess up their wall. I was a mural painter when Ed and I met."

They were introduced at a Valentine's Day party in 1938. Ed had been invited because a young woman from the South was to be in attendance, and he had a known penchant for "Southern girls with Southern accents." Seated with his prospective date on one side, Ed found Elizabeth on the other. "That was it," Elizabeth recalls. They were married one year later, on February 3, 1939.

After the marriage, Ed joined Elizabeth as a student of Christian Science. Faith soon became paramount in his life as well as hers, and he has come to rely entirely on prayer for his health and general well-being. "I'll give you an example," Ed says. "Right before Charles was born, I dropped Elizabeth off at the hospital and drove to my office on Liberty Street. I had just climbed the stairs when my secretary announced, 'There was a phone call for you. You're a father.'" Ed smiles broadly and continues. "I got back in the car, very excited to say the least, and drove back to the hospital. When I got there, a doctor came out and said, 'I have bad news for you, Mr. Horman. Your son's feet are terribly misshapen. I don't know if anything can be done to help him.' Under Christian Science treatment, it all worked out." Ed's voice trails off. "Somehow, with Chile, we've failed to understand."

Those four weeks in autumn, 1973, are as deeply scarred on Ed's mind as on Elizabeth's. "At the time of the coup," he recalls, "we were in New York preparing to leave for a two-week vacation on Cape Cod. Naturally, when we learned about the coup, everything was put on hold. Then we heard from Terry's mother, who relayed the message from Viña that all was well. We waited another day and, when everything seemed all right, we left. We went to Cape Cod with a completely free feeling or we never would have gone."

The Hormans drove to Wellfleet at the north end of the Cape and began to enjoy the crisp autumn weather which New Englanders so love. On Tuesday, September 18, the evening news carried word that telephone communication with Chile had been reestablished. Charles and Joyce did not have a phone, but were generally reachable through a neighboring couple named Mario and Isabella Carvajal. That night, Ed tried to call them, but was told that a three-day backlog existed. On the morning of September 21, he tried again. The American operator did not speak Spanish, so Ed instructed her Chilean counterpart on his own. Finally, Isabella Carvajal came on the line, and Ed asked to speak with Charles.

"Charles and Joyce don't live in this neighborhood anymore," she answered.

"Where do they live?"

"I don't know."

"When did they move?"

There was no answer.

"Right then," Ed recalls, "I realized there was a serious problem. I hadn't known Charles and Joyce were moving from 425 Paul Harris but, under any circumstances, I would have expected the Carvajals to know where they were. They had been good friends, and Mario Carvajal had even helped write background music for Joyce's animated feature project, 'The Sunshine Grabber.' "

"Please connect me with the American Embassy," Ed instructed the operator. Long minutes later, a man identifying himself as United States Vice-Consul Dale Shaffer, came on the line. Ed introduced himself and asked if the Embassy had any knowledge concerning his son, Charles.

"All I know," Shaffer told him, "is that your son is missing. His house was ransacked by soldiers, and he's gone."

Ed's stomach tightened. "What about our daughter-in-law?"

"She's been giving us a lot of trouble," Shaffer answered. "She's really pestering us."

"I couldn't believe what I was hearing," Ed remembers. "Here I was, asking about a missing son with the Embassy unable to tell me where he was, and Shaffer was complaining about Joyce being a pest." The conversation dragged on for several minutes with Shaffer offering no additional information. His face white, Ed hung up the phone. Elizabeth had been at his side in anticipation of talking with Charles. She heard fully one end of the conversation.

"It's probably not too serious," he reassured her. "My guess is that Charles was arrested by accident in some sort of dragnet, and it's just a matter of time before they sort people out and he's released. They wouldn't harm an American." He tried to smile but was unable. "We'd better go home to New York," he said at last, "and set up some sort of base for communications."

The three-hundred-mile drive from Cape Cod to New York took seven hours. Shortly before dusk, they arrived home and

Ed telephoned the Washington office of Senator Jacob Javits. Javits was out of town, but an aide promised to contact him and suggested that, in the interim, Ed telephone the Bureau of Special Consular Services at the Department of State. Doing so immediately, Ed was transferred to Charles Anderson at the Bureau's "Chile Crisis Desk." Their conversation lasted until 6:00 P.M., after which further calls to State Department officials and members of Congress proved futile. Most of official Washington had gone home for the weekend.

Thus began a vigil that lasted well into October. Ed in the bedroom by the telephone; Elizabeth and her sister Ruth hosting well-intentioned visitors and making certain there was food at home. On Monday, September 24, Ed learned from the morning news that a young American couple named Adam and Patricia Garrett-Schesch had been released from the National Stadium in Santiago and were returning to the United States. Tracking them down by telephone at the home of Patricia's parents in Virginia, he asked if they could offer any advice regarding Charles's welfare.

"Contact the most important people you can," Adam told him, "and have them send cablegrams to the American Embassy in Santiago. American pressure is the best way to get your son home alive."

That afternoon, Ed began telephoning one public figure after another. "I was desperate," he recalls. "With each call, I tried to be as brief as possible, since one seldom has an unlimited audience with the powerful. I simply introduced myself over the phone, stated my problem, and asked for help."

The list of notables who offered support to the Horman cause is impressive. Dozens of Senators and Congressmen sent cablegrams on Charles's behalf. So too did Harvard President Derek Bok and McGeorge Bundy, Chairman of the Ford Foundation. Ed tried to reach Arthur Ochs Sulzberger, publisher of the *New York Times,* but could not get through Sulzberger's secretary. Temporarily frustrated, he called the paper a second time and asked to speak with Harrison Salisbury, one of several Pulitzer-

Prize-winning reporters on the *Times* staff. Unlike Sulzberger, Salisbury came on the line.

"You don't know me," Ed told him, "but I need your help. My name is Ed Horman. My son Charles has been arrested without cause by the military in Chile, and I've been told that his safety may well hinge on the number of influential people who send cablegrams to the American Embassy in Santiago on his behalf. All I want is for you to send one cable asking that his welfare be given high priority. Will you do that for me?"

"Hell, yes," Salisbury answered.

Two years later, while crossing Third Avenue in Manhattan, Ed recognized a face he had seen on television several times. "Excuse me," he said, approaching Harrison Salisbury. "We've never met, but I want to thank you for a favor you once did for me."

"What was that?"

Ed told him.

"I'm sorry," Salisbury answered, "that we weren't more successful."

On Tuesday, September 25, Ed brought his plea for assistance directly to Washington. Boarding an early morning shuttle flight, he went to the offices of Senators Jacob Javits, Henry Jackson, Charles Percy, and Warren Magnuson, all of whom promised to send cables to Santiago. Representatives Edward Koch, Bella Abzug, Ed Medzvinsky, and Jack Kemp also agreed to help. The Washington trip offered hope, but it also produced one particularly disturbing moment. Congressman Robert McClory of Illinois was among the Congressmen Ed had counted on most for support. Both McClory and his wife were Christian Scientists and, when Ed had been Superintendent of the Third Church of Christian Science Sunday School in New York, Mrs. McClory had worked with him.

"I went to McClory's office confident that he would assist me," Ed recalls. "I told him what had happened and asked if he would send a cable on Charles's behalf."

The expected sympathetic response was not forthcoming. "What are your son's political opinions?" McClory queried.

Ed stared, dumbfounded at the suggestion that politics might play a role in determining whether McClory would try to help save his son's life. No matter what Charles's involvement at home or in Chile, it could hardly stand in the way of a simple cable asking the American Embassy to ascertain whether he was dead or alive and see that his rights were protected.

"He's a liberal," Ed answered. "But by no means radical. All I'm asking is that you do what a number of other members of Congress have already done."

"Well," McClory told him, "I will have to consider this very carefully before I act."

McClory eventually sent the cable and worked wholeheartedly on Charles's behalf. Later, during House Judiciary Committee hearings on the impeachment of Richard Nixon, he was to earn Ed's full respect. But, in September, 1973, the import of the Congressman's remarks was clear. Even so fundamental an issue as the protection of an American life could not be totally divorced from partisan politics.

Two days after Ed's visit to Washington, Charles Anderson of the Bureau of Special Consular Services telephoned the Horman home. "Our Embassy people have looked into the matter," he said, "and have found no sign of your son. Neither they nor the government of Chile know where he is. Our feeling is that Charles is probably in hiding because of his left-wing views and will surface when things calm down."

Anderson's statement was troubling, largely because it contradicted what Ed and Elizabeth had already learned. Several days earlier, the *New York Times* had printed a dispatch from a reporter in Chile, which included the following information attributed to Joyce:

She said neighbors told her the military had come two or three times to her home on Monday night . . . . Friends said that the Chilean Military Intelligence Service had called them to get information about Charles.

113

If the *Times* dispatch was true, then Charles was most likely not in hiding. He was probably in the hands of the Chilean military, and the American Embassy was either ignorant or doing nothing about it. "I remember being very puzzled by Anderson's remarks," Ed says, "but I assumed he was acting in good faith. It never occurred to me that our government might be deliberately camouflaging Charles's fate. When he told me that my son was in hiding, I assumed our Embassy in Santiago and the Department of State simply hadn't had time to coordinate all of the information at hand. I was upset at their apparent lack of efficiency, but I took it in stride. The last thing I wanted to do was lash out at someone and say, 'Listen, you son of a bitch, this is my son.' I was prepared to take any kind of guff to avoid stirring up some bureaucrat who might substitute petty revenge for Charles's best interests."

Ed's voice lowers. "One week after we learned that Charles was missing, Elizabeth and I had no choice but to face the possibility that something unspeakable had happened. Still, it was hard for us to believe that a foreign government would execute an American citizen. And it was inconceivable to us that our own government might have been directly involved."

CHAPTER XIII

JOYCE HORMAN– ELEVEN DAYS IN SANTIAGO

September 17–18, 1973

After leaving Charles and Terry at the bus station on September 17, Joyce had spent the better part of the day visiting friends to make sure they were well. By late afternoon, she wanted to return home, but transportation was unavailable. The buses wouldn't stop. Like everyone else, their drivers were racing to get home ahead of curfew. The collectivos were full.

Realizing she would be unable to reach Vicuña Mackenna before dark, Joyce began walking towards the Santiago apartment of two friends. The streets were teeming with troops, hundreds of Chileans rushing by. She was aware of standing out as a foreigner . . . the only woman in sight with Scandinavian features and blond hair.

Joyce's friends were not home, and she sat by the front door to wait. At six o'clock, she realized that they too had been caught in the curfew and would not be coming home. It was cold, and she had no coat. The neighbors were unwilling to let her in, refusing to open their doors to a strange foreigner. She spent the night huddled in the stairwell, praying that soldiers would not come by and hoping that Charles would not be too worried about her.

Tuesday morning, when curfew lifted, thousands of troops

launched a parade in celebration of Chilean Independence Day. Tanks rolled past the Moneda, with soldiers laughing and waving multicolored red, white, and blue flags. Joyce threaded her way home through the streets, arriving at 8:30 A.M. Opening the door, she stopped in shock. The house was in shambles. Books were strewn across the floor, Charles's desk was upended, and cushions had been ripped from the furniture. Sheets were torn from the bed and bureau drawers dumped out. No corner had been left unsearched.

A knock on the door broke the silence. Joyce looked up as a tall man entered. "Excuse me," he said, "I am the owner of several buildings in the neighborhood. Last night, soldiers were here several times. You must go now for your own safety before they return."

She nodded. Charles had probably been caught in the curfew too. Most likely, while she froze at the top of a stairwell, he had spent the night with a friend. She picked a sheet of paper up off the floor, and penned a short note, saying she would be at the home of Hector and Carlotta Manosa—friends in downtown Santiago. Then, after leaving it by the front door where Charles would find it, she left. Upon arriving at the Manosas' in late morning, she telephoned several friends in an effort to locate her husband. The last person she called was Mario Carvajal.

"I don't want to talk over the telephone," he told her. "Could you come here now?"

Joyce hung up the phone and readied to go, but Mrs. Manosa intervened. "You can't travel. You haven't slept in over a day. Our son will go instead." Agreeing reluctantly, Joyce went to sleep on a cot in the Manosas' extra bedroom. When she awoke, it was night. Hector Manosa was by her side.

"I have news that is difficult to accept," he told her. "The Carvajals have received a telephone call from Military Intelligence. Charles is in custody. His captors have demanded certain information about him. They say that he is an extremist."

Joyce's vision began to blur.

"I am sorry," he said. "My wife has telephoned a friend at

your Consulate and reported everything. It's after curfew. There is nothing more we can do tonight."

September 19, 1973

By morning, Joyce's fears had doubled. If Charles was in military custody, Terry could be too. When curfew lifted, she went directly to the American Consulate.

"I'd like to speak with someone who can help me," she told the receptionist. "My husband has been seized by the Chilean military."

"Is he registered with us?"

"I don't know."

"What's his name?"

"Charles Horman."

The receptionist began thumbing through a box of cards. "He never registered. Take this card and fill it out for him." Joyce completed the form and handed it back. "I'll see if someone can speak with you. Please sit over there."

Joyce took a seat by the door, and waited. Several minutes later, a nondescript-looking man appeared. "I'm Vice-Consul John Hall," he said. "Consul Purdy is busy at the moment. What seems to be the problem?"

Joyce explained Charles's seizure, and Hall listened impassively.

"Was there anything in the house that might have irritated the soldiers?" he asked when she had finished.

"Nothing."

"Are you certain?"

"Yes . . . with one exception."

"What was that?"

"About a year ago, Charles did some research on the assassination of General Schneider. Some of his material was at home."

117

Hall raised his eyebrows. "Where did he get his information?"

"Mostly from documents on file in the Public Library."

"What exactly did he write?"

"I'm not too familiar with it. Charles was more knowledgeable about Chilean politics than I am."

Hall began scribbling notes on a four-by-six-inch index card. "What else can you tell me about this research on the Schneider assassination?"

"Nothing."

The Vice-Consul finished writing and glanced up from his notes. "Where can you be reached for the next few days, Mrs. Horman?"

"Aren't I staying here?"

"Good heavens, no! We have no accommodations."

Confused and flustered, Joyce buried her face in her hands. "I have no place to go. . . . Do you have an address for someone named Terry Simon?"

Hall went to the registration card file and returned moments later. "She's at the Riviera Hotel."

Terry was bored. Since visiting the American Consulate two days earlier, she had been cooped up in a hotel. Now, she was eagerly awaiting Charles's arrival. At least then she'd have company. One o'clock passed . . . 2:00 P.M. . . . 3:00 P.M. It was unlike Charles to keep someone waiting this long. She considered going down to the lobby but discarded the idea for fear she would miss him if he called. With nothing better to do, she began rearranging her suitcase for the third time. A knock sounded.

"At last," she said, opening the door. "What kept. . . . " Her words broke off in midsentence. Standing in front of her, looking very much like death, was Joyce.

"What's the matter?"

Joyce lurched into the room and fell forward onto the bed. "Charles has been taken," she said, curling into a near-fetal position.

"Taken?"

"Arrested . . . by the military."

Terry draped an arm around her, and Joyce began to cry. It took an hour, broken by intermittent sobbing, for her to recount what had happened.

"There's someone who might be able to help," Terry suggested. "Ray Davis told me to get in touch if I had any trouble. Do you want me to call him?"

"I suppose so."

Davis was not at his office. Terry left her telephone number with a secretary and waited with Joyce until the call was returned. "Was this reported to Fred Purdy?" Davis asked after Terry told him what had happened.

"No, to a Mr. Hall."

"Purdy is in charge of the Consulate. I'll get in touch with him tomorrow. Was Charles involved in anything that might explain his arrest?"

"No."

"Did he have any weapons in the house?"

"No."

"Was he affiliated with any political party?"

"No."

"All right," Davis instructed. "I want you and Joyce to come to my office at the Embassy first thing tomorrow morning."

"What time is first thing?"

"Anytime after nine. And look! You have to remember, the situation in Chile is very confused right now. Sometimes these things take time . . . a lot of time."

September 20–21, 1973

Joyce awoke at dawn in a tiny hotel room with Terry at her side. The room was stuffy and her head ached. The periodic eruption of gunfire had kept her awake for most of the night. Putting on the same clothes she had worn since Charles's seizure three days earlier, she drank two cups of coffee and proceeded with Terry to the American Embassy. Davis arrived shortly after they did and ushered them inside his office. There, Terry introduced Joyce, who repeated everything she knew about Charles's disappearance. When she finished, Davis mulled the problem over.

"I'm friends with Admiral Huidobro of the Chilean Navy," he said at last. "Let me see what he knows about this." He picked up the telephone, and Terry made a mental note of the Admiral's name. Huidobro was the man Patrick Ryan had brought to the United States in July to purchase military supplies.

"The Admiral is busy," Davis announced, "but he'll stop by my house for a drink sometime this evening. I think you two should be there when he comes."

"What about curfew?" Joyce asked.

"That's no problem. I have plenty of room. You can stay for the night."

"Wouldn't it be better if we were at the hotel in case someone calls with news of Charles?"

"Take the day to think it over," Davis told her. "But, like I said, it would be better if you spoke with Huidobro yourself. And besides, I'll be called in the event anything develops."

Laying the issue aside, Joyce raised another question. "I have no clothes. Is there someone who can take me home and wait while I pull some things together?"

Checking with an aide to make certain that the Vicuña Mackenna neighborhood was militarily secure, Davis volunteered for duty himself. Accompanied by three Chilean soldiers, he drove Joyce and Terry home and waited while Joyce gathered some belongings.

"I'll drop the two of you off at the hotel," Davis told them as they reentered his car. "Then I'm going to a party at the Ambassador's residence. I expect to be home by five o'clock this evening." He looked towards them. "I still think it would be advantageous if you came for dinner and met Huidobro. If you want to do what's best for Charles, you'll come."

Viewed in that light, there was no other option. Back at the hotel, Joyce and Terry packed a small overnight bag, and left for Davis's residence an hour before curfew. His house was enormous, surrounded by a well-manicured lawn and thick stone wall. As they pressed a buzzer at the driveway gate, a maid exited from a side door and began walking towards them. Just before she reached the halfway point, Davis appeared in the main doorway and motioned her aside, indicating that he would escort the company in himself.

"It's time for the news from Panama," he announced after greeting his guests. "Come on upstairs." Leading them to a small room on the second floor, he turned on a large radio and began to listen. "Damn it!," he said, halfway through the broadcast. "They still don't understand what's happening in Chile. The military is getting bad press, and it's not fair."

When the news ended, he walked his guests downstairs. "These are my children," he said, pointing to a picture of an attractive teenage son and daughter. "Unfortunately, we're not together anymore." He paused, then picked the conversation up again. "I'm something of an art collector too, as you can see from these things around the house."

Joyce admired several pieces of Oriental art. "I was an art history major in college," she told him.

"At the University of Minnesota, wasn't it?" Davis responded.

Terry stiffened. Neither she or Charles had told Davis anything about Joyce's background. Whatever his source of information, it was from the outside.

"Come on into the living room for a drink," Davis instructed.

"Just sherry for me," Joyce told him. Terry accepted a glass of scotch, and their host mixed a large pitcher of martinis for himself, placing it on an end table within easy reach. "I don't understand why people are so steamed up about the coup," he said. "Everyone knew it was coming." He turned to Joyce. "You've been living here for a year. Didn't you know there'd be a coup?"

"It seemed likely," she answered. "But I didn't think it would be so violent."

"Then you just didn't understand what was happening down here. The military had to protect itself. When a person is backed into a corner, he lashes out with all the power he can muster."

A maid appeared and told Davis he was wanted on the telephone. Excusing himself, he left the room and returned moments later. "That was Admiral Huidobro," he announced. "He won't be able to come tonight after all."

Joyce sagged. The sole purpose of the evening had been to meet Huidobro. Now she and Terry were stuck with a man who made them extremely uncomfortable, and they were away from the hotel where someone might call with news of Charles.

"Dinner is ready," the maid announced.

Gathering his pitcher of martinis in one hand and a glass in the other, Davis led them to a table set with sterling silver, cut crystal, and expensive china. "How old are you?" he asked Terry as they were seated.

"I'll be twenty-nine tomorrow."

"In that case, a birthday celebration is in order."

Terry winced. Davis was treating the evening as a purely social occasion. He seemed to have forgotten why his guests were there. "Thanks, but I don't feel much like celebrating," she answered. "When we get Charles back, we can all celebrate."

Dinner consisted of turkey, salad, fresh vegetables, wine, and crème custard with caramel syrup for dessert—this in a country where housewives stood in line for hours to buy a loaf of bread. Joyce kept turning the conversation back to Charles. She desperately wanted Davis to know what a good person her husband was and how much she loved him.

"Just remember," Davis told her, "you have to stay ahead of the power curve."

"I don't understand," Joyce replied.

"It's a saying they have on aircraft carriers. If a pilot comes in ahead of the power curve, he can pull up and out safely if something goes wrong. If he falls behind the curve and something happens, he'll crash into the ship. You always have to look out for yourself and stay ahead of the power curve."

At the close of dinner, he offered his guests another drink. They declined. "Is there anything else you'd like?" he asked, pouring himself a glass of brandy.

"Only Charles," Joyce told him.

"Relax and don't worry about it. Are you sure you don't need toothpaste or soap or anything like that?"

"No, thank you."

"Okay. I'll take you to your rooms."

Lifting himself from his chair, Davis led his guests upstairs. At a large hall closet, he stopped. "Take anything you want," he urged, opening the door to reveal a collection of Johnson & Johnson baby powder, Colgate toothpaste, and a myriad of other drugstore items that were virtually unattainable in Chile. "Whatever you want, take it . . . . Okay, it's your loss if you don't want anything."

"This room is yours," he told Terry when they reached the middle of the hall. "I'll show you the inside." Leading her through the door, he strode past a large bed and dressing area into the bathroom. "You look tired," he said, turning on the bath water and pouring some liquid soap into the tub. "A bubble bath will do you good."

Then he left. Terry followed him to the door and locked it behind him, turning the tasseled gold key firmly to the side. Back in the bathroom, she undressed, turned off the water, and lowered herself into the tub. Charles was missing, quite possibly because he had taken her to Viña. In a country where people were literally starving, she had just gorged herself at dinner, during which time dozens of people had probably been shot. Crumpling a washcloth in her hands, she began to cry. The outer bedroom door opened.

"Oh God," she thought. "It's Joyce. I can't let her see me crying."

The bathroom door opened. Terry looked up and saw Ray Davis standing over her.

"Do you have everything you need?" he asked.

"I'm okay," she told him.

Davis walked past the tub and looked down at her.

"Captain Davis," she said, "I'm very tired, and Joyce and I are under a lot of pressure. I appreciate everything you've done for us, but I would like you to leave."

Without further conversation, Davis turned and walked out the door. Feeling terribly alone and vulnerable, Terry climbed from the tub, dried herself, and slipped into her nightgown. "I have to see Joyce," she thought. "Someone has to tell me that everything will be all right."

Very quietly, she opened the door to her room and peered down the empty hall. A light shone out from underneath Joyce's door. Adjusting her eyes to the dark, Terry walked towards it. "It's me," she whispered, knocking on the door. "Open up." There was no answer. "It's me," she said again, pressing her face forward. "Are you there?" Still no response.

Terry turned the handle and walked inside. The bedroom was empty. Crossing past the bed to the adjacent bathroom, she opened that door too. Huddled against the far wall, Joyce stood sobbing, her arms squeezed across her chest.

"Was he here too?" Terry asked.

Joyce nodded.

———⌄———

Davis was gone when the two women awoke on Friday. Shortly afterwards, an Embassy driver appeared and announced that he had been instructed to take them back to the Riviera Hotel. Joyce demurred, asking to revisit Vicuña Mackenna, where she might talk with neighbors who had witnessed Charles's arrest. Bowing to her demand, the driver dropped Terry off first, then drove Joyce to the home of Dr. Nuñez, the Hormans' landlord.

"I did not see your husband arrested," the doctor told her. "But I spoke with someone who did. Charles was taken by soldiers to the National Stadium."

"How do you know?"

"A woman followed in a car."

"Can I speak with her?"

"I will ask, but she is very frightened. I can promise nothing."

The home of Mario and Isabella Carvajal was next. "On the morning of September 18," Isabella told her, "we received a telephone call from Military Intelligence. They said that Charles was an extremist and demanded to know why he used our telephone. I told them that you were good neighbors and had no telephone of your own." Isabella trembled on the verge of tears. "Charles is not an extremist, but we are all in great danger. This man said that if Mario and I lied to him, we would lose our lives."

That night, Ed Horman telephoned from New York. "Elizabeth and I learned about Charles's seizure when we telephoned Santiago this morning," he told Joyce. "We're doing everything possible at this end to save him. Is there anything more we should know?"

"I don't think so," she answered. "The Embassy will relay whatever details you don't already have to Washington. That's safer than talking on the phone."

"All right. If you need any more help, you might contact James Goodsell. He's the Latin American reporter for the *Christian Science Monitor,* and I've known him a long time. He's in Santiago now at the Carerra Hotel."

Joyce scribbled Goodsell's name and address on a piece of paper.

"Take care of yourself," Ed urged. "And remember, we want you healthy and well when Charles comes home."

September 22–23, 1973

More than anyone else Charles had been friendly with in Chile, he trusted Steve Volk. The two met in late 1972 at the offices of FIN. Steve was a former Fulbright Scholar who had returned to Chile to complete his doctoral dissertation for Columbia University. Living with his wife in Santiago, he spent nine hours a day in the municipal archives researching nineteenth-century class development in Chile's northern mining region. Nights, he joined Charles and a dozen other Americans at the FIN office to compile the weekly review of North American news.

Five days after Charles's seizure, Joyce and Terry turned to Steve for advice. No constructive response had been forthcoming from the American Embassy or Consulate, and the Viña revelations weighed heavily on their minds. Inviting him to their room at the Riviera Hotel, Terry showed him her notes. "It was," Volk recalls, "a moment of incredible tension . . . as though someone had handed me the key to Pandora's Box. All the clues to American involvement in the coup were there. What was even more extraordinary, though, was the way Terry handled the situation. Joyce was falling apart. I had the feeling that she could collapse mentally at any moment, but Terry was calmer than any of us. She just sat there and kept asking, 'What's the best thing to do? Where do we go from here?' And her notes were unbelievably thorough."

"What now?" Terry asked when Steve had finished reading her notebook.

"It's been five days since Charles was taken," he said. "Let's visit the Consulate and see what they're doing." He smiled ruefully. "My guess is they're not doing very much. Today is Saturday."

His prediction was accurate. Despite the seizure and imprisonment of over a dozen Americans, the Consulate was virtually empty. Two Chilean secretaries and Consul Purdy were the only persons on duty. After they had waited for several minutes, the senior secretary motioned Joyce inside. Terry and Steve remained in the reception area.

"What can I do for you, Mrs. Horner?" Purdy inquired when Joyce was seated.

"Horman," she said, correcting the mispronunciation.

"That's right. I'm sorry. What can I do for you, Mrs. Horman?"

Joyce looked across the desk at the man who was legally responsible for the welfare of American citizens in Chile. Purdy had dark blond hair, sharp features, and a Southern military air which had probably served him well through fourteen years in the foreign service, the last three as head of the American Consulate in Santiago.

"I'd like to know the status of your efforts to find my husband."

"Oh yes. I understand from Mr. Hall that he disappeared on September 10, and you reported him missing on the nineteenth. Is that correct?"

Joyce was seized by a mixture of fear and anger. "Charles was arrested by soldiers on the seventeenth," she answered. "It's extremely imaginative of Mr. Hall to think that he was picked up by the military before the coup and I waited nine days to report it."

"I see, Mrs. Horman. Well, we're working on it."

"Have you been to the National Stadium to look for him?"

"Not exactly, but his name hasn't shown up on the prisoner computer lists released by the military. Do you have any other questions?"

Several awkward minutes later, Purdy walked Joyce back to the reception area, where Terry and Steve were waiting. "There is one other item that might help," the Consul suggested. "Could you give me your husband's passport number?"

Joyce stopped short. "Haven't you people coordinated anything? My husband has been missing for five days. I gave the passport number to Ray Davis on Thursday."

"Look, Mrs. Horner," Purdy shot back, "you can read whatever you want into this, but I'm doing the best I can. I haven't had a good lunch with my friends for eleven days. I missed my baby's birthday on the eighteenth, and I worked late two nights this week. If you don't like the job we're doing, you can go somewhere else for help."

Verging on emotional collapse, Joyce staggered from the Consulate, Terry and Steve Volk propping her up on either side.

"I don't know what to do," she sobbed. "I don't understand anything anymore. Why aren't they helping?"

"Pull yourself together," Terry urged.

"What do you want me to do?"

"I want you to keep trying." Terry was groping for something constructive to suggest. "Look," she said at last. "Let's visit the reporter for the *Christian Science Monitor* Ed mentioned last night. What's his name?"

"Goodsell."

"He's at the Carerra, isn't he?"

"I think so."

Taking a collectivo across town, they proceeded to the hotel lobby and came face to face with Ray Davis. "Hello," he said, looking somewhat embarrassed. "How are you?"

"Not so good," Joyce told him, fighting to keep her composure. "I just had a very unpleasant session with Fred Purdy."

"I know. He called to tell me about it."

"We were probably both very tired," she said.

"Maybe so. What are you doing at the Carerra?"

"We came to see James Goodsell."

Davis furrowed up his brow. "He's a reporter, isn't he?"

"Yes."

"Be careful about what you say to reporters. They can get you in trouble. And they won't help Charles much either."

Goodsell was not in his room, and the rest of the day passed uneventfully. The following morning, Terry went to Steve Volk's apartment and typed a summary of her notes from Viña. When they had finished, Steve folded the paper and inserted it in the base of a tube of chapstick. That night, as Terry and Joyce readied for bed, a tank rolled up to the Riviera and troops poured into the hotel. Fearing arrest, Terry tore the incriminating original pages from her notebook and flushed them down the toilet. The soldiers passed their door without incident. As she and Joyce went to sleep, gunfire sounded in the night.

September 24, 1973

"I thought of something important," Terry said when they woke up the next morning. "If Charles is in custody, I hope they have a newsstand in the National Stadium."

Her attempt at humor fell flat. "He's been gone a week," Joyce answered, "and I'm frightened. I want to go back to the Consulate and see if anything new has happened."

For the third time in as many visits, a different Consulate official spoke with them.

"I'm Vice-Consul Dale Shaffer," a light-haired, slightly overweight man announced. "Let's go inside where we can talk."

Joyce and Terry followed him to his office, and Shaffer began flipping through a series of four-by-six-inch index cards. "So far, we haven't had any luck," he said, looking down at the notes. "You might try contacting the Dutch Embassy. I understand that they've been able to send a representative into the National Stadium. Maybe they'll know something about your husband."

"I don't understand," Joyce told him. "Why can't you do something like that?" Terry wasn't listening. Her attention was focused on another item. "Could I see those notecards?" she asked.

Shaffer glanced up, surprised at the request. "I suppose so," he answered, handing them over.

One by one, Terry flipped through the cards as Joyce peered over her shoulder:

> Charles Edmund Horman
> wife Joyce
> address 4126 Vicuña Mackenna
> . . . .

A sloppily written entry caught her eye: "Journalist—working [illegible] extremist."

"What's this?" Terry asked, reading the phrase aloud.

"Oh," Shaffer answered. "That must refer to the Viaux-Schneider case. The people who killed General Schneider were extremists."

Not wholly convinced, the two women read on:

> Reported detained by friend of M.T. Perez de Arce
> 9/18/73

The "friend," Joyce knew, was Carlotta Manosa. De Arce was the Consulate employee whom Carlotta had called. Suddenly, she realized that when she spoke with Hall on the nineteenth, he never mentioned that Charles had already been reported missing. "Hector told me his wife had done it," she thought, "but Hall never said a word." She read on:

> Another [illegible] re Horman called in by Warwick
> Armstrong.

"Jesus," Joyce thought. "No one told me anything about that." Concealing her surprise, she read through the remaining cards and watched as Terry handed them back to Shaffer.

"There's one other possibility you might consider, Mrs. Horman."

"What's that?"

"Your husband might be in hiding because he doesn't want to see you."

"That's impossible, Mr. Shaffer," she answered.

Out on the street, Joyce had a new sense of direction.

"Where are you going?" Terry asked.

"To talk with Warwick Armstrong."

"I saw the card, but who is he?"

"A Regional Development Advisor for the United Nations. His wife and I met last fall in a Spanish class at the North American Institute. We've kept in touch ever since. Charles and Warwick were friends."

Joyce was greeted warmly by Armstrong when she arrived. "I'll tell you everything I know," he said. "My wife and I own a house in Nuñoa which we rent to a Frenchman. Last Tuesday morning, the eighteenth, he received a telephone call from the military. The caller mistook him for me. Naturally, he relayed the message as soon as the conversation ended."

"What did the military say?"

Armstrong shifted uncomfortably. "That an American friend had asked me to speak on his behalf, and I should go immediately to a nearby Carabiñeros station. When the Frenchman asked for the American's name, the caller told him only that the friend makes films. That could only have been Charles. I reported the call to the Consulate right away. I tried to reach you too, but I couldn't find you."

Leaving the Armstrongs' home, Joyce proceeded to the American Embassy. "I'd like to speak with Ray Davis," she demanded.

Davis came out to the reception area. After reporting what she had just learned, Joyce asked for the use of his driver and car.

"What for?" he queried.

"I want to visit the Dutch Embassy and possibly the National Stadium."

"Help yourself," he told her. "I'm always willing to offer any assistance possible."

An employee at the Dutch Embassy informed Joyce that she had been misled. No Dutch official had been allowed admission to the National Stadium. Acting out a last chance hope, she instructed the driver to take her to the Stadium itself. The entrance was barricaded by a phalanx of troops, her plea for admission denied.

"Can I at least see a list of prisoners' names?" she pleaded.

"Absolutely not," a guard answered.

Ray Davis telephoned her at the Riviera hotel that night. "Could Charles have been involved in some sort of political activity without your knowing it?" he asked.

"That's totally impossible."

"You sound more sure of yourself than you should be," he cautioned. "Did you ever read about the most famous Russian spy who ever lived?"

"No."

"Well, his wife didn't know what he was doing either."

"That," Joyce shot back, "doesn't say much for their relationship."

"Look," Davis told her with a modicum of irritation creeping into his voice, "you're an intelligent, young, pretty girl with your whole life ahead of you. Look forward, not back."

Joyce bit her lip. The words sounded very much like a declaration that Charles was dead.

"Don't forget," Davis added, "if there's anything more I can do for you, be sure to let me know."

September 25–27, 1973

Tuesday the twenty-fifth passed without incident. At noon the following day, Joyce walked to the Embassy and demanded to see United States Ambassador Nathaniel P. Davis. She went with great trepidation. Davis's reputation had preceded him to Chile. Born in Boston, like Charles a graduate of Exeter, he had joined the Foreign Service in 1947. In 1968, he was named Ambassador to Guatemala, where he was alleged to have supervised a "pacification program" that resulted in the deaths of twenty thousand opponents of Guatemala's right-wing regime. In October, 1971, shortly after Salvador Allende announced that Kennecott and Anaconda would not be compensated for their Chilean copper holdings, Davis replaced Edward Korry as Ambassador to Chile. Joyce expected little sympathy from him, but she knew that, by virtue of his position, Nathaniel Davis was one of the most powerful men in Chile. She felt he could help . . . if he wanted to.

Entering the Embassy, Joyce went directly to the reception desk. "The Ambassador's line is busy," she was told. "If you'd like, I'll leave word with his secretary that you wish to speak with him."

Joyce nodded and took a seat. Fifteen minutes later, she asked if the number could be rung again. "I'm terribly sorry," the receptionist said. "There's been a mix-up. The Ambassador just left his office and won't be back for another twenty minutes." Wearily, Joyce went to the canteen for a cup of coffee, then proceeded to Davis's office on her own. Several minutes later, the Ambassador appeared in the doorway.

"How do you do?" he asked in a resonant voice. "I understand that Captain Ray Davis has been working on your problem. Do you mind if he joins us?"

"It makes no difference," Joyce answered.

Buzzing his secretary, the Ambassador instructed that Ray Davis be sent in. When he arrived, the Ambassador asked for a status report on the case.

"Well," Captain Davis responded, "I've made inquiries with my friends in the Chilean military, and none of them have heard of Charles Horman. His name hasn't appeared on any of the prisoner lists released at the National Stadium. We're checking out all possible leads, but so far we haven't come up with anything."

Nathaniel Davis leaned back in his chair, hands clasped behind a mane of thick white hair.

"Is there anything more you would like us to do, Mrs. Horman?"

"I understand that Ambassadors from other countries have gone to the National Stadium in person and gotten their people out. I would very much appreciate it if you did the same thing, or arranged for someone else from the Embassy to search there for my husband."

"We really can't do that, Mrs. Horman," the Ambassador answered. "If we ask special favors of the ruling forces, everyone else will want them too. That might damage our relations with the new government."

"I don't understand," Joyce responded, her voice trembling. "Why can't someone from the Embassy go to the National Stadium and look for my husband?"

A patronizing look crossed the Ambassador's face. "Just what do you want us to do—look under all the bleachers and into every corner?"

"That's exactly what I want you to do, and I see nothing wrong with it."

"I'm sorry, Mrs. Horman. You'll have to be more patient."

When the meeting ended, Ray Davis drove Joyce back to the Riviera Hotel. "Remember," he urged, "if I can do anything more to help, let me know."

Back in their room, Joyce reported to Terry on her latest encounter. "Look," Terry said, "we're getting the grand stall. Charles has been missing for nine days, and, outside of bubble baths and dinner, we haven't gotten a thing from the Consulate or Embassy. No one is helping. One of us has to go back to New York and tell Ed what's happening. The best way to save Charles might be through pressure on Washington."

"You'll have to go," Joyce told her. "I'm not leaving Chile until Charles is located."

Santiago had been reopened to air travel several days earlier. Late on the afternoon of September 27, Terry took a collectivo to Pudahuel International Airport. Passing through a screen of barbed wire and several trenches which had been dug on the day of the coup, she boarded a Braniff plane for the long flight home. The past two weeks had been the most difficult of her life, and things threatened to become still worse. Hours before her departure, she had spoken with Fred Purdy on the telephone for the last time. "There's only one more thing to do," the Consul had said. "I'm going to check the morgue."

CHAPTER XIV

WAITING

In New York, Ed and Elizabeth Horman were guided by two considerations—Charles's welfare and the desire to spare each other as much suffering as possible. As devoted spouses, they were bearing up with tremendous strength, but the pressure of events continued to mount.

On the morning of September 28, Ed telephoned Charles Anderson at the Bureau of Special Consular Services and asked to meet with him that afternoon. Arriving in the nation's capital, he went directly to the State Department's Chile Crisis Desk, where the diplomat was waiting with a press spokeswoman named Kate Marshall.

"We still think your son is in hiding," Anderson reported, "or perhaps concealing himself in a mass of prisoners. In any event, we have no real leads to go on."

"What exactly is being done to find him?" Ed pressed.

"Our Embassy is in regular contact with the Chilean military. We know of several Americans who were arrested and then released as a result of our efforts. In fact, one of them, a fellow named Frank Teruggi, was released just three days ago."

"That's right," Marshall added. "And he never even stopped by the Embassy to say thank you."

Ed looked across the table. "How do you know he was released?"

"The Junta told us," Anderson explained. "He was arrested on the twentieth. They told us on the twenty-fourth that he was in custody at the National Stadium, and he was released a day later."

"I'd like to talk with him," Ed answered, "if he gets out of Chile alive."

Terry's flight from Santiago arrived at Kennedy Airport in midafternoon. Proceeding by cab to the Hormans' apartment, she was greeted by Elizabeth, who hugged her tearfully. An hour later, Ed returned from Washington, put his arms around her, and voiced relief that she was safely home.

"I have a lot to tell you," Terry said. "Some very strange things have been going on in Chile." For three hours, she recounted what had happened in Viña, the telephone calls by Military Intelligence to Warwick Armstrong and the Carvajals, and what she and Joyce had learned from neighbors who had witnessed Charles's seizure. As she spoke, Ed's face reddened. For over a week, he had been led to believe by the Department of State that Charles was "probably in hiding." Joyce, in several telephone conversations, had expressed a view to the contrary, but she had been extremely frightened and not a very good communicator. Now, in very cold, matter-of-fact fashion, Terry was laying out a series of events that suggested that he and Elizabeth had been deliberately misled.

Ed typed up a summary of the newly received information. The following morning, he telephoned Charles Anderson and read portions to him. Anderson promised a thorough investigation. That night, Ed telephoned Joyce in Santiago.

"They've checked the morgue without finding anything," she told him.

"Try not to worry," he urged. "Terry briefed us fully on what's happened, and the State Department promises it will get things in the Embassy moving."

"Ray Davis told me today that he's been placed in charge of the investigation."

"There you are," Ed assured her. "The senior United States military man in Chile is running the show. What more could you ask for?"

"Charles," she answered.

Meanwhile, the interminable wait continued. "That," Elizabeth recalls, "was the worst part of the entire experience—waiting by the phone, knowing we were unable to control what happened in Chile. We did everything in our power to move people on Charles's behalf, but nothing worked."

On the evening of September 30, the Hormans were visited by Reverend William Wipfler of the National Council of Churches. As head of the Council's Latin American Division, Wipfler had monitored the Chilean situation since the early days of the Allende administration. Having learned of Charles's seizure, he came to offer his support, bringing with him a young man named David Hathaway.

Tall and good-looking, Hathaway had moved to Chile following his graduation from Amherst College in 1972. After taking a job in a Santiago factory to study worker participation in nationalized industries, he became engaged to a Chilean woman and developed a close circle of American friends. One of them, who eventually became his roommate, was Frank Teruggi.

At the mention of Teruggi's name, Ed's interest grew. "The State Department told me that he was arrested, held in the National Stadium, and then released. Is that true?"

"I don't know," Hathaway answered. "All I can tell you is what happened to the two of us."

As Ed and Elizabeth listened, Hathaway told them about his former roommate. Frank Teruggi was the son of a printer from Des Plaines, Illinois. After attending college at the California Institute of Technology, he moved to Santiago where he enrolled at the University of Chile School of Political Economy. Friends described him as very reserved and something of a loner, but he was extremely conscientious in his work and never sought to slough off boring tasks on others.

Shortly after arriving in Santiago, Teruggi joined a group of Americans who were distributing the weekly newsletter FIN. There, he met Steve Volk and David Hathaway, who were to become his closest friends in Chile. Later, he was introduced to

Charles Horman, with whom he shared a passing acquaintance.

On the evening of Thursday, September 20, 1973, Teruggi and Hathaway were in their Santiago apartment. At 8:15 P.M., a dozen troops barged in and began searching their personal belongings. Discovering several "Marxist" books, they arrested the two Americans and loaded them on a police bus headed towards downtown Santiago.

"We were the only prisoners on the bus," Hathaway recalled. "The streets were deserted except for other military vehicles. The soldiers all sat in back where heavy bales of hay were pressed up against the windows to protect against sniper fire. Frank and I were forced to sit up front, our faces pressed against the glass."

Hathaway and Teruggi were brought to a Carabiñeros station, where the commanding officer slugged them both in the solar plexus and ordered them detained. Two hours later, they were driven to the National Stadium. Passing through the main gate, they were unloaded at a registration center, where their request to call the American Embassy was denied. Shortly after midnight, they were interrogated, then sent to a small cell with several other prisoners.

"We were both nervous," Hathaway recalled, "but Frank didn't expect that anything would happen to us. We agreed that whoever was released first would go directly to the American Embassy and seek protection for the other. We even bet on how long it would be until we got out, and the one who lost would have to buy dinner for the winner." At 6:00 P.M. the following evening, Frank Teruggi was called from the cell. He never came back.

Five days after his seizure, Hathaway was brought to a small dressing room underneath the stadium stands. Four plain wood tables stood along the far wall, each one with an officer and prisoner on opposite sides. When the first prisoner chair became vacant, Hathaway was seated.

"Your name," asked his interrogator, looking up from a long questionnaire.

"David Hathaway."

"Address?"

"2575 Hernan Cortés."

"What did you think of the Allende government?"

Hathaway portrayed himself as a student who had come to Chile as an observer and grown disillusioned with the Allende experiment. As the examination closed, his interrogator placed the questionnaire on the table and readied himself to insert one of three symbols in a space at the bottom. "LC" (*libertad condicional*) would mean conditional liberty. Prisoners so graded were generally released within twenty-four hours. "S" stood for *sospechoso* (suspicious) and required further consideration. "P" (*peligroso*—dangerous) meant that additional interrogation, torture, and death were likely. Shrugging his shoulders, the officer moved his pen to the bottom of the sheet and wrote "S."

"One day later, I was released," Hathaway told Elizabeth and Ed. "The morning after that, I went to the morgue but, if Frank was there, I couldn't find him. I don't know where he is or what happened to him."

"The State Department says he was freed on September 25," Ed answered.

"That's what the government of Chile told them. I'm not sure any of us will see Frank alive again."

David Hathaway's visit had a sobering effect on Elizabeth and Ed. Throughout their ordeal, they had considered it unlikely that Charles was in hiding but had allowed themselves the luxury of hoping that he was in custody without Chilean or American officials knowing it. Their image of the National Stadium had been one of thousands of prisoners milling about with no organization or order. Hathaway had punctured their balloon. The prisoner registration and interrogation systems made it likely that the military knew exactly where Charles was.

The first two days of October passed without incident. On October 3, Joyce called from Santiago. Following their conversation, Ed handed the phone to Terry, who was visiting for dinner. She and Joyce chatted a while longer.

"You're not telling me something," Terry said. "I can hear it in your voice. What happened?"

"They've found Frank Teruggi," Joyce answered.

The search for Teruggi had begun and ended with Steve Volk. Shortly after the coup, Steve and several friends had organized a system of telephone checks to monitor each other's welfare. On September 24, he learned that Frank and David Hathaway had been arrested and reported their seizure to the American Consulate. Later that day, the Chilean military responded to a Consulate inquiry with the statement that both Americans were being held in the National Stadium for "curfew violation." The following morning, the Consulate was informed that Teruggi's interrogation was complete. Hours later, Consul Frederick Purdy received a telephone call from the Santiago morgue reporting that a body tentatively identified as Teruggi had been found three days earlier.

Purdy chose to discount the report from the morgue, which was in direct conflict with the assurance of military authorities that Teruggi had been alive and well earlier that morning. Then, with Hathaway's release from custody, the military changed its story. Teruggi, it now claimed, had been released in good health on September 21.

On September 27, Purdy reluctantly accompanied Hathaway to the morgue. There, the recently freed American viewed a hundred and fifty corpses, failing to identify any of them. However, the reliability of his review was subject to doubt. He had been in detention for six days and was tired, tense, and emotionally fatigued. In addition, he was upset about an ultimatum to leave Chile within forty-eight hours or face reimprisonment.

Returning to his fiancée's home, Hathaway was troubled by the memory of a body he had seen in the morgue. It had looked very much like Frank . . . thinner and with darker hair than he remembered his roommate as having, but the height and facial features were similar. Several hours before departing from Chile, he telephoned Steve Volk and asked him to visit the morgue.

On October 1, Volk went to the Consulate and told Vice-Consul James Anderson about Hathaway's doubts.

"What are you suggesting?" Anderson asked.

"I'd like to go to the morgue and confirm David's findings for myself."

"Just a minute," Anderson told him. "I'll talk with the Consul."

He rose from his chair, and disappeared into an adjoining room. Listening through the open door, Volk heard Frederick Purdy explode: "I don't care what Hathaway told Volk. He told me that it wasn't Teruggi, and that's the end of it."

Moments later, Anderson returned. "I'm afraid that another visit to the morgue is impossible. It's very difficult to gain admittance, and we don't want to pressure the new government by asking for too many favors."

"That's unconscionable," Volk shot back. "Frank has a family that's desperate to find out what happened to him. If those bodies are buried, they'll never know."

"I'm sorry. We just can't do it."

One day later, Volk received a telephone call at home. "We've changed our minds," Anderson told him. "I'd like you to come down to the Consulate so we can visit the morgue."

"I went to the Consulate," Volk recalls, "and was driven to the morgue by Anderson and a second official named Donald McNally. We stopped briefly in the business section, and then went down into the basement area. We pushed through a pair of double doors and walked into a corridor lined with bodies on either side. From there, we shoved through another set of double doors into a high-ceilinged room with a white tile floor that sloped from either wall towards a long sluice filled with water that split the room down the middle.

"The whole room was white. White floor, white tiled walls, white ceiling; and there, lying next to each other, were four rows of corpses from one end of the room to the other, two rows on either side of the water. I started at one end and began walking up and down the aisles. The bodies were nude although, in some instances, there were piles of clothes beside them. Most had parts of their heads crushed or blown away. They had all been shot in the head at close range or machine-gunned in the body. All except two were young and, judging by their hands and clothes, most of them appeared to have been workers. They had been slit open from the chest to the genitals in a pro forma autopsy, then sewn back together with some sort of rough cord."

Each body had a little tag with a cadaver number attached to it. All of them were unidentified . . . Anderson called them "no-names." Off to the side, Volk saw another room with still more bodies. Midway down the third aisle, he recognized Frank.

"This is him," Volk said.

McNally looked down at the tag. "Yep, that's the one we thought."

Learning from Terry about the discovery of Frank Teruggi's body, Ed got back on the phone. Several days earlier, he had proposed coming to Santiago to assist in the search for Charles but had been told by Joyce that it was unnecessary. Now he reextended the offer.

"I'd like you to come," she told him, "but you don't have to."

"Yes, I do. The only reason I've stayed in New York this long was the belief that I could do more up here than in Chile. Maybe I've been wrong. If I don't come to Santiago, I won't be able to face you or Elizabeth again."

CHAPTER XV

THE ODYSSEY OF ED HORMAN— OCTOBER 4-7, 1973

On the evening of October 4, Ed and Elizabeth retraced the route to Kennedy Airport where, five weeks earlier, Charles had said good-bye. "It was an emotional moment," Elizabeth remembers. "Despite everyone telling me to have hope, deep down inside I knew my son was probably dead. Then I watched Ed board the same Lan Chile flight Charles and Terry had taken when they left New York, and a horrible feeling of déjà vu swept over me. Suddenly, I thought I might not see Ed again either."

In the wake of the coup, few travelers were flying to Santiago, and the plane was virtually empty. After boarding, Ed settled by the left rear window only to discover that his seat would not adjust backwards. He gathered his belongings and moved forward several rows to a chair that worked.

He hardly looked like a man with a mission. Balding . . . round-faced . . . dressed in baggy slacks with a blue-and-red horizontally striped shirt open at the collar, he could have passed easily for a retired vacationer en route to Miami. His face belied the fact that, for two weeks, he had shuttled between Washington and New York, made frantic telephone calls, and done everything possible to save his son. Now, for the first time since learning of Charles's seizure, he was alone. There was no one to talk with . . . no telephone calls to make . . . only waiting until the plane landed in Santiago five thousand miles and sixteen hours later.

"I tried very hard not to indulge in sorrow," Ed remembers. "Certainly, my hopes had dwindled, but I was committed to pursuing every last chance that Charles might still be alive. When the plane took off, I sat back, relaxed, and tried to think about what I could do to help. Maybe I fantasized a little about where our relationship would go if Charles were rescued and brought home alive. Fortunately, I had the satisfaction of knowing that, while we suffered the wear and tear that was normal between members of our respective generations, the bonds between us were strong."

In some respects, the plane ride was reminiscent of a journey Ed had taken six years earlier. After graduating from Harvard, Charles had grown extremely bitter about the war in Vietnam and hostile towards "the establishment." Ed, as an available representative of the older generation, had become a target for more than occasional abuse.

"We were cordially noncommunicative on many subjects in those days," he recalls, "and it troubled me greatly. Charles was living in Portland at the time, and, when he decided to move back East, I asked if I could fly out and drive back with him."

"I'll let you know," Charles told his father. "I'll have to think about it." Several days later, he called back and said he would like it very much if Ed came.

The drive cross country to New York took seven days. "We talked all the way," Ed remembers. "I didn't completely satisfy him and he didn't completely satisfy me, but it helped a lot. We grew closer from that point on. When Charles and Joyce quit their jobs and went to Chile, I didn't approve completely but at least I understood and was able to accept what they were doing."

The Lan Chile flight to Santiago stopped in Miami, Cali, Quito, and Lima. Waking from a fitful sleep, Ed sat silent in the dark predawn hours and listened to the sounds of the plane in the night. Slowly, the horizon brightened and the sun rose over the Andes Mountains, their tall, craggy peaks pushing upward through the clouds. Severe valleys spotted with patches of green followed, giving way to the fertile fields of Peru. Then the Atacama Desert of northern Chile stretched out below.

Half an hour before arriving in Santiago, Ed went to the toilet to change shirts and shave. When the plane landed, he proceeded to the terminal building, where a blond-haired man with sharp features approached.

"Are you Ed Horman?"

"I am."

The man extended his right hand. "I'm Fred Purdy, the United States Consul in Santiago. Charles Anderson cabled from Washington and told us you were coming. I understand you'd like to meet with the Ambassador as soon as possible."

"That's correct."

"Well, Mr. Horman, he'll be available this afternoon. You have to understand though, the situation is very confused down here."

"I'm aware of that," Ed told him. "I don't expect results overnight, and I realize that you people are running the show. I simply want to do whatever I can to help find my son."

Purdy was polite but with a distinct military air that Ed found slightly grating. "I've been in Santiago for three years," he said, leading Ed through customs. "It's not a bad city, but I'm looking forward to reassignment."

"Where will you go next?"

"I don't know. I've been in the Foreign Service for fourteen years. So far, I've served in Mexico, the Azores, and Jamaica. I'd like to go to Brazil, but that's not my decision."

Joyce had made reservations for Ed and herself at the Crillon Hotel. "I'll drop you there," Purdy told him. "Once you've unpacked and had lunch, I'll pick you up for your meeting with the Ambassador."

"That will be fine. What's the Crillon like?"

"It's not bad; a little nicer and more secure than the Riviera, where your daughter-in-law was staying at first." There was irony to Purdy's remark. If the Crillon was secure, it was only because the sympathies of its management were well known to the military. On the afternoon of Allende's death, the hotel had hoisted flags and served complimentary champagne in celebration of the coup.

Joyce met Ed at the hotel when he arrived. Wearing a rumpled cotton dress that was badly in need of ironing, her hair askew, she looked awful. Ed comforted her as best he could, then began to unpack. Two lightweight suits . . . several shirts . . . a pair of slacks . . . Joyce spied a bottle of Woolite among his belongings and confiscated it immediately. Then they went to the hotel dinning room for lunch, and she recounted what had transpired since Terry's departure.

In essence, Joyce's efforts had amounted to a week of frustration. On Sunday, September 30, she learned that the National Stadium would be open to visitors for eight hours. She rushed to the site, but was informed that only soldiers on duty were allowed visitors. The prisoners were to have none. The following morning, she went to see Ray Davis, who had just been assigned to head the investigation into Charles's disappearance.

"I used to work as a research analyst for the Pentagon," Davis told her. "I know how these things operate, and the best way to start is with some very basic facts. How tall is your husband?"

"Five-nine."

Weight?"

"About a hundred and fifty pounds."

"Eye color?"

"Green."

After running through Charles's physical characteristics, Davis turned to another area. "I'd like to learn all I can about your husband's personal associations. It would be very helpful if you gave me a list of his friends with information about what each of them has been doing in Chile."

Joyce shifted nervously in her chair. That was precisely the sort of information she did not want to give Ray Davis. Her distrust had grown daily, and she feared that any names she provided would be converted into a military arrest list.

"Is that really necessary?" she asked.

"I think it is."

"All right. I'll make the list up tonight. What else do you want to know?"

"That will give us a start." Pausing, he looked directly at her. "What's your husband really like?"

"You drove him back from Viña. What was your impression?"

"He seemed like an introvert," Davis answered, speaking very slowly. " . . . something of a semi-intellectual . . . . He didn't talk much."

Leaving the Captain in his office, Joyce took a collectivo to Vicuña Mackenna in search of further witnesses to Charles's seizure. True to his word, Dr. Nuñez had arranged for a meeting with the woman who followed the arresting soldiers to the National Stadium.

"I was leaving my mother, who lives across the street," the woman told Joyce. "A car came for me just as the soldiers put your husband on the truck. My home is past the stadium, so I followed the same route the soldiers took to get to my home. They drove right to the stadium and went inside."

That night, Joyce telephoned Davis to report her findings. "Be at the Embassy tomorrow at one," he instructed. Arriving as told, she went to his office, where he greeted her less than warmly. "Did you bring the list of Charles's friends?"

"I didn't have time to prepare it," she told him. "I thought it was more important to interview neighbors and identify what military group arrested Charles."

"Have it your way, but it would be in your husband's best interests for you to prepare that list."

Knocking on the door, a young Chilean entered. "This is Luis Blamey," Davis explained. "He's a local investigator who's been employed by the Embassy from time to time. I've arranged for him to drive you back to your old neighborhood, which seems to be what you intend to do anyway. He'll handle your problems for the rest of the day."

Out on the street, Joyce turned to her new escort. "What do you know about my husband's case?" she asked.

"Everything."

"What do you mean by everything?"

"That he disappeared."

"What else?"

"Nothing."

Joyce slumped back against the front seat of Blamey's car and repeated everything she had told both Davises and three Consulate personnel before him. "Can we go right to Vicuña Mackenna?" she asked.

"First I have to get gas," he told her. The next hour was spent in search of an open gas station. In mid-afternoon, they arrived at Vicuña Mackenna, and Joyce began questioning her former neighbors.

"I saw the soldiers come," one woman told her. "I work in a store two doors from your home. Ten to fifteen soldiers came in a green truck. The captain came into the store to ask questions about a parking lot. Then they left."

"I saw them too," a second woman volunteered. "They put your husband in a truck with a box of books and took him away."

"Did they say why they were taking him?" Joyce asked.

"I don't know, but our neighbor next door talked with the officer in command. She's at work now, but you can see her if you come before nine o'clock tomorrow morning."

Joyce turned to Blamey and asked if he would meet her at eight-thirty the following morning. The investigator agreed reluctantly and suggested that it had been a long day and was time to go home. Taking a bus to the home of Warwick and Rosalie Armstrong, where she had been staying since Terry's departure, Joyce arrived in time to receive a telephone call from Ray Davis.

"Would you like to have dinner with me this evening?" he asked.

Rather firmly, she declined.

Blamey arrived an hour late the next morning. By the time he and Joyce reached Vicuña Mackenna, the neighbor who had reportedly spoken with the soldiers was gone. "I suppose we can come back and talk with her at the end of the day," Joyce suggested.

"Not me," Blamey answered. "No one at the Embassy works past 5:00 P.M."

Further interviews proved futile, and Blamey drove Joyce back to the Armstrongs', where she called Fred Purdy. "I'd like another investigator," she said.

"All right. We'll give you an American named Donald Mc-Nally. You can start working with him tomorrow."

The next morning, McNally and Joyce interviewed the woman who had talked with the arresting troops' commanding officer. She confirmed earlier descriptions of the soldiers but was unable to provide more. "I asked questions," she explained, "but he would not answer."

"And that," Joyce told Ed as they finished lunch in the dining room of the Crillon Hotel, "is where things stand."

"It's not very good, is it?"

"No, it's not," she answered.

Purdy arrived at the hotel in midafternoon to drive Ed and Joyce to their meeting with Ambassador Davis. The streets were teeming with soldiers. Passing the smashed façade of the Moneda, Ed gazed out the car window at their warlike apparel . . . long, heavy German-style coats . . . plastic eye shields . . . steel helmets with leather flaps extending down below the neck.

When they reached the Embassy, Purdy ushered them inside, where they were introduced to a defense attaché named William Hon. Then they proceeded to the Ambassador's office.

"It's a pleasure," Nathaniel Davis declared, shaking hands with Ed. "Won't you sit down?"

Lowering himself onto a sofa to the Ambassador's left, Ed glanced around. The room was extremely large and luxuriously furnished with richly upholstered black leather chairs. Everything seemed in order down to the neatly piled papers on the Ambassador's desk. Purdy and Hon took seats to the right, and the meeting began with Joyce at Ed's side.

"Let me tell you what's been done so far, Mr. Horman," the Ambassador began. "Since your son was reported missing, we have exhausted every realistic lead and searched down every possible avenue. Embassy personnel have called local Carabiñeros stations and checked with the Chilean Department of Investigations without success. Consul Purdy has twice visited the National Stadium, spoken with the officer in charge of detainees, and reviewed prisoner lists for your son's name. He's also visited other detention centers and been told that no Americans are being held there."

As Ed and Joyce listened, Nathaniel Davis continued his recitation of events. "On September 24, Captain Ray Davis had lunch with Admiral Huidobro, the Junta's Chief of Staff. Several days later, I spoke with the Admiral myself. He assured us both that the Chilean military has no knowledge of Charles's whereabouts. I raised the issue personally with Chile's Ambassador-designate to the United States, and another Embassy official discussed it with Frederick Willoughby, Press Secretary for the Junta. Colonel Hon has checked with Chilean Military Intelligence and exhausted each of his contacts. The Chilean Embassy in Washington has formally advised the Department of State that your son is not in detention. Our conclusion, Mr. Horman, is that your son is most likely in hiding."

"That's not plausible," Ed answered.

"Why do you say that?"

"Because everything I've heard points to a contrary conclusion. Charles had no reason to go into hiding and, even if he did, he would have sent word to Joyce that he was safe. Your entire investigation rests on self-serving statements by the government of Chile. You've done nothing to follow up reports by witnesses to my son's seizure, and you've ignored the most important piece of evidence that shows Charles to be in military hands."

"And what might that be?"

"The calls by Military Intelligence to two of Charles's friends the day after his seizure. Both friends were told that Charles was in military custody, and both calls were reported immediately to the American Consulate."

Without changing his expression, Davis turned to Purdy. "What's this about telephone calls?" he asked.

"I know of none," Purdy told him.

"That's a lie," Joyce interrupted. "I saw notations concerning both calls at the Consulate when Dale Shaffer showed me your file cards."

Purdy looked towards Davis as if seeking help, and the Ambassador averted his eyes. "Oh yes," the Consul said at last. "I remember them."

The Ambassador leaned back in his chair and looked dignified. "He's a real professional," Ed thought. "There's no trace of surprise or emotion about him."

"I wonder, Mr. Horman," the Ambassador began, "do you think that these so-called inquiries from Military Intelligence were really as you've described them?"

"You've had over two weeks to investigate," Ed answered. "I suggest you find out."

"The Consul will do that immediately, won't you, Mr. Purdy?"

"Yes, sir," came the reply.

"Is there anything more you would like done, Mr. Horman?"

"I would like the most thorough investigation possible and will do anything I can to assist in it."

"We all understand your sentiments," Davis answered. "Our primary concern is finding your son."

"I wish I was more certain of that," Ed thought.

The next morning, October 6, Ed began the routine he would follow throughout his stay in Chile. Rising early, he shaved, showered, ate breakfast, and read the morning edition of *El Mercurio*. The paper's right-wing bias irked him considerably, but there was no alternative. Chile's other newspapers had been shut down in the wake of the coup.

After finishing the paper, he slipped several pages of notes into a slender attaché case and began walking towards Santiago's Christian Science Reading Room. Half a mile from the Crillon Hotel, he came to a small commercial building and entered a study at ground level.

Several desks and a dozen chairs were evenly spaced on the hardwood floor. Copies of the Bible, the *Christian Science Monitor,* and most of Mary Baker Eddy's writings lined shelves on the wall. Sitting by the window, Ed read a lesson of passages from the Bible and prayed. Then, after lunching with Joyce at the hotel, he went to the Embassy and spoke by telephone with Fred Purdy. "We've interviewed Warwick Armstrong and the Carvajals," the Consul told him. "Their accounts match what your daughter-in-law reported."

"I know," Ed answered. "I called them myself last night."

"Well, we're going to look into it thoroughly. Colonel Hon will ask Military Intelligence for a full report."

For reasons Ed did not fully understand, the Embassy and Consulate still appeared to accept the word of the Chilean military at face value. "There are several other things I'd like done," he told Purdy. "I've heard that a number of foreign embassies have been more active than our own in pursuing the matter of political prisoners. Could you find out whether any of them has knowledge of Charles?"

"That's a pretty broad request," Purdy answered.

"This is a very broad problem. However, if it will help, I'm particularly interested in the Swedish Embassy and its Ambassador, Harold Edelstam."

"That will be difficult, Mr. Horman. There's some bad blood right now between the American and Swedish embassies. But I'll follow up with the other embassies as soon as possible. Are there any other requests?"

"Yes," Ed answered with some hesitation. "I would like you to make a definitive check of all bodies in the morgue which might possibly be Charles. I will go with you, if you'd like."

"That's another problem. We've had difficulties in dealing with people at the morgue. There's a doctor down there we don't get along with at all. Maybe you should go alone."

The following day was Sunday, and all Consulate activity ground to a halt. Ed accompanied Joyce to the Armstrongs' for lunch, and listened as Warwick recounted his feelings about the coup. "It's been a numbing period," the United Nations advisor said. "And the personal tragedy we feel is matched by the suffering in Chile as a whole."

Midway through the meal, a friend telephoned to warn that soldiers were proceeding from house to house on a neighboring street in search of Marxist literature. "That," said Armstrong, "is the sort of thing I was referring to. I'm afraid that no one is safe here any longer."

Later in the afternoon, Ed and Joyce visited 4126 Vicuña Mackenna. "I was pretty choked up when we got there," Ed recalls, "partly because I realized what had happened inside and, I suppose, partly because the place was pretty crummy. The bathroom wasn't finished. The shower consisted of an iron head coming out of the wall with a drain in the middle of the floor. There was no shower stall. I'm sure it was more than adequate by Chilean standards, but it upset me to think that this was where Charles might have spent his last days."

The living room was still in shambles. Papers littered the floor, and furniture lay overturned against the wall. Bending over, Joyce sorted through the debris until she came to several sheets of paper clipped together and marked "The Sunshine Grabber." Slowly, she began to read:

Once upon a time, there was a country so far north
It was further north than The North Pole.
It was further north than The Big Dipper.
It was even further north than The Milky Way
(and that's pretty far north).
Nobody knew the name of the country
except the folks who lived there
because the ink in the explorer's pens froze
before they could write it down.

Biting her lip, she read on:

This is a picture of the country.
If you peer hard you might see a sign with the country's name

NORTH OF NORTH.
You might also see 5 rabbits or 15,000 yaks.
But you will have to look very hard because they're all
covered with snow.
Also, very far under the snow in an igloo
lived a family named Sharn.

Ed returned from the bedroom and began to read over Joyce's shoulder:

The father was named Erg
The mother was named Zerg
And the little boy and the little girl
were named Zibbon and Gluck.

Everyday Erg and Zerg tunneled up through the snow
to catch Yaks.
They were the best Yak-catchers in all the land.

But the Yaks were sneaky.
Sometimes they hid behind one snowdrift.
Sometimes they hid behind another . . . .
And sometimes they just stood against a lamp post
disguised as John Lennon.

Gathering the pages, Ed slipped them into his attaché case and walked outside. "Then we saw the duck," he remembers. "And, as strange as it might seem, that silly duck moved me as much as anything I saw the entire day. When Charles was in New York, he told me how he and Joyce had trained it to come. They'd yell, 'Here Duck,' and it would waddle towards them, quacking like mad. Now, here I was in the heart of Santiago with my son missing and, when Joyce stepped from the house, this enormous duck waddled over, acting like a dog. It remembered her, and all it seemed to want out of life was to be patted."

That night, several reporters questioned Ed at the hotel concerning his efforts to locate Charles. Ike Pappas of CBS, Charles Murphy of ABC, and Bill Nicholson of the Associated Press had all learned of his search and were anxious to help as well as looking for news. "Do you think the United States government is doing everything it can to save your son?" one of them asked.

Mulling the question over, Ed considered several answers. His doubts as to the Embassy's good faith had grown. There was no reasonable explanation for the Consulate's neglect to date. Yet, when all was said and done, he still harbored hope that Charles was alive and feared saying anything that might prejudice his welfare. He had no doubt that Charles had been taken into military custody. But maybe the Junta was looking for a way to gracefully release him. Perhaps he'd been beaten and they were holding him until his appearance and health had returned. Maybe, just maybe, something less than fatal had happened. Ed wanted the Embassy on his side.

"The only reason I'm here in Chile," he answered, "is to find my son. I have no interest in challenging what our government has done in the past. I'm interested only in the future."

CHAPTER XVI

THE ODYSSEY CONTINUES— OCTOBER 8-12,1973

On the morning of October 8, Ed went to the Embassy, borrowed a typewriter, and prepared a request that the Consulate take six specific steps on Charles's behalf. He had just returned to the hotel when Purdy and William Hon knocked on his door. Greeting them both, he handed the freshly typed letter to Purdy, who glanced at it, then stuffed it in an inside jacket pocket.

"We've rechecked all our leads with the Chilean military," Hon said, "and they still deny knowledge of your son's arrest. Maybe some more information would be helpful. What kind of work was he doing in Santiago?"

Ed described "The Sunshine Grabber" and several of Charles's other projects. When he mentioned a film script that touched on the War of the Pacific between Chile and Bolivia, Hon broke in with a detailed description of several battles fought in 1879.

"You have an impressive store of knowledge," Ed told him.

"I have to," the Colonel responded. "I've been in the Army since 1941. It's my job."

Hon's historical review continued several minutes longer. Then Ed changed the subject. "Look," he said. "I'll be as frank with both of you as I know how. I've read quite a bit lately about Latin America, and one of the names I've come across is Dan Mitreone."

His visitors shifted awkwardly.

"There's no need to play games with each other," Ed continued. "I know full well that Dan Mitreone was an agent for the CIA. He was assigned to the American Embassy in Uruguay, and assassinated by Tupamaros guerrillas because of his role in repressing the Uruguayan left. I assume that there is a Mitreone-type operation in Chile. I don't know what it is, I don't care who runs it, and I don't even want an affirmation that it exists. All I ask is that you use this organization to find my son."

"I hear what you're saying," Purdy answered. Then he and Hon left.

Minutes before noon, Ed's telephone rang. "This is Fred Purdy," the Consul said. "Ambassador Davis would like to see you this afternoon."

"What for?"

"He wants to discuss the six points raised by your letter."

Proceeding to the Embassy, Ed went directly to Davis's office, where the Ambassador and Purdy sat waiting. "I understand there are some political questions you wish to discuss with me," Davis said.

"That wasn't my understanding," Ed answered. "The Consul told me that you wanted to discuss the requests for assistance raised by my letter."

Reaching for the document, Davis read through it in a manner suggesting that he was studying it for the first time. "Well," he said going down the first page, "you'd like us to check detention centers other than the National Stadium, contact other embassies, and report more fully on the results of Colonel Hon's investigation. That should be no problem. You also want a check of fingerprints at the morgue, a reward offered for information concerning your son's seizure, and further interviews of all possible witnesses. All of that can be arranged."

"Thank you," Ed said. "I would appreciate it."

"Well then," the Ambassador asked, "is there anything more you wish to discuss?"

"No, sir."

"I believe you raised a question earlier today with Mr. Purdy.

157

As I understand it, you suggested that there might be some sort of police assistance program run by American operatives in Chile. Is that correct?"

"We had a discussion along those lines."

Davis's voice hardened. "I would like you to know that nothing of that sort exists in this country. Does that satisfy you?"

Choosing his words with care, Ed responded. "I understand what you're telling me, Mr. Ambassador. I brought the matter up because I assume that such an operation does exist. I won't contest what you've said, but I want you to know that, if there are resources available to find my son that remain unused, I hope you will utilize them."

"Mr. Horman, no such operation exists."

"Mr. Ambassador," Ed continued, "there's something that I would like to make very clear to you. Over the past few days, it has become apparent that my son's disappearance is not being pursued by this Embassy in a proper manner. Telephone calls from Military Intelligence to Warwick Armstrong and the Carvajals were ignored for over two weeks. Witnesses to Charles's seizure aren't being properly interrogated. You seem to accept the word of the Chilean military as Gospel. I don't know whether this is the result of ineptitude or something far more serious and, quite frankly, I don't care. My sole concern is for the welfare of my son. I'm in Chile for one purpose and one purpose only. Nothing else matters to me. I want you to find my son."

"We're doing everything we can, Mr. Horman. You'll simply have to be more patient."

"My patience has been exhausted."

"I'm sorry to hear that."

Driving back to the hotel, Purdy appeared anxious to sooth ruffled feathers. "You have to remember," he explained, "this is only one of several cases we're working on. We have to consider the welfare of all the American citizens in Santiago."

"I understand that," Ed told him, "but this is the case I'm concerned with."

"You and a lot of other people. We've gotten an extraordinary number of cables from Washington about your son. What kind of in do you have there, anyway?"

"I'm an American citizen," Ed answered.

The following morning, Tuesday, October 9, Ed and Joyce went separate ways. Rising early, Joyce visited the office of *El Mercurio* in the hope of placing a reward offer for information concerning Charles's seizure. Meanwhile, Ed readied for a tour of Santiago's hospitals.

Shortly after 10:00 A.M., Donald McNally arrived at the Crillon in an Embassy car. Ed liked McNally. Most of the Embassy-Consulate personnel projected as cold, pasty-faced bureaucrats. McNally had bright red cheeks and an open smile. More important, he seemed to care about Charles and gave the impression of genuinely wanting to help.

"I have a list of nine hospitals I'd like to visit," Ed told him.

"Where do you want to start?" McNally asked.

Ed took a map of Santiago from his pocket and listed the hospitals in geographic order. Then the search began. At each stop, the procedure was the same. McNally would inquire whether a patient named Charles Horman was registered, after which he and Ed viewed the "no-names" and, finally, visited all male patients in the hospital ward. One of Ed's hopes was that Charles was in a state of amnesia or had sought treatment under an assumed name. At each stop, he showed a picture of Charles to hospital personnel. Always, the results were negative.

Midway through the day, it began to rain. Buttoning his coat against the storm, Ed offered his umbrella to McNally.

"You keep it," the young man said.

"I insist," Ed told him. "The coat will keep me dry."

As the rain grew in intensity, they came to a psychiatric hospital on the outskirts of Santiago. The main building looked very much like a converted farmhouse surrounded by a collection of outhouses. The rooms were virtually without furniture; many of them with only dirt floors. The patients reeked of urine. Moving from bed to bed, Ed viewed the inmates . . . men drooling, laughing, babbling . . . others lying in a semiconscious state. There was no sign of Charles.

Late in the afternoon, they reached the ninth and final hospital. McNally went to the reception desk to explain their mission, and Ed leaned against a far wall. Suddenly, a rifle barrel jammed against his ribs. Looking up, he saw a soldier standing over him, gun in hand.

For five days, Ed had watched soldiers with guns. Each morning, he had walked past armed troops to the Christian Science Reading Room. At night, gunfire had punctured his sleep. Now after a futile search through nine hospitals, his breaking point was at hand. Reaching out, he grabbed the rifle from the soldier's hands and pointed the muzzle downward. Before his adversary could react, McNally rushed between them. Then the search resumed.

Returning to the hotel at dusk, Ed found a stranger in his room. "I'm here to fix the telephone," the man said.

"It works fine," Ed told him.

"No! It has to be fixed." Taking the receiver apart, the stranger toyed with its inner mechanism. "Now it will work better," he announced.

That night, as usual, Ed and Joyce dined together. "He did the same thing to my phone this afternoon," Joyce said.

Ed shrugged his shoulders. "I assumed when I came down here that our phones would be bugged, but I thought they'd started long ago and I never dreamed they'd be so clumsy about it." He paused, picking at his food. "Also, I assumed that it would be the Chilean government that did it, not our own. Now I'm not so sure."

Fred Purdy telephoned the following morning to report on the Consulate's fingerprint check at the morgue. "It turned up negative. There's no trace of your son."

"Would dental records help?" Ed inquired.

"I don't know why. If the fingerprints don't match, teeth won't either."

Purdy's answer made sense but, for lack of anything better to do, late in the day Ed and Joyce visited Dr. Abud Tapia, Charles's dentist in Santiago. "I'm terrible sorry," Tapia said when informed of their purpose in coming. "Charles's file was destroyed two days ago."

"Is that normal procedure?"

"Of course," Tapia answered. "Let me tell you, though, I work sometimes for the military. I will ask my friends there if they have knowledge of him."

The remainder of the day passed without incident. The following morning, Purdy reported a call to the Consulate from a man who claimed to have seen Charles boarding a plane for southern Chile. Checking the airport log, a Consular official determined that the informant was mistaken. Late in the day, Ed and Joyce accidentally passed by collectivo through a sector of Santiago cordoned off by police, who were combating sniper fire. No harm resulted. "In reality," Ed says, "I felt quite safe. I assumed that I was the last person in Chile the Embassy wanted anything to happen to. They guarded me well."

That night, Ed restocked the supply of apricot juice he kept in his room for guests who happened by. Late in the evening, Purdy telephoned. "I've made arrangements for you to visit the National Stadium," the Consul said. "Be ready at one o'clock tomorrow."

Ed expressed his gratitude. "I'll be on time," he promised.

"Fine, but let me warn you now. I don't think anything will come of it."

On the afternoon of October 12, Ed, Purdy, and Dale Shaffer drove to the stadium. When they reached the chain-link fence surrounding the edifice, the Consul stepped from the car and handled all necessary detail work with the soldiers on duty. Then, motioning for Ed and Shaffer to follow, he walked past a Sherman tank towards an entrance at the rear of the stadium.

"This is the command post," he explained. "We'll need Colonel Espinoza's approval before we can go inside."

"Will we have trouble getting it?" Ed asked.

"I don't think so, but you can never tell."

Despite his tough looks and fierce black mustache, Espinoza seemed anxious to please. Welcoming his guests, he produced a series of release forms signed by a dozen Americans previously held at the stadium. Leafing through them, Ed saw the names of Joseph Francis Doherty, Jim Ritter, and David Hathaway. There was no reference to Frank Teruggi or Charles. Handing the forms back, he eyed the octagonal-barreled pistol at Espinoza's side and awaited further instructions.

"Come with me," the Colonel said. With Purdy and Shaffer at his side, Ed followed through a wide gate into a long passageway beneath the stadium stands. Forty yards down the runway, they emerged near midfield.

Adjusting his eyes to the sun, Ed looked around. Some two thousand prisoners were seated in the seats, a hundred soldiers sprinkled among them. The playing field was empty. Climbing to a platform ten rows into the stands, Espinoza took hold of a microphone and announced that an American had come to the stadium in search of his son and would be permitted to speak.

Shaking with anticipation, Ed stepped to the microphone and began:

Charles Horman, this is your father. I'm here in the hope that you can hear me and, in order that you may know who I am, I'm going to mention the names of several friends from your past.

Pausing after each surname, Ed spoke the names of Roger Lipsey, Orland Campbell, and Tom Vachon—friends from Allen-Stevenson Grammar School and Exeter. Then he continued:

If you are here, I would like you to take my word that it is safe and come to me now.

"I really didn't have much hope," Ed later recalled, "but right then a young man came out of the stands and started running towards me. He was quite a distance away and I couldn't see him well, but he ran in the same disjointed manner as Charles . . . arms and legs flapping all over. For one glorious moment, I thought I had found him. Then the fellow got closer, and I realized that it wasn't my son—just someone who looked like him, with a question to ask Espinoza. Right then, I knew I'd never see Charles again."

CHAPTER XVII

THE ODYSSEY ENDS—
OCTOBER 13-21, 1973

Painfully, the search dragged on. On Saturday, October 13, Ed toured a Chilean refugee village. The following morning, he attended church and lunched with the Armstrongs at noon. On the morning of October 15, he revisited Nathaniel Davis. "We were on a treadmill," he later recalled. "Nothing constructive was being done, and I had begun to feel that I was being out-and-out lied to. A confrontation with the Ambassador, however distasteful, seemed the only solution."

Ushered into Davis's office, Ed was seated opposite the large desk from which the Ambassador reigned.

"What can I do for you, Mr. Horman?"

Choosing his words carefully, Ed began: "Mr. Ambassador, I have been in Chile for ten days. I now know enough about the country to have a feel for its size and government. There is no doubt in my mind that the Chilean military knows exactly where Charles is, and I see no reason why you can't force them to reveal it. I know something about your past and why you were sent to Santiago. None of that matters to me. What does matter is that, as the primary representative of the United States government, you are probably the most powerful man in Chile. All the power is on your side. One telephone call from you can end this entire matter.

"My assumption," Ed continued, his voice quavering, "is that my son is dead. But I cannot go home and face my wife without the truth. I'm asking you on grounds of simple common humanity to help."

"I understand your feelings, Mr. Horman," Davis answered. "And I assure you that we are doing everything we possibly can."

Leaving the Ambassador's office, Ed rejoined Joyce and readied himself for another encounter. Three weeks earlier, while Terry was still in Chile, Joyce had received a telephone call from Major Luis Contreras Prieto of the Chilean Army. Explaining that a friend of the Hormans' had contacted his brother, who worked for the Irving Trust Company in New York, Prieto had questioned Joyce on Charles's disappearance and promised to report back to her the next day. On the evening of September 26, Prieto's wife called. Major Prieto, she explained, was in bed as the result of a foot wound suffered in a helicopter attack on a leftist-controlled factory. However, he had checked with military sources and learned that Charles was alive. As soon as the charges against him were settled, he would be released.

Bubbling with euphoria, Joyce reported the news to Fred Purdy. The following afternoon, the Consul called her back. "I've checked with Prieto," Purdy said, "and there's been a mis-understanding. He has no information about your husband."

"That's impossible," Joyce cried.

"Check for yourself, Mrs. Horman. I talked with him just ten minutes ago."

Joyce dialed Prieto's number. "You did not misunderstand me," Mrs. Prieto said, "but my report was wrong. I told you about the wrong person."

"But I wrote Charles's name on a piece of paper and gave it to your husband."

"I know. I'm very sorry. The report was wrong."

Thereafter, Prieto was of little help. On October 3, Joyce visited his home. "I have no further information," he told her. "The best I can do is give you a letter of introduction to Colonel Ewing, the Secretary General of our government. Perhaps he can help you." Accepting the letter, Joyce went to Ewing's office but was refused an audience. Two subsequent attempts to meet with him also failed. She had not heard from Prieto since.

Now, having leveled his broadside at Nathaniel Davis, Ed wanted to visit the Major as well. Perhaps a face-to-face appeal would spur him to action.

Prieto lived in a five-story apartment house inhabited largely by military officers and their families. A well-guarded machine-gun nest embellished the front lawn. Arriving with Joyce at 2:30 P.M., Ed was greeted by Mrs. Prieto and brought to the Major's study. Because his Spanish was shaky, Ed suggested that Joyce carry on most of the conversation.

"I'm sorry for the confusion," the Major told them. "My original report was based on what I had learned from friends. Now they tell me that they were wrong. This is proved by those who witnessed your son's seizure. The truck that took him had no military markings. Soldiers in Chile travel only in military vehicles and never in one truck alone."

"Major Prieto," Ed interrupted, "I don't think you understand the anguish my family and I are suffering. My son has been missing in your country for almost a month. His mother, his wife, and I desperately love him. I appeal to you as one man to another for help."

Opening his mouth as if to answer, Prieto rose instead and walked to the far end of the room. Picking up the telephone, he dialed SIM—the Chilean Army branch of Military Intelligence. For about ten minutes, he spoke with a man named Sala, then returned.

"Be in your hotel room tomorrow morning," he told Ed. "Two men from Military Intelligence will come to see you."

After leaving the Major's home, Ed telephoned Fred Purdy to report on his most recent venture. Expressing skepticism as to Prieto's reliability, the Consul nonetheless agreed that his efforts could do no harm.

"Let me ask you something else," Ed queried. "Has the Chilean military used civilian trucks these past few weeks?"

"With the present shortage of operating vehicles," Purdy answered, "they use anything that runs."

"What about the possibility that leftist extremists or looters masquerading as soldiers might have seized Charles?"

"They'd have to be crazy to try something like that. It's much too dangerous."

"Thank you," Ed replied. "That's what I thought."

The next morning at 10:30 A.M., two agents from Military Intelligence appeared at the Crillon Hotel. Proceeding to Ed's room, they identified themselves as Raul Manesas and Jaime Ortiz of SIM and began to ask questions about Charles. Manesas was the taller of the two, with a sallow complexion, shining black hair, and a bushy mustache. Ortiz, who was ruddy-faced, short, and stocky, was the more vocal. Ed and Joyce spent the next ninety minutes answering questions about Charles's disappearance.

Later in the day, Purdy telephoned. "I'd like you to come down to the Consulate if you could." Arriving at 5:15, Ed was introduced to Vice-Consul James Anderson and a man named Timothy Ross.

"Mr. Ross is a journalist from Great Britain," Purdy explained. "He has good access to left-wing circles in Chile, and has come up with some interesting information about your son. Nothing has been confirmed, of course, but Ambassador Davis thought a meeting between the two of you might prove fruitful."

"I'm interested in pursuing every lead possible," Ed said, turning to Ross. "What is it that you've learned?"

"That your son is alive and well," the journalist answered. "Let me explain. Four days ago, Mr. Anderson asked if I would inquire of my associates whether they had any knowledge of Charles's whereabouts. At his request, I spoke with someone currently involved in helping political refugees escape from Chile. He told me that his organization had secured credentials for three Americans seeking to leave Santiago by clandestine means. One of them was your son."

"Where is he now," Ed asked.

"In northern Chile."

"When will he be out of the country?"

"Sometime next week."

"Is there any way I can contact him to confirm your story?"

"No."

Weighing what he had just heard, Ed addressed the British journalist: "Mr. Ross, I would like very much to believe what you've just told me, but I cannot. My son had no reason to flee Chile. Also, I don't think that a serious leftist organization would run the risk of transporting a political neophyte like Charles in its escape pipeline. I hope with all my heart that you're right and I'm wrong, but I doubt it."

"I guess only time will tell," Anderson said.

"I guess that's right," Ed answered.

A week earlier, Ross's story would have been received with hope. However, by mid-October, Ed sensed that his odyssey was nearing an end. The hour and place of resolution were still unknown, but their coming seemed inevitable.

On the morning of October 17, Ed visited the Ford Foundation office in Santiago. McGeorge Bundy, President of the Foundation, was one of the people he had spoken with in New York while soliciting cables on Charles's behalf. Bundy had been extremely supportive and suggested that the Hormans enlist Peter Bell, head of the Foundation's Chile office, if they needed local assistance. Then, after Ed had flown to Santiago, Bundy had telephoned Elizabeth weekly to inquire about Charles's welfare.

With no leads left to follow, Ed felt a courtesy call on Bell was in order. Proceeding to the Foundation office, he was greeted by an aide named Peter Hakim.

"Mr. Bell is out of the country," Hakim explained. "Can I be of any help?"

"Not really," Ed told him. "I just wanted to thank you people for the Foundation's efforts on my son's behalf. My family and I are extremely grateful."

"Why don't you come inside?" Hakim suggested. "We can talk for a while."

Following to his host's office, Ed was introduced to an Economic Program Advisor named Lovell Jarvis. They shook hands, and Ed was seated.

"What do you think of the American Embassy's performance in your son's case?" Hakim asked.

"Speaking confidentially, it has not been good."

"In what respects?"

As fairly as possible, Ed recounted some of the problems he and Joyce had suffered. "I realize you people are very busy," he concluded, "but any assistance you can offer would be appreciated."

At the meeting's end, Jarvis walked Ed from the room. "Will you come with me, please?" he said. Not knowing what lay ahead, Ed followed down a short hall to a large conference room with dark paneled walls. A huge oval table surrounded by ten chairs dominated the floor.

"Have a seat," Jarvis instructed.

Ed obeyed.

"I have a friend whom I play tennis with regularly," Jarvis began. "I won't identify him other than to say that he works for an English-speaking Embassy in Santiago and is close to someone with good contacts in the Chilean military. *Your son was executed in the National Stadium on September 20.*"

Ed sat silent. "Is there anything more you care to tell me?" he said at last.

"I'm sorry. I'd like to, but I can't."

"Would it be possible for me to meet your friend or his Chilean contact?"

"I doubt it. I understand your feelings, but these are very dangerous times."

"I'll go anywhere. You can take me blindfolded with my hands tied behind my back."

"I'll see what can be arranged," Jarvis said. "But it's doubtful. I feel awful. I'm sure you understand that. This is a terrible tragedy."

Suppressing his emotions as best he could, Ed left the office and telephoned Fred Purdy at the Consulate. "I have just received a credible report," he began, " . . . a report that my son was executed in the National Stadium on September 20. I would like your fullest attention to the matter."

"Who told you that?"

Ed didn't answer.

"Who was the report from?" Purdy pressed.

Ed deliberated with the receiver to his ear. For twelve days, he had relayed every last scrap of information he had gathered to the Embassy and Consulate, and nothing had come of it. The thought of this last lead evaporating was unbearable. "From a source I do not wish to reveal," he finally answered.

Then he returned to the hotel and reported to Joyce on his meeting with Jarvis. "Don't give up hope," he urged. "It's not conclusive."

"Maybe not," she said, her eyes brimming with tears. "But it's probably true."

The reappearance of Manesas and Ortiz interrupted their conversation. "We are investigating a body that was brought to the morgue several weeks ago and later buried," Ortiz explained. "It was the same height and weight as your son and dressed in a white shirt, brown trousers, and print underwear. What was he wearing at the time of his disappearance?"

Ed turned to Joyce. "Those aren't his clothes," she answered. "Maybe the underwear, but not the rest."

"We will check the fingerprints again," Ortiz told them.

Events were moving towards their inevitable climax. The following morning, Ed went to Joyce's room after breakfast and found her in tears, two men standing over her.

"I am Inspector Mario Rojas of Investigaciones," the taller man said. "I have instructions to bring Mrs. Horman to headquarters for full interrogation."

Ed picked up the telephone and asked the hotel switchboard to connect him to Purdy's number. "I don't want Joyce taken anyplace against her will," he told the Consul after explaining the situation.

"Let me speak with Rojas," Purdy ordered. Handing the receiver to the Inspector, Ed listened to one end of the conversation: "Yes, Consul Purdy . . . I understand . . . certainly . . . I will do as you say." Then the receiver was returned. "Rojas and his friend will leave now," Purdy told Ed. "Don't go anywhere until I get to the hotel."

Half an hour later, the Consul arrived. "Investigaciones is the Chilean equivalent of our FBI," he explained. "Why don't you and I visit Rojas alone?" Leaving Joyce behind, they drove to agency headquarters, where Purdy engineered their quick admission. Walking down a long corridor and up a stairwell, they came to a small, starkly furnished office with a floor-to-ceiling beam jutting from a side wall. Inside, Mario Rojas sat hunched over a large, battered desk.

"Forgive me for the earlier disruption," he apologized. "I have been ordered by the Foreign Ministry to exert every effort in solving the unfortunate problem of your son's disappearance, and I am expected to do so quickly. I only wanted to question Mrs. Horman. Perhaps you could bring her here later this morning."

Ed agreed and returned with Joyce at noon. Rojas was unavailable. "Come back in several hours," they were told. Reappearing at 4:00 P.M., they proceeded upstairs, where the Inspector inserted a questionnaire in an old-fashioned typewriter and began clumsily pecking away at the keys.

"Your husband's name?"

"Charles Edmund Horman."

"Date of disappearance?"

"September 17, 1973."

"Your address in Chile?"

"4126 Vicuña Mackenna."

Twenty minutes into the interrogation, a second agent appeared. "There is a telephone call for Mr. Horman," he announced.

Excusing himself, Ed followed down the hall to a small spare

171

office with empty beer bottles littering the floor. "This is Ed Horman," he said, picking the receiver up off the desk.

"Hello, Mr. Horman. This is Fred Purdy at the Consulate. How are things going?"

"About the same. What about at your end?"

"Not so good, I'm afraid. We've just been told that a body has been identified through a morgue fingerprint check as that of your son. I'd like to talk with you about it. Is it all right if I come over to Investigaciones?"

"I'll be here," Ed told him.

The second-floor corridors formed a long "L" with the stairwell at their point of intersection. Rojas's office was at the far end of the longer hall. Ed waited at the top of the stairs until Purdy arrived, then led him twenty feet down the right angle so Joyce, who was still in the Inspector's office, would be unable to see them talking.

"I'm terribly sorry, Mr. Horman," the Consul began.

"When was he killed?" Ed asked.

"September 18."

"In the National Stadium?"

"Yes . . . he was buried on October 3."

"Where?"

"The Municipal Cemetery."

"In a grave?"

"No . . . in a wall. They do that sometimes."

"Are you certain it's Charles?"

"I'm afraid so. The morgue ran a positive fingerprint check this afternoon."

Experiencing a swell of emotion, Ed again forced his feelings down. Then, very deliberately, he walked back to Rojas's office, where the Inspector continued his questioning.

"I'd like you to leave," Ed told him, "so I can talk with my daughter-in-law alone." Rojas stepped outside. "Charles is dead," Ed said.

Purdy drove them back to the hotel. When they arrived, Ed telephoned Elizabeth's brother in New York. "There's something you have to do for me," he said. "Charles is dead, and I can't bring myself to tell Elizabeth . . . not over the phone at a distance of five thousand miles. I'd lose control. I want you to do it for me."

That done, he telephoned Joyce's father in Minnesota, then went down to the dining room with Joyce to eat dinner.

The following morning, October 19, Ed walked to the Christian Science Reading Room for his daily lesson. Later in the day, Manesas and Ortiz came to the hotel to confirm Charles's death.

"They have verified his fingerprints," Ortiz reported. "He was shot in the Stadium. I'm sorry. Things like this should not happen."

While they were there, Purdy telephoned. "I've been to the morgue," he said. "The fingerprint check is absolute. The autopsy card and our own match completely."

"Why wasn't this revealed by the fingerprint check you ran earlier?" Ed asked.

"There was a misclassification at the morgue. We'll check dental records from the United States tomorrow, but there's really no doubt. It's your son."

"I'd like to go home as soon as possible," Ed told him.

"We'll make immediate reservations for you and Mrs. Horman."

"Not on Lan Chile. I've had enough of this stinking country. I want to fly home on an American airline."

"Fine," Purdy answered. "We'll make reservations with Braniff."

The next morning, Ed returned to the Christian Science Reading Room for the last time, then brought a large suitcase of Charles's clothing to Warwick and Rosalie Armstrong for distribution at a United Nations refugee center. Back at the hotel, he was visited by Mario Rojas of Investigaciones, who confirmed Purdy's report. "This is a horrible tragedy," the Inspector said. "Your son was killed without reason."

Shortly after lunch, Purdy arrived to drive Ed and Joyce to their flight. Passing the Moneda, they saw two busloads of troops dressed for combat. At the airport, they threaded their way through barbed wire and troops to the terminal building, where Ed used the last of his Chilean currency to buy coffee for the Consul. Then he and Joyce boarded Braniff flight 988 and departed.

The journey home took fifteen hours. Wandering through the Lima airport on a layover in Peru, Ed chatted with a passenger who was changing planes from Miami. Learning that Archibald Cox and Elliot Richardson had fallen victim that evening to Richard Nixon's Saturday Night Massacre, he reboarded the plane and reported the news to Joyce.

"I don't feel well," she answered, oblivious to the dispatch. "I think I've been poisoned."

"That's silly."

"No, really! I think I'm going to die . . . . Promise me that, if I die, you'll have an autopsy."

"Don't worry," Ed told her. "You'll be all right."

"No! Promise me, you'll have an autopsy."

"All right! I promise."

She fell asleep with her head on his shoulder.

The plane landed at Kennedy Airport in New York at 9:00 A.M. Elizabeth was there to meet them. In some ways, the past two weeks had been even more difficult for her than Ed and Joyce. They at least had been afforded the opportunity to act. She had been left at home, able only to wait for her husband's nightly telephone calls from Santiago and fantasize in romantic moments about Charles climbing the Andes Mountains to safety.

Standing with her brother, Elizabeth sorted out disembarking passengers in the sterile airport lounge. Then she saw Ed. "I almost didn't recognize him," she remembers. "He looked like a different person. The color in his face was gone . . . his eyes were distended to the point where I was afraid they'd pop out of his head."

Rushing forward, she clung to him, oblivious to everyone and everything around them. Then, she remembered Joyce.

"I wasn't sure I wanted to face her," Elizabeth later admitted. "My son was dead. Nothing in the world is harder for a mother to accept, and Joyce had been a part of his passing. Then, I realized that she was the one who had come back from Chile with no husband, no job, and no home. I thought about how much Charles loved her and how she loved him. I turned towards her and, in that moment, I knew she belonged to Ed and me as much as Charles ever had."

Elizabeth held out her arms. Joyce rushed forward and began to cry.

CHAPTER XVIII

REMAINS

Terry arrived at the Hormans' apartment shortly after noon. Joyce and Ed were still unsettled, their luggage in the foyer. "I'm glad you're home," she said, embracing them both. "It's good to see you."

Ed's retelling of the past two weeks in Santiago took the remainder of the day. Elizabeth roasted a leg of lamb and, afterwards, Jerry Cotts, who had been best man at Charles and Joyce's wedding, paid a condolence visit. With his appearance, Joyce again began to cry. The ensuing year would be far more difficult for her than anyone else. Frenetically, she would jump from one social cause to another . . . wanting to be an artist, a filmmaker, and, at times, a revolutionary. Ultimately, she returned to computers as a systems analyst. In the interim, she lived with Elizabeth and Ed, who awoke frequently to her screams in the night.

A sense of guilt, however unwarranted, was the common denominator for them all. Terry felt that Charles had traveled to Viña and been seized as a consequence of her visit to Santiago. Joyce bore the knowledge that the move to Chile was, in part, the result of her urging. Ed and Elizabeth were plagued by doubts that only a parent can have when an only child has settled in another culture in another land. Their self-flagellation was understandable, but also unjust. Charles himself had once written, "We have no more right to accuse ourselves than to accuse others. Guilt feelings are like fear—given us for survival, not destruction."

Four days after returning to New York, Ed requested that the Department of State transport his son's remains back to the United States. On October 27, Charles Anderson of the Bureau of Special Consular Services responded by telephone:

"We have a problem, Mr. Horman. Your son's body was exhumed for positive identification on October 18. It's been under refrigeration since then but, before that, it was unpreserved for a period of thirty days. It's too decomposed for embalming, and the Chilean government won't permit shipment in its present state."

"I want my son's body home."

"I understand that, Mr. Horman, but the Chilean government has a strict policy about this sort of thing. Their Department of Sanitation will not authorize shipment. Your alternatives are cremation or reduction of the skeleton to bones. Then we can ship the remains."

"Tell them to waive the regulation."

"We'll try, but I don't know how much we can promise."

One month later, when nothing more had been forthcoming from Washington, Joyce wrote directly to Anderson: "It seems an unnecessarily long time since either Edmund Horman or I have heard any word regarding the return of my husband's remains to New York. Perhaps you could keep us better informed about the development of this situation." There was no reply.

On January 3, 1974, Nathaniel Davis was replaced as Ambassador to Chile by David Popper, and the Hormans resumed their efforts. In response to their plea, Popper cabled Henry Kissinger, explaining the Junta's reluctance to act: "[Minister of the Interior] Bonilla says he has delayed authorization to ship Horman remains out of concern that release be so timed as to minimize use of event to detriment of Chile in U.S. media and public opinion."

Eight days later, after testing the Congressional waters, Kissinger cabled back: "Cannot guarantee that return of remains will not receive publicity. However, continued Chilean failure to authorize shipment will keep incident alive and fan family's resentment."

Kissinger was right. Fueled by a series of letters coordinated from the Hormans' Manhattan apartment, Congressional interest was growing—not only in the return of Charles Horman's body but also in the circumstances surrounding his death. In early March, several Senators, led by New York's Jacob Javits, threatened to block shipment of further military aid to Chile unless the remains were returned. Sensing a hardening of public sentiment, the Junta responded.

At 11:30 A.M. on March 21, 1974, Rafael Gonzalez of the Chilean Intelligence Service and United States Vice-Consul James Anderson drove to the Municipal Cemetery in Santiago. Gonzalez, in particular, was troubled by the Horman affair. In late September, 1973, he had been present when General Augusto Lutz ordered the American's execution. Now, half a year later, the death still preyed on his mind.

Stopping first at the Civil Registry, the Chilean obtained three copies of Charles Horman's death certificate. Next, at the morgue, permission for exhumation of the body, which had been reinterred during the winter, was obtained. The two men then proceeded to plot 9, space 188, at the Municipal Cemetery. Too many bodies had been buried in the midst of too much chaos. The markings were inexact. "We had to open a couple of graves," Gonzalez remembers. "Then I recognized him. He was already more or less, you know, but we recognized a little bit of him."

That afternoon, D. S. Candey of the Department of State telephoned Elizabeth in New York. "Your son's body has been removed to a local mortuary," he said. "Prior to shipment, we'll need a destination address and nine hundred dollars."

"I'll call you back," she told him. "I have to talk with my husband and daughter-in-law first."

The following morning, Candey telephoned again, speaking this time with Ed. "Shipment is scheduled for tomorrow," he said, "but we need the instructions and nine hundred dollars first."

"I'll notify you as soon as our decision is made," Ed replied.

"This is our daughter-in-law's decision, and some very deep wounds are being reopened."

"Maybe I should call her myself," Candey suggested.

"To the contrary," Ed answered, his voice rising, "I forbid it. She's had enough of your bureaucratic tripe."

One day later, a telegram addressed to Elizabeth and Ed was delivered to their home:

Subject—Disposition of Horman Remains

This is to confirm the government of Chile's decision to approve your request for the release of the remains of Charles Horman for return to the U.S. In order for the American Embassy at Santiago to arrange shipment, you will recall that a deposit of nine hundred dollars is required to cover the estimated cost for preparation of the remains and transportation to New York City. Funds and instructions should be sent to the office of Special Consular Services. Please accept our deepest condolences in this tragic affair.—Kissinger

Later that week, Joyce telephoned Candey. "The body should be sent to the Chief Medical Examiner of the City of New York," she told him.

"All right," he answered. "It will be shipped from Santiago at 6:30 P.M. on Saturday March 30. You have until nine o'clock that morning to get the money to us."

The memorial service in Charles's honor was simple and unadorned. Robert Louis Shayon, a friend of the Horman family for almost forty years, recalled Charles listening to an old radio program called "You Are There." Shayon had been Executive Producer of the show. Charles, who was then a small boy, was fascinated by it. The dramatic recreation of historic events enthralled him.

"In one particular script—'The Monitor and the Merrimac,' " Shayon told the gathering, "I gave a young naval officer the name Lieutenant Charles Horman. I can still see the entranced grin with which the boy heard his own name in the annals of his country's history."

179

As Shayon spoke, others sat with their own memories. "I went to see him on campus during his first year at Exeter," Charles's aunt recalled. "He was fifteen—an age when most boys are forbidden to acknowledge women relatives. Charles tried to hide me. When we walked along the street, he separated himself by several yards. He led me down as many back roads and hidden paths as possible. Finally, I asked to see his dorm and Charles hesitated. 'Okay,' he said at last, 'but I'm going upstairs to look around first.' Then he came back down and announced, 'The coast is clear but, if anyone sees us, tell them you're the maid.' "

Others focused on more troubling times. For several hours in August, 1973, Simon Blattner had sought to persuade Charles not to return to Chile. Wracked by the consequences of his failure, he found himself speculating much against his will on the manner in which Charles had died: "I think he faced death bravely," Blattner opined, " . . . with great strength and a sense of irony. At the last moment, he must have thought, 'Jesus, what a stupid way to die!' "

On April 13, 1974, Elizabeth, Ed, Terry, and Joyce drove to Greenwood Cemetery in Brooklyn. "We didn't want anyone else there," Elizabeth recalls, "just the four of us. The moment was near intolerable, and we wanted to be alone."

Passing through the huge sandstone arch at the cemetery gate, they disembarked from Ed's car and walked towards the family plot. As if on signal, the cold gray drizzle overhead turned to a hard, driving rain. "Then," Elizabeth remembers, "we saw the hearse and, out of the back, comes this thing . . . not a coffin, but a thing . . . a crate made of lousy wood slats with writing in magic marker on the side. Nothing but a crate with the words 'Charles Horman from Santiago' written in black."

Two men lifted the makeshift coffin from the back of the hearse and carried it to the freshly dug grave. As the rain pelted down, its side markings began to run. Elizabeth leaned forward to touch it, then pulled away. Very deliberately, as her son's remains were lowered into the earth, she took a small bouquet of flowers from her purse and divided it in four . . . one flower to Ed . . . one to Joyce . . . one to Terry . . . the last for herself.

They threw the flowers on the crate, and then they left.

PART THREE

CHAPTER XIX

ED HORMAN'S
THREE QUESTIONS

It's midday and the doorman won't be on duty until 4:00 P.M., so a visitor can pass unimpeded to the Hormans' eighth-floor apartment. Inside, at a bedroom desk, Ed Horman sits leafing through a sheaf of papers. To one side, a dozen books on Chile, Allende, and the CIA lie piled on the floor. To the other, stands a file cabinet containing several thousand pages of documents, newspaper clippings, and assorted memoranda concerning the death of his son, Charles.

"I began collecting documents shortly after I returned from Chile," Ed explains. "As you know, Joyce and I were extremely disenchanted with the performance of our Embassy in Santiago and felt that someone should be called to task. The nature of the Nixon administration was to cater to big corporations like Kennecott and Anaconda. There was no room for the individual, and this lack of consideration for little people had clearly filtered down to Embassy level. I began my ad hoc review suspecting only arrogance and an absence of care. Then, as things progressed, I became aware of something far more serious. I am now convinced that the United States government had foreknowledge of and possibly planned my son's execution."

These are strong words, but Ed Horman is not a man given to irresponsible charges. He is a fairly conservative industrial designer, who lives a life of moderation and frequently votes Republican. For over four years, he has sought to learn how and why his son died. In painstaking fashion, he has written hundreds of letters, made innumerable telephone calls, interviewed scores of witnesses, pressured dozens of Senators and Congressmen, and exhausted every other avenue that might effect a thorough investigation into the causes of Charles's death. If no active lead exists, he returns to old files and reads through them a fourth and fifth time. His professional life has been largely ignored. Searching for "the truth about Charles" has become the dominant motivating force in his life.

"I now see Charles's death as incidental to a far larger conspiracy," Ed explains. "But to understand what I'm driving at, you have to put things in perspective. You have to realize what our government did in Chile . . . focus on the nature of the government we helped to overthrow and the Junta we now so actively support."

Salvador Allende took power without a shot being fired. He was the freely elected President of a democratic government in a country with a longstanding tradition of constitutional rule. He repeatedly disavowed the Communist Party's obedience to world strategy and sought instead to create a new type of socialism which would maintain constitutional freedoms without revolutionary violence. His administration brought social reforms, not socialism, to Chile and was more reformist than revolutionary. Allende sought better health care, better housing, better jobs, better education, and a better way of life for his people. In most respects, his programs were far closer to Franklin Roosevelt's New Deal than Marxist dogma. Indeed, had he carried out the same programs from an anti-Communist or neutralist pulpit, it is doubtful that the United States would have moved against him.

Allende was not above criticism. His nationalization of Chile's copper industry was a pseudolegal "grab" which should have resulted in some form of compensation for Kennecott and Anaconda but did not. His administration was wracked by economic mismanagement. But an act of nationalization hardly justifies the covert subversion of a nation's economy by a foreign power. And it will never be known how much of the economic turmoil that beset Chile was caused by Allende's leadership and how much was the result of economic sabotage by the United States. For the fact of the matter is that the United States brought to bear its economic might against a nation with fewer people than the state of Ohio. If one ponders the disruption to the American economy (the strongest in the world) caused by a few Arab sheiks who decreed a short-lived, ineffectual oil embargo in 1973, the devastating effect of our nation's full economic might crushing down upon Chile becomes obvious.

And what of the Junta? Economically, even with American support, its record has been one of dismal failure. In the year following the coup, the price of bread rose from three to twenty-four cents per kilo, milk from three to twelve cents a liter. The cost of living rose 145.6 percent in the first six months of 1974 alone. By 1976, real wages had dropped 21.5 percent below their precoup level. During his thirty-four months in office, Allende had presided over a lowering of unemployment from 8.3 to 3.1 percent. After three years of military rule, that figure had sextupled.

As for the larger issues of political freedom and human rights, the record speaks for itself. Allende was committed to governing within a constitutional framework. Under his administration, Chileans were free to read and write what they chose. They could petition their government and demonstrate in the streets. Free elections were a way of life, as they had been for decades. By contrast, the Junta presides over what Senator Frank Church has called "the desolation of Chile."

The reign of book-burning, torture, and death which enmeshed thousands in the aftermath of the coup has continued unimpeded. Returning from a 1974 study mission to Santiago, former American Ambassador to Chile Ralph Dungan testified before a Senate subcommittee on political refugees as follows: "I am morally certain that tortures are taking place systematically and to a substantial extent. It is not an episodic thing where an individual soldier or intelligence agent went off and did something on his own. You have systematic torture being used in connection with interrogations with substantial numbers of persons. And, when I say substantial, I am talking about 10 or 20 percent of the total number of people detained. Electric shock, psychological tortures of one kind or another, plastic bag tortures, immersion of the head in water or oil, all kinds of tortures . . . . There was evidence of people being hung up by the wrists, of needles or other instruments under the fingernails . . . . The situation reminds one of the 1930s in Germany."

A report by the Economic and Social Council of the United Nations General Assembly continues this theme, citing "the transformation of Chile's intelligence services into a secret police which is omnipotent and immune from responsibility . . . . Persons suspected of opposing or potentially opposing the regime are described as Marxists. This term is applied to anybody expressing views not corresponding to those officially held. The adjective is used not only in connection with personalities who had a political role in the past, but with those whose functions place them outside politics, who are members of moderate or centrist movements, writers, students, and even Catholic or Protestant bishops. Legal procedures have been bent to follow these concepts. 'Subversion' is given as a reason for arrests and imprisonment. The expression 'offenses against the state of siege' is commonly used to describe unspecified charges."

A 1977 report by the Inter-American Commission on Human Rights—an agency of the twenty-five-nation Organization of American States—confirms that arbitrary arrest, torture, and murder remain rampant in Chile. Moreover, the Chilean people have been stripped of all possible defense against these abuses by the restructuring of political institutions to consolidate military rule.

On September 11, 1973, the day of the coup, the Junta ordered Chile's Congress "indefinitely" closed. Ten days later, it banned all Marxist political parties, declared non-Marxist parties "in recess," and announced the formation of a "distinguished committee" to formulate plans for a new Constitution. On September 25, 1973, all freely elected mayors and city councilmen were removed from their posts pending the appointment of replacements by the military. Two weeks later, the "recess" imposed on non-Marxist parties was changed to a "suspension." It subsequently became a permanent ban.

On October 17, 1973, a decree forbidding all political activity by individuals, parties or other organized groups was put into effect and the Chilean Constitutional Court abolished. Thereafter, electoral registers containing the names of 3.5 million Chileans entitled to vote were destroyed. "I never said this was a transition government," explained Junta President Augusto Pinochet. "It may last ten or twenty years." In June, 1975, Pinochet amended his statement: "There will be no elections in Chile during my lifetime, nor the lifetime of my successor."

Not content with controlling Chile's political structure, the Junta has moved to suppress freedom of choice in virtually every other area of public life. In the wake of the coup, Chile's largest labor organization—the eight-hundred-thousand-member Central Workers' Confederation—was abolished. The university system has been placed under tight supervision, with professors required to submit their teaching programs for military review on a weekly basis. Mail and press censorship are common. Indeed, the Junta has gone so far as to ban use of the term "compañero," which had been a traditional greeting among Allende supporters.

"There is a new order in Chile," Ed Horman says bitterly, "and that order is fascism. Let me tell you what our government has done about it. Two weeks after the coup, the United States recognized the Junta as the legitimate government of Chile. While Charles's body was still in the morgue, the new Ambassador from Santiago arrived in Washington and was met by Henry Kissinger, who threw his arms out and hugged him. Then the Director of the CIA went before the House Foreign Affairs Committee and testified that the postcoup executions in Chile had done 'some good' because they reduced the possibility of civil war. Not once did our government issue an expression of disapproval, forceful or otherwise, against the Junta's conduct in 1973. Not once has it exerted pressure to bring to justice those persons responsible for Charles's death."

The facts bear Ed Horman out. In the last full year of the

Allende government, the United States extended a meager $2.5 million in Food for Peace assistance to Chile. For fiscal 1974, that total was multiplied fifteenfold. Shortly before the coup, the Nixon administration refused a Chilean request for credit to buy much-needed wheat to combat a food shortage. Less than a month later, a $24.5-million credit was granted, prompting Senator Edward Kennedy of Massachusetts to declare: "I am shocked. The credit offered by this administration in a single day to the military junta is eight times the total commodity credit offered Chile in the past three years when a democratically elected government was in power."

Yet Washington's receptivity to military rule should have surprised no one. For three years, the Nixon administration had violated virtually every precept of international law in an effort to foment a military coup in Chile. Only the scope of the administration's efforts was unknown, and this as a consequence of lies to Congress and the American people.

The case of Richard Helms is an example on point. Speaking before a student group at Johns Hopkins University in 1972, the CIA Director responded to a student who asked whether the United States had sought to influence the 1970 Presidential election in Chile with the answer, "Why should you care? Your side won." Testifying before the Senate Foreign Relations Committee in February and March, 1973, Helms was somewhat less candid, categorically denying American involvement. Caught in his lie when the Church Committee Report revealed the scope of CIA conduct, Helms escaped indictment for perjury by threatening revelations that would endanger national security. Ultimately, he was permitted to plead "no contest" to a misdemeanor charge of "failing to testify fully before Congress." His government pension intact, he was fined two thousand dollars and announced that his plea would be worn "like a badge of honor." Hours after sentencing, the fine was paid by a group of former CIA employees, who met at a party and tossed checks into a wastepaper basket placed on top a piano.

The Justice Department's handling of the Helms case

prompted Senator Frank Church to comment, "I thought there was to be an end to the double standard of justice for big shots." "What Church failed to perceive," Ed Horman observes, "is that there is no inclination on the part of our government to rock the boat on Chile. The prevailing view, even in the Carter administration, is that the matter should be laid to rest."

Indeed, one State Department official recently went so far as to suggest that Allende was "not really a democratically elected President," since he was elected with only 36 percent of the popular vote. This, of course, overlooks the fact that, in ten of the past twenty-seven American Presidential elections, minority Presidents have been elected, the most recent being Richard Nixon who captured the White House with 43.4 percent of the popular vote in 1968.

Thus, it is hardly surprising that the only expression of regret to be heard from the Nixon administration regarding Chile's fall from constitutional rule was the most perverse. Seven days after the coup, Jack Kubisch—then Assistant Secretary of State for Inter-American Affairs—declared, "It was not in our interest to have the military take over in Chile. It would have been better had Allende served his entire term, taking the nation and the Chilean people into complete and total ruin. Only then would the full discrediting of socialism have taken place. The military takeover and bloodshed has confused this lesson."

Kubisch's remarks warrant special attention because, at the time he made them, he was the public official with primary responsibility for American relations with Latin America. Perhaps Richard Fagen (a Professor of Political Science at Stanford University and former President of the Latin American Studies Association) has put them in context best:

[Kubisch evinces] no regret about the coup other than it interrupted his preferred scenario for Allende's demise; no shame in equating the U.S. national interest with the destruction of the socialist experience in Chile; not even any sense of irony that discrediting Allende's constitutional revolution lends support to the argument that structural change will come about only through violence and the rejection of democratic practices; just decades-old cold warriorism, twisted logic, total lack of concern for the Chilean people, and a single-minded commitment to the destruction of the Chilean way by the most convincing means possible.

So much for hemispheric cooperation, social justice, democracy, nonintervention and other fine phrases. What really matters to people who think this way is that the hemisphere be made safe for "the American way of life," and this in turn implies that socialist experiments must be destroyed as convincingly as possible. Given this mission, it follows that human lives don't count for much—especially if they are relatively young and think "wrong thoughts." It is in this context, permeated by a mentality of destruction, that the death of Charles Horman must be placed.

"Fagen was half-right," Ed Horman declares. "In limiting United States responsibility for Charles's death to the creation of a climate in which the coup occurred, he overlooked something far more sinister. From the day I returned home on, the actions of our government have convinced me that the American Embassy in Santiago was very much involved in Charles's murder. Let me tell you why."

Straightening the papers on his desk, Ed pulls one file folder aside. "If anything was certain when I left Santiago, it was that Charles had been executed in the National Stadium by the Chilean military. Then, two days after I returned, the *New York Post* ran an article which quoted Kate Marshall, the woman I met in Washington with Charles Anderson, as taking a completely contrary position. Here! Look for yourself."

Reaching into the folder, marked "Miscellaneous 1973," Ed extracts a clipping from the October 23, 1973, *New York Post,* and points to a paragraph bracketed in ink:

State Department officials said they had requested an investigation of Horman's death and suggested he may have been killed by left-wing groups masquerading as soldiers and parading around in uniforms after the coup . . . . "really wicked people who would kill him just to make the military look bad," said Department spokeswoman Kate Marshall.

"The moment I saw that," Ed explains, "I telephoned Kate Marshall and asked her how she could possibly make a statement like that. Fred Purdy himself had told me that Charles was executed in the National Stadium. Mario Rojas of Investigaciones and two agents from SIM had confirmed the report. What I didn't know then and do now was that Nathaniel Davis had begun to circulate a far different version of events. The very same day Purdy told me my son was dead, Davis had cabled Henry Kissinger, saying that Charles's body had been picked up, not at the National Stadium, but on the street by a passing military patrol. From the time I saw that clipping in the *New York Post* on, all I've gotten from our government are denials. Purdy now denies telling me that Charles was executed in the National Stadium. Rojas, Manesas, and Ortiz deny confirming the report; and the State Department has adopted the Junta's story that Charles was killed by left-wing extremists. I'm up against a stone wall."

His dismay clearly visible, Ed Horman returns the sheaf of papers he has been holding to their proper file. "Neither the Ford or Carter administrations has seen fit to reopen the matter of Charles's death," he says, annoyance present in his voice. "Well, I'm not going to let the matter die. There are three issues to be publicly resolved. One, was my son killed by the Chilean military? Two, did the United States government knowingly seek to cover up facts surrounding his death? And three, did our government have foreknowledge of or possibly even order his execution? I want a satisfactory response to each of these questions. Unfortunately, I think I already know the answers."

CHAPTER XX

WAS CHARLES HORMAN EXECUTED BY THE CHILEAN MILITARY?

For the record, the government of Chile now says that Charles Horman's body was found on a street in Santiago by a passing military patrol, and delivered to the morgue at 1:35 P.M. on September 18, 1973—the day following his disappearance. His corpse was received by Angel Carrasco, a morgue official who allegedly recalls nothing about the occasion, but does recognize his signature on the Certificate of Receipt of Corpse. The body was fingerprinted and held for sixteen days before burial in the Municipal Cemetery in Santiago. Through an "error in classification," the fingerprint card was misplaced, only to be rediscovered the day after Ed was told by Lovell Jarvis that Charles was dead.

The Chilean government further asserts that it is not possible for Charles to have been seized by troops as claimed by neighbors because military regulations required troops to travel in clearly marked military vehicles and never in one vehicle alone. In a December 13, 1973, report to the United States Embassy, the Junta declared, "The competent authorities of the Ministry of National Defense consider it highly probable that the death [was] due to the action of snipers or extremists using military uniforms."

194

An alternative explanation comes from Enrique Guzman, Sub-director of International Relations for the Chilean Foreign Ministry, who reported to the American Embassy on December 5, 1973, that Horman was "deeply involved in leftist activities" and "perhaps had been shot by his own comrades for betraying the cause." Guzman's report was based in part on a memorandum prepared by General Augusto Lutz—the head of Chilean Military Intelligence—who is identified by others as having ordered Charles Horman's execution. In relevant part, the Lutz report states:

American citizens Frank Randall Teruggi and Charles Horman were accurately investigated by officials of the Military Intelligence Service in order to establish cause of death as a special deference to the American Embassy. Available information on both persons leads to the conclusion that they were involved in extreme leftist movements in our country which they supported both materially and ideologically. Available and well-supported data evidences . . . that both Americans died out of military control.

Incredibly, the United States Department of State now accepts the Junta's version of events and refuses to place blame on the government of Chile for the death of Charles Horman. On July 24, 1974, Linwood Holton, Assistant Secretary of State for Congressional Relations, declared, "The Chilean government has addressed the question of responsibility in its Foreign Ministry note of December 13, 1973. That official response asserted inter alia that the competent authorities of the Ministry of National Defense consider it highly probable that the death was due to the action of snipers or extremists using military uniforms . . . . We are unable to establish a legal basis for attributing an international wrong to the Chilean government for the death of Mr. Horman."

Given this Orwellian stand by the Department of State, it is necessary to search out the original actors in the Horman drama.

Colonel William Hon spends much of his time these days relaxing at his home in Falls Church, Virginia. Retired from the

United States Army in 1976 after thirty-three years of service, he fondly recalls, "It was never dull."

According to official records, at the time of Charles Horman's disappearance, Hon was a defense attaché assigned to the American Embassy in Santiago. The scope of his duties is unclear, but he acknowledges that they required maintaining good relations with the Chilean military. One source quotes Lieutenant-Colonel Patrick Ryan, second in command of the United States Naval Mission in Valparaiso, as suggesting that Hon was "a spy." Ryan denies making the remark but qualifies his denial by saying, "I would never use the word spy . . . . Spy is a word you use in James Bond things. But anybody with any political intelligence or diplomatic background knows that one of the functions of an attaché is to gain information that would be beneficial to the United States. You won't see it written anyplace, but that's one of the functions of an attaché."

A State Department memorandum entitled "Résumé of Embassy Actions on Horman Case" indicates that Hon was extremely active in attempting to secure information concerning the whereabouts of Charles Horman. Beginning on September 20, 1973, he is reported to have questioned General Augusto Lutz, the head of Chilean Army Intelligence, on at least six occasions, and made numerous inquiries of other "intelligence contacts" within the Chilean military. One of these contacts was General Camilo Valenzuela, later named by the Church Committee as a prime mover in the 1970 plot against the Army Chief of Staff, Rene Schneider.

Hon is "tired of talking about the Horman matter" and reluctant to discuss it further. "This thing has gone on and on," he says, "and been questioned and questioned. It's one of those things where, no matter how it comes out, it's not going to benefit anybody. I think it's just a case that's been overworked and will ultimately be ho-hum, so what."

Ed Horman is understandably irked by Hon's attitude. Having lost his son, he is disinclined to treat the matter in "ho-hum" fashion. However, there is significance to Hon's comments in that, while he steadfastly denies any American role in Charles's death, he does appear to hold the government of Chile responsible: "I did what was possible under the circumstances," Hon says. "There was not much else I could do. Naturally, it's impossible to move a government when you have no control over them at all as to what they should or shouldn't be doing. They considered their actions necessary, and obviously certain people were going to get caught up in that sort of thing."

Hon's statement is at odds with official State Department pronouncements that there is no basis for attributing guilt to the Chilean government with regard to the death of Charles Horman. However, it is fully consistent with several unrebutted facts.

Half a dozen neighbors saw Charles taken from his home by Chilean troops. One witness followed the arresting soldiers directly to the National Stadium, which was then in use as a prisoner detention center. On the day following Charles's seizure, telephone calls in the name of Military Intelligence were made to the home of Warwick Armstrong and Mario and Isabella Carvajal. Two additional witnesses, to be discussed in this and the following chapter, also place Charles Horman in Chilean custody. One of them, Rafael Gonzalez of Chilean Military Intelligence, claims to have been present when Horman's execution was ordered. Another, Enrique Sandoval, says he spoke with a military officer who saw Horman being led out to be shot.

In response to these charges, the government of Chile argues that Charles Horman could not have been arrested by the military because he was seized by soldiers from a solitary truck and Chilean troops never traveled in one vehicle alone. It also notes that the truck was reportedly without official military markings. This denial is nonsense. The great majority of Americans detained in the aftermath of the coup were transported by soldiers who arrived in a single vehicle. Joseph Francis Doherty, Jim Ritter, and David Hathaway were all arrested in this fashion. As for the absence of military markings, Dr. Philip Polakoff, a physician serving in Chile with the United States Public Health Service at the time of the coup, testified before Congress as fol-

197

lows: "We would see on numerous occasions troops coming in, and they did not come in with fancy troop carriers. They came in taxi cabs and rented vehicles and anything else they could take."

The refusal of the Chilean government to return Charles Horman's remains prior to March, 1974, is another indication of culpability. "I'll tell you why," Ed Horman explains. "First, the Junta said it didn't want the remains shipped to the United States because of health regulations. Then that excuse went by the boards, and we were told that fear of bad publicity and exploitation by the U.S. media was the reason. Still, that didn't prevent the Junta from offering to send back a skeleton, which would have been just as bad from a publicity point of view.

"This is not a pleasant subject," Ed continues, "but I suspect that the real reason Charles's body was held for so long is that the Junta wanted time and decay to erase any sign of torture. That's the only explanation I can think of. All this talk about health regulations and media exploitation is hogwash. It's no more credible than the discovery of a so-called fingerprint misclassification at the morgue. The Junta was afraid that, if Charles's remains were returned too soon, an autopsy would show conclusively that he had been tortured."

The Junta's denial of responsibility for the death of Charles Horman appears particularly flimsy when matched with a similar disclaimer with regard to Frank Teruggi. Teruggi, the Chilean military claims, was arrested for "curfew violation" on September 20 and released one day later. Thereafter, his body was found "in the streets" by a passing military patrol and brought to the morgue on the evening of September 22.

The Junta's version of Teruggi's death is clearly fabricated. Teruggi was not arrested for curfew violation. He was dragged from his apartment with David Hathaway in the presence of the latter's fiancée. The supposed September 21 release date is in conflict with assurances of the Junta, now recanted, that he was in good health and undergoing interrogation at a later date. Moreover, it is highly unlikely that Teruggi or any prisoner would have been released from custody just one day after his arrest, as the Junta now claims. Except in instances of summary execution, interrogation and prisoner evaluation took a minimum of several days. By way of example, David Hathaway, who was arrested with his roommate, was detained one day shy of a week. Also, Hathaway reports that Teruggi was taken from his cell late on the afternoon of September 21. Given the paperwork that accompanied an end to detention, release before the evening curfew would have been impossible.

The Junta's credibility with regard to the death of Frank Teruggi is further undermined by Steve Volk, who identified his friend's body in the Santiago morgue. Recalling that moment, Volk remembers, "Frank's body was completely nude and uncovered. There were two gunshot wounds in his head and a long slash on the neck. No other wounds were present."

Four days after Volk's visit to the morgue, the government of Chile issued an autopsy report citing seventeen bullet wounds in Teruggi's corpse. "Given the stress of the moment," Volk says, "it's possible that I overlooked one or two wounds, but not over a dozen. The autopsy report is nothing but an attempt to lead people to believe that Frank was gunned down in the streets. I saw two bullet wounds in his head. That, to me, is indicative of an execution."

Frank Teruggi's body was identified by Steve Volk on October 2. The very next day, Charles's Horman's corpse was taken from the morgue and buried in the Municipal Cemetery. "Clearly," Ed Horman says, "someone didn't want my son's body to be discovered." Nor, apparently, did the government of Chile want to be linked to his death, and, to avoid this, it engaged in a clumsily transparent attempt to place Charles as being alive after the time of his execution.

On the afternoon of October 3, the Chilean Foreign Ministry sent two notes to the American Embassy. One of them restated in formal fashion the Junta's earlier claim that Frank Teruggi had been arrested for curfew violation on September 20, released the following day, and later found dead in the streets. The other note contained a remarkable declaration. In it, the Foreign

Ministry stated that Charles Horman had also been arrested for curfew violation on the twentieth and released one day later. Clearly, the note was at odds with the facts. Charles Horman was seized on September 17, not the twentieth. But its contents are important because they are the sole admission by the Chilean military that Horman was ever in custody.

Predictably, the note was later withdrawn. On October 17 (the day Ed Horman met with Lovell Jarvis), Junta Press Secretary Frederick Willoughby informed the American Embassy that its contents were "in error." A formal retraction followed five days later, accompanied by the statement that the note "did not correspond to actual events."

Factual discrepancies in the government of Chile's treatment of the Horman and Teruggi cases are clearly lies. Both Americans were arrested by the Junta and, from all appearances, executed while in military custody. Indeed, the official cover is so fragile that, in a November 13, 1973, cable to the American Embassy in Santiago, Secretary of State Henry Kissinger warned Nathaniel Davis, "There is continued strong Congressional and public interest in the circumstances leading to the Teruggi and Horman deaths. Interested parties and press here are dwelling on factual discrepancies . . . indicative of official cover-up."

Still, despite the Kissinger message, the Department of State has consistently refused to take public issue with the Chilean military regarding Charles Horman's death, and this leads to Ed Horman's second question: Did representatives of the United States government seek to cover up information concerning the fate of his son?

CHAPTER XXI

WAS THERE A UNITED STATES GOVERNMENT COVER-UP?

On July 14, 1977, New York Congressman Jerome Ambro summed up Department of State conduct in the Horman case with the declaration, "Lack of answers, false answers, incorrect answers by State after the fact smack of severe cover-up." Before the Congressman's charge can be fully evaluated, it must be viewed in its proper context.

United States relations with those foreign countries with which it has formal diplomatic ties are the responsibility of an Ambassador. He or she is a personal representative of the President and is charged with representing United States interests before the local government and protecting American citizens who reside in or are traveling through the host nation. In carrying out these duties, the Ambassador has control over resident Department of State personnel and representatives of all other United States agencies with programs in the country, exclusive of military operations.

Embassy organization varies slightly from post to post, but diplomatic missions are generally divided into four sections. The Political Section negotiates agreements between governments and analyzes local developments of political interest. The Economic-Commercial Section gathers data on the host country's economic condition, formulates economic development programs, and works to advance United States trade interests. The Administrative Section is responsible for the day-to-day functioning of the Embassy, including such matters as budget planning, housing, and security. The fourth mission subdivision is the Consular Section. It provides visa, citizenship, passport, and related service assistance. More important, it is entrusted with the protection of American lives.

Linwood Holton, former Assistant Secretary of State for Congressional Relations, has sought to put these responsibilities in context with the statement, "The welfare of our citizens abroad in whatever circumstances they may find themselves is our first and most important responsibility." Yet, despite this obligation, it is clear that the American Embassy in Santiago fell far short of maximum performance in the case of Charles Horman.

At the time of Charles Horman's seizure, every United States Consulate in the world was subject to a century-old statute known as the Act of 1868. This law, which is still in effect, requires that whenever any United States citizen is wrongfully deprived of his liberty in a foreign land, the President through his representatives must immediately demand that the local government state the reason for imprisonment. Then, if the detention appears unjust, the President must demand the citizen's release and use all "necessary and proper" means to effectuate that end.

The arrest of Charles Horman was reported to the American Consulate on September 18, 1973. The immediate demand for information required by law was not forthcoming. Instead, the Embassy made inquiries of local Carabiñeros stations and Investigaciones, followed by other low-level military contacts. It was not until September 26—nine days after Horman's seizure—that Ambassador Davis first broached the subject with Chile's Foreign Minister. No explanation for this failure to act in conformity with law has ever been given. Instead, the Department of State has repeatedly fallen back on the excuse that no harm resulted from violation of the statute because, "It appears that Charles Horman died sometime before noon on September 18, [and the] Embassy did not receive word that he had been detained or was in difficulty until he was already dead."

"That excuse," Ed Horman says, "is poppycock. In the first place, our Embassy claims it didn't learn Charles was dead until late October. If that's true, it should have followed the statute when first informed of his seizure. Second, there's no proof that Charles was, in fact, killed on September 18. Lovell Jarvis told me that the execution took place on September 20, and nothing contradicts that date except the Junta's claim that Charles's body was found in the streets two days earlier. I think my son was alive on September 18, and I think that rapid, forceful action by our Embassy could have saved him, if they had wanted to. Instead, they did virtually nothing. Don't take my word for it. Look for yourself."

Reaching into the pile of books at his side, Ed withdraws a 1975 report by the Comptroller General of the United States, entitled "An Assessment of Selected U.S. Embassy-Consular Efforts to Assist and Protect Americans Overseas During Crises and Emergencies." "In Chile," the report reads, "prompt and effective protests by high-level U.S. officials on behalf of arrested and detained Americans were not always made."

"Keep reading," Ed instructs.

The report goes on: "There is no evidence that the U.S. Embassy during this period discussed with top officials of the Chilean government the arrest and detention of American citizens [at all]."

To say that Embassy and Consulate personnel did nothing on Charles Horman's behalf would be unfair. Some well-motivated people within the American diplomatic community tried to save him. Nonetheless, the record of neglect is obvious. The United States Consulate was informed of his seizure on September 18 in separate telephone calls from Warwick Armstrong and Carlotta Manosa. The only step it took that day was to telephone several local Carabiñeros stations and Investigaciones headquarters.

"Why," Ed Horman wants to know, "didn't Fred Purdy go directly to the National Stadium? It was common knowledge that prisoners were being held there. Why didn't he contact the Chilean Army, Navy, and Military Intelligence? The fact of the matter is that, once the telephone calls to Charles's friends were reported, our Consulate ignored them."

Here again, the charge is strong, but the record appears to bear Ed Horman out. When Joyce met with John Hall on September 19, the Vice-Consul gave no indication of prior knowledge concerning Charles's seizure. It was not until Terry and Joyce saw Dale Shaffer five days later and requested access to the file cards he was holding that they even learned of Warwick Armstrong's telephone report. When Ed arrived in Santiago on October 5 and met with Nathaniel Davis, the Ambassador disclaimed any knowledge of the calls. Not until October 6—eighteen days after the inquiries by Chilean Military Intelligence were first reported— did the Consulate question Armstrong and the Carvajals. Indeed, the official attitude towards the calls was perhaps best summed up by Fred Purdy several weeks after Charles's body was discovered in the Santiago morgue. In response to an inquiry about them, the Vice-Consul told an associate of newspaper columnist Jack Anderson, "I don't remember the details. We don't have tapes like the White House."

In her first three trips to the Consulate, Joyce was interviewed by three different officials, all of whom manifested substantial ignorance of the case. At times, it appeared as though the Embassy and Consulate had stopped trying altogether. On Saturday, September 22, when Joyce, Terry, and Steve Volk visited the Consulate, it was virtually empty. On a day when over a dozen American citizens were missing, the only persons visibly present were two secretaries and Fred Purdy. One former Consulate employee now seeks to excuse this apparent misfeasance by arguing, "Things in Santiago shut down over the weekend. There was nothing we could have done on a Saturday." However, this excuse fails to explain another item revealed by the Embassy calendar for the proceeding Thursday, September 20.

The twentieth was a day of particular significance. By Lovell Jarvis's account, that was when Charles Horman was executed.

It was also the day Frank Teruggi and David Hathaway were arrested. Yet Department of State documents show that, on the afternoon of the twentieth, United States Embassy, Consulate, and military personnel attended a party at the home of Ambassador Nathaniel Davis. "That says something to me," Ed Horman contends. "If the Department of State had displayed the same sense of urgency for Charles's welfare that it displayed in collecting nine hundred dollars for the shipment of his remains, my son might be alive today."

"The protection of American lives," Ed continues, "is the rationale most often given in support of the United States invasion of foreign lands. From the Dominican Republic to Cambodia, that was our justification for military intervention. Yet rather than take firm steps to save my son's life in Chile, our Embassy held a party. If Charles and Frank Teruggi had been arrested and executed by the Allende government, you can bet Nathaniel Davis would have acted. Yet, here, the Ambassador went so far as to refuse Joyce's request to visit the National Stadium on grounds that he didn't want to ask too many favors of the Junta. That," Ed concludes, "is significant in the extreme because it shows what Nathaniel Davis is made of. The United States was in a position to ask as many favors of the new government as it wanted. The Junta's primary source of military supplies was Washington, D.C. Its sole hope for economic recovery was Washington, D.C. The Generals were hardly in a position to turn to the Soviet Union or China for help. Nathaniel Davis could have asked for and received as many favors as he wanted."

Needless to say, the Department of State vigorously disputes Ed Horman's contention that its efforts were less than total. While conceding that the Act of 1868 might not have been followed to the letter, it cites "intense informal efforts" on Charles Horman's behalf followed by later contacts of a more official nature. It also points to conditions extant in Santiago in the aftermath of the coup and, in a letter sent to several Senators and Congressmen, declares:

During the period when Embassy personnel were attempting to locate Charles Horman, they were also involved in protection efforts on behalf of the entire American community in Chile, numbering somewhere between 2,200 and 2,800 persons. In the process, Embassy personnel checked on the welfare of over 600 American citizens and reported the results to relatives or friends in the United States. They were instrumental in securing the release of seventeen Americans who had been detained by the Chilean authorities, and obtained safe conduct passes and helped arrange transportation for more than forty Americans who would have been unable to leave Chile otherwise. This was accomplished in the midst of street violence and Chilean administrative disorganization, and with efforts impeded by difficulties in communication, a strict curfew and severe military restrictions on personnel movement and activity.

Much of what is contained in the above quote is true. However, there are disturbing reports that Embassy and Consulate assistance was administered on a partisan basis and that diplomatic support was withheld from "certain types" of Americans. These reports, if accurate, remove United States government handling of the Horman case from the category of negligence and place it with a far more serious group of offenses.

The American community in Santiago was significantly divided at the time of the coup. Half of its members were United States government employees and their dependents. Traces of a once-substantial business community also remained. However, a large number of Americans in Chile were cut from a far different mold. They were young, liberal, and intent on experiencing the Allende experiment. Their resentment towards established institutions was, on occasion, ill-concealed, and far too often the American diplomatic community responded in kind.

Peter Bell arrived in Santiago in September, 1970, to assume command of the Ford Foundation office for the southern cone of South America—an area encompassing Argentina, Paraguay, Uruguay, and Chile. "Prior to the coup," Bell says, "there had been an attitude of hostility towards the Allende government. Americans who were in Chile and did not share the Embassy attitude were regarded as troublemakers. I think the attitude was a fairly pervasive one within the Embassy."

Professor Richard Fagen observed a similar posture. On leave from Stanford University, he was in Santiago as a visiting Professor at the Latin American Faculty of Social Sciences. "While in Santiago," Fagen recalls, "I met a number of young Americans who were living and working in the city and were, in varying degrees, sympathetic to the Allende experiment. I had not been in Santiago long before it became quite evident that the expressed hostility of the American Embassy toward the Allende government extended to those members of the American community who were known to cooperate, sympathize, or even take a neutral stance toward the regime. Words such as 'traitorous,' 'commie,' and 'fellow traveler' were bandied about in reference to many of my American friends and acquaintances."

The experience of Terry Simon and Charles Horman on September 17, 1973, confirms Fagen and Bell. Fearing for their safety, the two young Americans went to the Embassy for information on flights out of Chile and were referred to the Consulate, one mile away, by a switchboard operator who refused to call ahead to ascertain whether assistance would be forthcoming there either. When Charles returned home to avoid being caught in the curfew, Terry entered the Consulate alone.

"Four days earlier," she recalls, "I had been in Viña del Mar, where the British Consul offered me money out of his own pocket. In Santiago, our own people wouldn't give me the time of day." At one point, Terry remembers, she asked a Consulate official how many United States citizens there were in Chile. "I don't know," came the reply. "They never visit us in normal times but, at times like this, they come crawling out of the woodwork."

Steve Volk, who dealt with the Embassy and Consulate on several occasions in the aftermath of the coup, describes their attitude as "cold, certainly not helpful, laden with the message that you were wasting their time. I saw it on several occasions," Volk says, "once when I went to the Consulate to see Purdy with Terry and Joyce, again when I told James Anderson that David Hathaway had asked me to look for Frank Teruggi's body in the morgue. Those were personal experiences," Volk continues. "Other incidents were worse."

One event related by Volk concerns an American citizen who voluntarily presented himself to military authorities in Temuco (a town in southern Chile) pursuant to a directive that all foreigners report to the local police. The American was in Chile on a tourist visa which had expired several days earlier. The military held him for four days, beat him, and finally dumped him on the street. When he went to the American Consulate for protection, he was told to report back to the military and ask for a new visa. Not one person in the Consulate offered assistance, even though it was common knowledge that foreigners without visas were being incarcerated.

Most of Steve Volk's time in Santiago had been spent researching a doctoral dissertation for Columbia University. By the time he left Chile on October 6, 1973, he had amassed a huge quantity of notes. "We had all heard that books and papers were being seized at the airport," he remembers, "so I went to the Embassy and asked the Cultural Affairs Attaché if he would send my papers back through the diplomatic pouch. He said yes, and I gave him a stack of notes that amounted to a year of my life. I never saw them again."

Philip Wohlstetter was a young American who had spent the better part of a year traveling through Latin America writing "A Guidebook for Wanderers." Four days after the coup, he and two companions were stopped at gunpoint by Carabiñeros in the heart of Santiago. Pushed against a building wall, they were frisked, ordered inside a nearby station house, and instructed to lie face down on the cold marble floor.

For twenty minutes, Wohlstetter and his friends lay with their hands behind their heads, a soldier with a submachine gun standing over them. Then they were interrogated. Who were they? Why had they come to Chile? Had they ever been to Cuba? Following interrogation, another hour passed. Still face down, Wohlstetter turned his head slightly to examine the faces around him. As he did, a short, pudgy man with longish blond hair, wire-rimmed glasses, and a blue suit entered the room with two soldiers. After talking briefly with a third officer, the man left.

Several hours later, following a second interrogation and the confiscation of one hundred dollars in cash, Wohlstetter and his friends were released. On Monday, September 17, they went to the American Consulate to report the incident.

"Just a moment," the receptionist told them. "Vice-Consul Shaffer will be out shortly."

When Shaffer appeared, Wohlstetter stared. Before him stood the same blond-haired, blue-suited man who had walked in and out of the station house during his detention.

"Can I help you?" the Vice-Consul asked.

"Remember us . . . the police station the other day?"

Shaffer shook his head. "I've never seen you before."

"Yes you have. We were lying on the floor when you walked in."

"Oh yes . . . I, uh, didn't see your faces."

"Yeah . . . . We had to keep them down against the floor."

"Yes . . . well, uh," Shaffer began to fidget. ". . . They uh, they said they were going to release you, so I didn't bother to do anything."

Several years later, Wohlstetter remains shaken by his experience. "There was a horrible feeling of helplessness in being an American," he says, "and not being able to go to the Embassy for protection. When things get hot, people should be able to go to the Embassy for safety. Instead, we were told to go home. That's where most of the Americans who got picked up were arrested—not on the streets, but at home."

Not every misstep by Embassy and Consulate personnel should be attributed to ill will towards "certain types" of Americans. Some United States officials appear simply to have suffered from inexperience. Vice-Consul Dale Shaffer is a case on point. Prior to January, 1973, Shaffer had been with the Peace Corps in

Nigeria. Santiago was his first diplomatic assignment. Subsequent to the coup, he was, by his own admission, extremely nervous.

"I suppose," Ed Horman agrees, "that Shaffer is not a bad sort. My impression of him was of someone put in a job he could do in normal times, but without the maturity and judgment to perform in a time of crisis. But that excuse doesn't justify conduct by our more seasoned diplomats in Santiago. And, from what I saw, they were far more interested in protecting the image of the Junta than saving American lives. Their main interest seemed to be in promoting an air of normalcy so people would believe that everything was all right.

"Look at the report of the Comptroller General," Ed continues. "Emergency evacuation plans for Americans in Chile were revised in April, 1973, but never activated. The Junta stressed the theme that so-called foreign extremists should be reported to the government and dealt with harshly, yet our Embassy took virtually no measures to protect its own citizens. Normalcy was the watchword for our people in Santiago."

Support for Ed Horman's charges is contained in a September 20, 1973, cable sent by the Department of State to Nathaniel Davis in Santiago. In relevant part, the cable states, "Department spokesman having difficult time with questions if Embassy officers have seen detained Americans and what we are doing to assure their welfare. Imperative that consular officers gain access to detainees *so spokesman can say so*. We note Junta . . . trying to improve their image in foreign press. Refusal to allow access by consular officers to detainees runs counter to this effort."

The case of Jim Ritter is also worth examining in the context of Ed Horman's remarks. Just prior to his arrest, Ritter went to the Consulate for advice. There, Fred Purdy told him, "We're trying to discourage Americans from leaving Chile. There's no need for it. You'll be safe at home." At the time he visited the Consulate, Charles Horman's detention had already been reported.

The handling of released prisoners by the American Consulate is another apparent indication of its desire to protect the image of the Junta. When an American is released from detention by a Communist country, he or she is subjected to debriefing of the most detailed nature. By contrast, almost without exception, Americans who were detained in the National Stadium report no debriefing at all upon their release. "That's no surprise," says Frank Manitzas, the former CBS newsman in Santiago. "Our government didn't want to know what was happening."

Manitzas's impression is bolstered by Joseph Francis Doherty, the Maryknoll Priest who was freed from custody on September 26. Doherty reports "no debriefing at all" and recounts the moment of his release when he was met by Consul Purdy at the stadium gate. "Mr. Purdy," the priest says, "informed us that the condition of our release was that we had to leave the country. He was not sure if we had to be out in twenty-four or forty-eight hours, but he knew that it definitely meant within one week of our release. He informed us that, if we could not accept this condition, we could go back into the Stadium at which time the United States Consulate would not be responsible for us."

The aforementioned episodes are significant because they provide the setting within which belief in a conspiracy flourishes. "Given the attitudes that were prevalent in Santiago," Ed Horman says, "I am convinced that certain persons seeking to protect the image of the Chilean military covered up facts surrounding Charles's death. There is no doubt in my mind that, while I was being led through the National Stadium and one hospital ward after another, there were people in our Embassy who knew exactly where Charles's body was."

Whether Embassy personnel knew "exactly where Charles's body was" is a matter for debate. However, it is clear that some people suspected, and in a few instances knew, quite a bit more than Ed Horman was told.

Judd Kessler was born in Newark, New Jersey, in 1938. Educated at Oberlin College and the Harvard Law School, he served as an attorney-advisor to AID's East Asian and Latin American Bureaus before being assigned to the agency's Santiago office. In

1970, Kessler authored a memorandum to the AID Director, Deane R. Hinton, suggesting ways in which Salvador Allende might be deposed in the event he took office. In part, the memorandum stated:

The U.S. might decide that the Allende regime [is] vulnerable to being deposed by democratic Chileans "with a little help from their friends" . . . . We would then through our intelligence operators provide arms, money, printing presses, etc. to Allende's enemies . . . . I don't believe the argument that some overt cooperation with Allende would significantly discourage those Chileans bent on ousting him. If any important group here really believes that we favor him, they can't be too bright—and in any event, I would guess that word could be put out to them discreetly to the contrary.

Shortly after the memorandum was written, Kessler was named "expropriations expert" for AID's office in Santiago. Thereafter, he was appointed Acting Director of the United States AID mission to Chile.

Caught in the United States at the time of the coup, Kessler returned to Santiago as soon afterwards as possible. He was not among the Embassy-Consulate personnel who met with Ed Horman but, as a member of the Ambassador's staff, he was in regular contact with those who were.

"Inside the Embassy," Kessler recalls, "we thought Horman was dead. We had asked the Chileans to tell us where he was and they hadn't, so we figured they were probably stalling to cover up . . . . We knew that they knew he was dead, not from the time he was reported missing but when he didn't turn up in a few days."

Vice-Consul Dale Shaffer admits to having similar sentiments before Ed Horman ever arrived in Chile: "You could figure that, Charles having disappeared in that period of time, there was a very, very strong chance he was dead. It didn't take a great deal of intelligence to surmise that. Let's face it. Let's be frank about it. People were being killed in those days."

State Department documents show that, from Charles Horman's seizure on, most Embassy personnel disbelieved the Junta's denial of responsibility but were reluctant to make their doubts public. On September 23, 1973, Herbert Thompson (the Deputy Chief of Mission in Santiago) reported by cable to Henry Kissinger that Charles was "missing and assumed to be detained," despite the fact that "Chilean authorities report no information." Six days later, following a telephone conversation with Ray Davis, Colonel Carlos Urrutia (Chief of the Army Subdivision of the United States Military Group in Chile) prepared a memorandum that stated, "Available information indicates Horman was removed by personnel in uniforms (Army and/or Carabiñero) and loaded in a vehicle (Army or Carabiñero) . . . . It is believed that Horman suffered bodily harm." On October 1, 1973, Vice-Consuls James Anderson and Donald McNally prepared a memorandum that included the testimony of neighbors that Charles had been arrested by a truckload of soldiers. Shortly thereafter, Nathaniel Davis cabled the Department of State that a witness to the arrest had followed Charles and the arresting soldiers to the National Stadium.

In sum, throughout the latter half of September, the American diplomatic community was telling itself that Charles had been arrested. Yet it persisted in telling the Hormans that he was "probably in hiding." On September 27, 1973, Charles Anderson of the Bureau of Special Consular Services spoke with Ed Horman on the telephone and told him, "Our feeling is that Charles is probably in hiding because of his left-wing views and will surface when things calm down." The following day, Anderson and Kate Marshall told Ed the same thing in person. When Ed arrived in Santiago on October 5 and met with Nathaniel Davis, the Ambassador voiced a similar sentiment.

Possibly, there were those within the Department of State who believed that Charles Horman was in hiding. Others may have thought him dead but wanted to protect his family until every last hope had been exhausted. Such judgments, if made in good faith, need not be questioned. However, in at least two instances, there is proof that relevant facts were deliberately withheld from Ed Horman, and these incidents merit close scrutiny.

The first such incident concerns the earlier mentioned October 3, 1973, note in which the government of Chile advised the United States Embassy in Santiago that Charles had been arrested for "curfew violation" and released one day later. When Ed and Joyce Horman met with Nathaniel Davis, Fred Purdy, and William Hon in the Ambassador's office on October 5, the note was not mentioned to them. Instead, despite the fact that the Embassy was in possession of an admission by the Chilean government that Charles had been taken into custody, Davis and Purdy persisted in the claim that they had no knowledge of his whereabouts. The State Department explanation for this delinquency is contained in a November 18, 1973, memorandum drafted by Purdy in response to a series of questions from New York Senator Jacob Javits. The memorandum states that the October 3 note was not received by the Embassy until late in the day on October 5. Thus, the Department claims, Davis and Purdy were unaware of its existence when they first met with Ed and Joyce.

The State Department's explanation is logical, but it is also patently false. The government of Chile note was not received late in the day on October 5, as later claimed by Purdy. It was received on October 3, as evidenced by a recently discovered memorandum written by Purdy himself for Secretary of State Henry Kissinger. In relevant part, the Purdy memorandum states, "Embassy received a [Foreign Office] note evening of 3 October saying Horman was detained at the National Stadium on 20 September for violation of curfew. . . . " The "drafting date" on the Purdy memorandum is October 4, 1973—one full day before the Consul later claimed that the October 3 note was received.

The second instance where relevant facts appear to have been deliberately withheld from the Horman family is even more compelling. As earlier noted, Ed Horman arrived in Chile to search for his son on October 5, 1973. It was not until October 18 that he was told by Fred Purdy that Charles was dead. "I am convinced," Ed says, "that the decision to tell me about Charles was made on the afternoon of October 17. That was the day I reported to Purdy that a source I chose not to reveal had told me Charles was dead—executed in the National Stadium. As far as I'm concerned, it's more than coincidence that one day later a so-called fingerprint misclassification was discovered at the morgue and my son's body found. Obviously, what happened was that somebody somewhere said, 'Hell, we can't keep this thing covered up any longer. Let's give Horman something he'll buy so he'll go home.' "

The starting point for an investigation of Ed Horman's thesis is Lovell Jarvis—the Ford Foundation Program Advisor who first told him that Charles had been executed. Jarvis has since left the Foundation and is a Professor of Economics at the University of California at Berkeley. He is now willing to identify his source of information concerning Charles—Mark Dolguin, First Secretary to the Canadian Embassy in Santiago at the time of the coup.

Dolguin now lives in Ontario, Canada, and acknowledges passing the information to Jarvis. "It was told to me in confidence," he explains, "which is why I didn't go to the U.S. Embassy through formal channels. I felt that the Foundation had the resources and attitude to handle the matter discreetly."

Who was Dolguin's source? Initially, he is reluctant to reveal it, fearing for the safety of persons still in Chile. Eventually though, a name is forthcoming.

"I was told by an Advisor to the Chilean Ministry of Education named Enrique Sandoval. We had been introduced several months earlier by a correspondent for the *Montreal Star* named Glenn Allen, and Sandoval was a useful guy to know. He was also a very nice fellow who, many years earlier, had studied at McGill University in Montreal. In fact, Sandoval's son was born in Canada.

"After the coup," Dolguin continues, "Sandoval was concerned for the safety of his family. He wanted to leave Santiago as soon as possible, so he telephoned my home and asked if he could come and see me. You didn't talk over the phone in those days. When he arrived, we discussed his problem and, during the conversation, he mentioned that an American named Charles Horman had been interrogated and shot in the National Stadium. I told Lovell Jarvis several days later."

The trail from Dolguin to Enrique Sandoval is easy to follow. The former advisor to Chile's Ministry of Education fled his native land in November, 1973, and has been living in Montreal ever since. "The days following the coup were terrifying," Sandoval remembers. "Like many former public officials, I feared for my life."

Hours after the bombing of the Moneda, Sandoval was arrested and taken to the Chile Stadium. There he was thrice interrogated and held for a period of five days before his release. Once freed, he began to seek a way out of Chile and, in the process, spoke with Dolguin. However, Sandoval did not meet with Dolguin and tell him about Charles Horman's fate until the first week of October. *Prior to that, in late September, before Ed Horman ever left New York for Chile, Sandoval informed the United States Embassy in Santiago that Charles Horman was dead.*

Sandoval's contact in the American Embassy was Judd Kessler. No evidence currently available indicates that either man acted improperly. Sandoval was simply transmitting information, and Kessler, who had no dealings with Ed or Joyce Horman, appears to have passed that information on to the proper authorities. However, their encounter forms a vital link in the chain of evidence surrounding Charles Horman's death and must be examined.

Kessler still works for AID. Of his contact with Sandoval, he recalls, "Enrique had been head of the Cabinet for the Ministry of Education for about six months before the coup. I had official dealings with him as Acting Director of the AID Mission, and we were friends . . . . Having read all this stuff about wholesale slaughter and so forth, I went around and made an effort to contact every person I knew. Enrique was one of them. I went to his house . . . and told him about Horman and Teruggi, that the Embassy was upset and was trying to find out what happened but hadn't had any satisfactory answers, and could he find out anything and let me know . . . . A few days passed, and he told me that he knew someone who was in the military at the National Stadium, who said that Horman had been in the stadium and was dead."

Sandoval confirms Kessler's account of their meetings, adding that he learned from three separate sources that Charles had been executed. One source was a close relative serving with the Chilean military in the National Stadium. Another was an officer, who claimed to have been present when Charles was taken from his cell to be shot. Sandoval places the date of death as September 20, 1973, and adds that he reported to Kessler as soon as he learned the facts, which was eight to ten days later. The crucial question thus becomes, "What did Kessler do with the information he received from Sandoval?" The answer, says Kessler, is, "I told Fred Purdy." And what did Purdy say when told that Charles Horman had been executed by the Chilean military? Again, Kessler's response: "Purdy said, 'I'll bet that's right.' "

In short, before Ed Horman ever left New York, the United States Consul in Santiago was told that Charles Horman had been executed by the Chilean military. Yet he chose not to share this information with the Horman family. Instead, he sat silent while Ed Horman flew to Santiago and searched through hospital wards, refugee centers, and the National Stadium for his son. For almost three weeks, Fred Purdy maintained a stony silence despite what he had learned. Why?

Purdy concedes that Judd Kessler told him about Charles Horman's death, and admits that he considered it more likely than not that Charles had been "killed by the Chilean military." However, he defends the withholding of information from Ed Horman on the following grounds: "Judd Kessler didn't identify the veracity or possible reliability of his source. At that time, we were getting all sorts of suggestions as to what might have happened. . . . When Kessler mentioned it to me, he did not either identify the source or give it to me as something that deserved consideration, and so I wasn't given anything upon which to act."

Purdy's explanation displays less than exemplary judgment.

He was the man legally responsible for the welfare of United States citizens in Chile. If Kessler failed to identify his source, then the Consul had an obligation to press for further identification. Moreover, it is hard to understand why an unconfirmed story from British journalist Timothy Ross to the effect that Charles Horman was alive and well in a "leftist pipeline" necessitated a special trip to the American Embassy by Ed Horman, when a far more credible report from the Acting Director of the United States AID Mission in Chile was never mentioned to him.

Some persons have sought to excuse Purdy's conduct by reference to the press of events. "At that particular time," Dale Shaffer notes, "he was under a great deal of pressure. It's very hard for people who only knew him then to formulate a true picture of him." To that, Ambassador Nathaniel Davis adds, "Fred Purdy was obviously frayed in the weight of what he was trying to do . . . . I have a clear conscience that we told Mr. Horman what we knew for sure at every stage of the investigation. You have to make a distinction between what you know, what is reported, and what is alleged. In terms of what we knew, we shared with Mr. Horman the information at our disposal."

However, Ed Horman holds to a different view: "I can tell you why Fred Purdy didn't tell me about Kessler's report. He was trying to cover up Charles's death. He did so for as long as he could and then, after it became clear that I wouldn't leave Chile until I got some answers, he admitted the truth—that Charles had been executed. That burst of candor," Ed continues, "lasted less than a week. After he told me in the corridor of Investigaciones Headquarters that Charles had been shot by the Chilean military, someone got to Purdy and told him to change his story. Now he denies ever telling me that Charles was killed by the military."

"Are you absolutely certain," Ed is asked, "that Fred Purdy told you Charles was executed in the National Stadium?"

"Yes."

"Is it possible that you misunderstood him?"

"Absolutely not!"

Fred Purdy vigorously denies telling Ed Horman that his son was executed in the National Stadium. "I have on all occasions tried to be very frank and honest with everybody," he says. "I was that way with Mr. Horman, and he unfortunately did not return the favor." Despite intense questioning, the Consul does not waver from this stand and reaffirms the position that he did everything possible to save Charles Horman's life. "A lot of people," he says, "now forget what the situation was in those days. We had a curfew that ran as long as twelve hours. The Chilean military had absolute control over everything, and our ability to go out and look for people was very limited. . . . It may be plain to Mr. Horman that Charles was picked up by Military Intelligence and killed at the National Stadium, but it is certainly not plain to me or to many other reasonable people who know something about the case."

Thus, the question of who is telling the truth—Ed Horman or Fred Purdy—remains. Certainly, the Consul's claim that he never said Charles was shot in the National Stadium must be weighed against his withholding of Judd Kessler's report. "Also," Ed Horman adds, "I have no reason to lie. I'm interested solely in finding out what happened to my son. I have no reason to misstate the facts." But the most compelling piece of evidence tending to support Ed Horman's claim that Fred Purdy and others suppressed certain information concerning Charles's execution comes from the mouths of Embassy and military personnel. For over four years, the Department of State has steadfastly refused to hold the government of Chile responsible for Charles Horman's death. Yet, in private, very different sentiments are expressed.

John Tipton was serving as a Political Officer in the American Embassy in Santiago in September, 1973. In that capacity, he met regularly with those persons charged with investigating the disappearance of Charles Horman.

"Do you have any personal belief as to what happened to him?" Tipton is asked.

"Yes, I do," he answers. "In fact, I'll go you one better. It's not only my own personal belief, but it was the general impression of Americans who were in the Embassy at the time . . . . I believe and I think most people believe that it was the Chilean military that killed him."

"Do you recall discussing this case at the time with Fred Purdy?"

"Oh yes."

"Was that his belief also?"

"Yes, I suppose so . . . . It isn't deeply etched in my memory who said what when. I do recall that it was the majority belief that the Chilean military did him in."

Judd Kessler voices a similar view with regard to the then-prevailing belief among Embassy personnel. "Is it fair to say," he is asked, "that the general impression in the Embassy was that the Chilean military was responsible for Charles Horman's death?"

"Yes," Kessler answers. "Somebody in the military killed him. He wasn't accidentally shot on the street."

Dale Shaffer concurs: "He was executed . . . by a military patrol. I don't think there's too much doubt, really."

Even Lieutenant-Colonel Patrick Ryan, second in command of the United States Naval Mission in Valparaiso, holds the Chilean military responsible: "My guess on Charlie is that, being the type of young fellow he was, he may have had the wrong friends. He may have been associated with the wrong people and, at the time of a revolution in South America, that can be a bad thing . . . . The United States had its My Lai—a young First Lieutenant gone berserk and he shoots some people. It happens. The same analogy could have taken place in Chile. Some young Captain gets carried away in the emotions of the day; this American is not cooperating and his Spanish was not that good. If I had to throw a dart at the wall, that to me would be the most logical explanation."

Given what is now known about Charles Horman's death, it is obvious that the Department of State has good cause to hold the government of Chile responsible. That it has not done so raises serious questions. One possible explanation is that the United States government is seeking to save the Junta from public embarrassment and repercussions in Congress. Another is that, having initially covered up certain facts surrounding the death, the Department has been forced by circumstances into "a cover-up of the cover-up." However, Ed Horman holds to an uglier theory: "I have spent over four years of my life investigating the death of my son. Reluctantly, I have reached the conclusion that the government of Chile is being shielded from blame for a very simple reason. If the finger of guilt is pointed at them, they will point it right back at Washington. Our own Embassy was responsible for Charles's death. His life was sacrificed to cover up American actions in Chile."

Did the United States government have foreknowledge of, or possibly even order, Charles Horman's execution? This is Ed Horman's ultimate question.

CHAPTER XXII

THE ULTIMATE
QUESTION

The room in the Italian Embassy in Santiago is small and square. Several religious icons stand in the corner next to a pile of boxes. Two chairs, a battered table, a small sofa, and single bed are the only pieces of furniture. There are no windows. A young boy suffering from anemia sleeps on the sofa. The bed is shared nightly by his parents. For over two years, this room has been "home" to Rafael Gonzalez and his family.

A card in Gonzalez's pocket identifies him as a member of the Junta's intelligence network. "I worked for more than twenty years in the highest security service in Chile," he says. "I was in the Estado Mayor de la Defensa Nacional. Sometimes they would call me for information for the Navy, for the Army, for the Carabiñeros because I was in the top service and I knew a lot."

While technically a civilian, Gonzalez maintained a reserve military rank. In 1969, he was transferred to New York City and placed in charge of security for the Chilean Consulate. Then, as coup planning progressed, he was brought home. "In March, 1973," he recalls, "General Baeza, who was the former military attaché in Washington, D.C., told me that something was coming and I was transferred back to Santiago."

"I am not on the right politically," Gonzalez explains. "I am not on the left. I was in the center, and I fulfilled my duties as an intelligence officer with many different governments in Chile. When Allende came, I fulfilled my duties in the same way because I was working for the security of the country and not for Allende's government. I used to work just as I always did for any kind of government."

On September 11, 1973, Gonzalez was among the troops who took over the Presidential Palace. As the fighting ended, he went directly to Allende's office. "My only duty there," he says, "was to collect the papers. In other words, I didn't shoot anybody. It was my duty as an intelligence officer to pick up the papers and bring them back to the Ministry of Defense."

While in the Moneda, Gonzalez saw the dead President, "his head wide open and some of his scalp on the back of the wall." For the next two weeks, he was all but consumed by intelligence duties. "For ten days," he remembers, "I almost did not sleep. If I could sleep, I slept not much more than two hours in a day. The first two days, the only thing I ate was some bread and water. I didn't have time even for eating because they sent me here, they sent me there. My wife, she didn't see me for a week."

In the months following the coup, Gonzalez's allegiance to the Junta wavered. Despite his apolitical posture, he was troubled by the role of DINA—the government's newly formed secret police. "All my life," he says, "I fought against Communism, but not for that reason am I going to support a fascist government like we have today . . . . DINA is a repressive apparatus created by this government in order to arrest everybody who is not in accordance with the new rules. It is something completely different than what is a real intelligence service. DINA is like a Gestapo."

On September 2, 1975, Gonzalez decided to leave Chile. That night, he visited a friend, who suggested that he request asylum at the Italian Embassy. "The American Embassy is supporting this government," the friend advised. "The Italian Embassy receives more refugees than any other in Santiago."

The following morning, Gonzalez went to the Italian Embassy. His wife and infant son followed five minutes later. Since then, they have been seeking safe passage to America. "I want to go to the United States," Gonzalez says, "because it is a great country. It is a country of freedom, of great possibilities."

Gonzalez has a valid alien resident reentry permit to the United States. His son, who was born in New York on April 20, 1970, has dual citizenship and an American passport. Yet, as of this writing, Gonzalez remains at the Italian Embassy in Santiago. He says that leaving its protective shelter "means death for me . . . . The police have orders to grab me and kill me."

The Junta does not want Gonzalez to leave Chile and, from all appearances, neither does the Department of State. Gonzalez says he was present when the execution of Charles Horman was ordered.

The Italian Embassy in Santiago has a policy against refugees receiving visitors. Telephone calls are strictly forbidden. However, on June 7, 1976, two reporters gained access to Gonzalez and taped an interview with him. Thereafter, it became known that United States Consulate officials had met with Gonzalez on five separate occasions. The Department of State refuses to divulge what was discussed at four of these meetings, but a transcript of the fifth has been obtained. Gonzalez's testimony is chilling: *"I knew that Charles Horman was killed because he knew too much. And this was done between the CIA and the local authorities."*

Gonzalez's declaration centers on a meeting he claims to have attended in late September, 1973. Present were General Augusto Lutz (the Director of Chilean Army Intelligence), Colonel Victor Hugo Barria (Lutz's second in command), and a third man who Gonzalez believes was an American. This third man sat silent throughout the discussion.

"I can't remember [the exact date]," Gonzalez says, "because in those days I didn't know when was Monday, Tuesday, Wednesday, or Saturday. I worked like a dog, night and day . . . . I was on the ninth floor of the Ministry of Defense in the office of General Lutz. There was General Lutz, Colonel Barria, and me, and an American but I don't know his name. Horman was in the next room . . . . They called me because I was to act as an interpreter if they were to question Horman . . . . I know English fluently more or less so I could serve as an interpreter."

"Are you sure," Gonzalez is asked, "that you saw Charles Horman alive in the Defense Ministry?"

"Yes, I am positive."

"You knew him, as to who he was?"

"Yes, because General Lutz said who it was."

"Who else was present when Lutz said that?"

"It was an American and there was Colonel Barria, the second man of the Army Intelligence."

"What was the conversation that you remember?"

"They told me this guy was an American whose name is Charles Horman. And I was told that this guy sitting outside in the next room, Horman you know, knew too much and that he was supposed to disappear . . . . I knew that they received the order to shoot him because I heard that order . . . ."

"Charles Horman," Gonzalez continues, "was brought from Valparaiso to Santiago. I saw the guys that brought him here . . . . I wouldn't say that the trigger was pulled by the CIA, but the CIA was mixed up in this. It was the Chileans who got rid of him, but the CIA was behind that."

Gonzalez's charges have been formally denied by the governments of Chile and the United States, but their impact remains. CIA ties with Chilean Military Intelligence are known to have been strong, and these same American agents could have held cover jobs as Embassy and Consulate personnel. One man who has made a study of the CIA in Chile is Steve Volk, who suggests that three men—Fred Purdy, James Anderson, and John Tipton—were covert agents.

"There is a certain type of methodology," Volk explains, "that can clue you in on whether a person is working for the CIA. It involves going through their backgrounds in the State Department Biographical Register and several other sources to see what their training was. If you find a lot of intelligence training, which is not normal for a Department of State official, it's a pretty good key. If you combine an intelligence background plus some period of time unaccounted for and they keep popping up in hot spots, you can come to a pretty fair conclusion. Purdy, Anderson, and Tipton all qualify."

Purdy and Tipton both deny working for the CIA. James Anderson does not.

Anderson joined the United States Air Force in 1953 at age nineteen and served overseas in an intelligence capacity until 1957. After returning home, he graduated from the University of Oregon in 1960, then rejoined the Air Force as an information analyst. In 1962, he began his career with the Department of State as a political officer in Mexico and was transferred to the Dominican Republic one month before the American invasion of 1965. In 1966, he returned to Mexico, serving as a political officer until March, 1970. Ten months later, he was reassigned to Santiago as a Vice-Consul.

Anderson refuses to confirm or deny having worked for the CIA in Chile. However, several Embassy and Consulate personnel, John Tipton among them, imply that the allegation is true, and Rafael Gonzalez, who accompanied the Vice-Consul to the Municipal Cemetery in search of Charles Horman's body, concurs.

If correct, the charge raises questions of a serious nature. A Vice-Consul's job is to protect the lives of American citizens abroad. Yet suppose, by way of example, that an American in Santiago uncovered proof of a CIA plot against Allende. And suppose further that this same American, fearing for his life, sought assistance at the American Consulate. If he spoke with a Vice-Consul who was an agent for the CIA, a case of severely divided loyalties would exist. Protection for the American might well be considered secondary to the "broader national interest" as perceived by the CIA agent.

James Anderson denies being torn by competing faiths. Of his alleged dual role in Santiago, he says simply, "There was no conflict of interest." Also, it should be noted, the mere fact of employment by the CIA is not evidence of negligent or criminal conduct. Still, the accusations of Rafael Gonzalez remain, and at least one former Embassy employee is willing to go on record as suggesting that they might be valid. That man is Judd Kessler, and his comments are troubling.

"Do you have any feeling," Kessler is asked, "as to why Charles Horman was picked up and executed?"

"I don't," the former Acting Director of the United States AID Mission to Chile answers. "There are all kinds of rumors and stories. I just hope that no American played any role in fingering him for the Chileans, for DINA, or for anybody else."

"You sound as though you have doubts on that score."

"Look," Kessler continues, "I'm prepared to believe some pretty ugly things about people in the American intelligence community—at least about individuals . . . . The CIA station and Chilean intelligence did have a certain amount of interchange of information and, if Horman's name had shown up in any of their files, they could have picked him up."

Kessler is not alone in his doubts. However, before the fears of others are catalogued, one critical question must be answered: Why would American military, diplomatic, or intelligence personnel knowingly permit or order the execution of Charles Horman? In formulating that answer, several facts are evident.

First, the case of Charles Horman was clearly regarded as "special" by the Chilean military. He was arrested at home rather than on the streets, which indicates planned detention. Unlike Frank Teruggi, the Garrett-Schesches, David Hathaway, Jim Ritter, Joseph Francis Doherty, and other detained Americans, he was taken directly to the National Stadium as opposed to a Carabiñeros station for preliminary interrogation. While in the stadium, according to Enrique Sandoval, Horman was held in a secluded area apart from the other prisoners. Even more important, he was then transferred to the Ministry of Defense, where only a select group of detainees were taken. One such prisoner was Enrique Kirberg, the former President of the Santiago Technical University and an Allende confidant, who says, "There were very few prisoners at the Ministry of Defense—all of them special in one way or another. Most of them were killed shortly after interrogation." Gonzalez concurs, as illustrated by the following colloquy:

> *Q.* I was wondering why Horman was in that building. There were many other prisoners all over the place. They didn't all go through that office.
> *Gonzalez:* Through that office? No! No! No!
> *Q.* You are saying he was a special case, then?
> *Gonzalez:* He must be a special case.

What made Charles Horman special? Certainly not his activity in FIN. Steve Volk, who was perhaps the most active member of the news-clipping organization, was never arrested. David Hathaaway, who was also involved with the group, was detained but then released. Nor is it likely that Charles's limited research into the Schneider assassination was the cause of his arrest. The soldiers who seized him most likely would not have known about the research until after reading the papers taken from his home and, before this was done, they had already taken the unusual step of bringing him directly to the National Stadium.

"Reread Gonzalez's testimony," Ed Horman suggests. "The answer to why Charles was murdered is there. Gonzalez says that Charles was killed 'because he knew too much,' and that he was 'brought from Valparaiso to Santiago.' Clearly, someone thought that Charles's stay in Valparaiso and Viña del Mar was significant. Otherwise, it would never have been mentioned in front of Gonzalez. If you want to find out why Charles was killed, take a look at what he and Terry learned in Viña."

Ed Horman's theory is quite simple. While in Viña, he believes, Charles and Terry stumbled on evidence of United States involvement in the coup. Initially, their presence was ignored, and American military personnel spoke freely in front of them. However, within a week, someone in a position of power grew concerned that they had seen and heard "too much." In 1973, the media were quite naive about the scope of covert American operations in Chile, and the Nixon administration, beleaguered by Watergate, was strenuously denying wrongful intervention against the Allende government. Charles's observations might have changed that. Accordingly, his name was passed to the Chilean military for arrest and interrogation. Subsequently, he was executed. Had Terry been home when the troops came, she too would have been taken. However, as luck would have it, she had checked into the Riviera Hotel earlier in the day. Once Charles was arrested, she was safe, since the coincidence of separate arrests and executions would have been too great to cover.

The first building blocks for Ed Horman's thesis are the remarks of Arthur Creter. The day after the coup, he met Charles and Terry on the patio of the Miramar Hotel and told them, "I'm here with the United States Navy. We came down to do a job and it's done." Subsequently, Creter volunteered the information that he had been on a ship in the harbor for about a week and was in Chile at military invitation; also that "a United States Consulate is the last place I'd go. They don't like to know too much about the military."

The day after meeting Creter, Charles and Terry encountered Lieutenant-Colonel Patrick Ryan, who introduced them to Roger Fraunfelder, Ed Johnson, and, eventually, Ray Davis. These men displayed extensive knowledge of the coup—how it was organized, that the former Mayor and city officials of Valparaiso were being held on ships in the harbor, and other military data. Ryan admitted taking Admiral Huidobro to the United States to purchase over a million dollars' worth of supplies and, like Ray Davis, he moved freely through the countryside despite roadblocks and a lengthy curfew.

Viewed in a vacuum, these facts hardly prove that United States military personnel were directly involved in the coup. Moreover, such participation, even if established, would not necessarily mean that American officials were responsible for the death of Charles Horman. However, Charles's and Terry's observations necessitate further study of events in Valparaiso and Viña, starting with the man who hosted them for much of their stay—Lieutenant-Colonel Patrick Ryan.

Ryan retired from the United States Marines in 1976 and now lives in La Jolla, California, where he is active with a real estate brokerage firm. Unlike some Americans, he has few if any regrets about the coup. "One important thing to remember," Ryan says, "and a lot of people forget it, is that Chile is the only country in history to have defeated Communism. We tried to do it for ten years in Vietnam and lost, ran away with a bloody nose. Chile stands out as a black eye for the world Communist movement. Chile beat 'em.

"For ten years," Ryan continues, "the United States fought Communism in Vietnam at a cost of fifty-five thousand American lives, six times as many wounded, and 150 billion dollars. We lost the war. Chile fought Communism without B–52s, the Seventh Fleet, or even a Bob Hope visit. No American fingers squeezed M–16 triggers, no parade of American flag-draped caskets was airlifted daily from Santiago. One of our best allies, one of the strongest pro-U.S. countries in South America, defeated Communism, which I've been taught over the past twenty-odd years is the enemy and, instead of supporting them, our country throws rocks at the Chileans. Now this humanitarian business that Carter is on carries it further. Human rights aren't all they should be in Chile today if you're a Marxist, but they aren't all they should be in America either if you're a black in Mississippi. Until the skirts of our Statue of Liberty are clean, I suggest we not preach to the world. I think the Junta is doing a very good job."

"That sounds like Pat Ryan, all right," Terry Simon says when apprised of his remarks. "You really have to look at him on two levels. Personally, Ryan was extremely helpful all our time in Viña. He brought us to his home. He took us out. He took us to Paul Eppley's house so we could wire my parents—all done in a very generous spirit. On a one-to-one basis, Ryan is a nice man.

"Still," Terry continues, "I'm convinced that Pat Ryan helped plan the coup. He and the other Americans Charles and I saw kept dropping hints about their role in things. I got the feeling that we arrived just as the celebration was starting, and they were delighted to have someone to brag to. It was as though, because we were Americans, they considered us automatic allies in anything the United States might do. I realize that Ryan acted in what he perceived to be the best interests of the United States and that he was just doing his job, but I think far more of his personality than his politics."

Whether or not Ryan actually played a role in planning the coup has been the subject of modest debate in recent years. He denies learning that the coup had actually occurred until six o'clock on the morning of September 11, 1973, when a Chilean sailor knocked on his door to inform him that all of Chile was under martial law. Asked whether or not he had advance knowledge that a coup was coming, Ryan concedes that he was "unofficially advised of various contingencies which might occur," but adds, "Everybody knew a coup was going to take place. You'd have to be a goddamn blithering idiot not to know that. It was obvious . . . . Even to sideline observers, it was not a question of would Allende's regime fall, but when."

Ryan also admits to knowing quite a bit about how the coup was planned, but contends that this information comes from after-the-fact conversations with his friend Admiral Huidobro of the Chilean military. Still, at least one report indicates that Patrick Ryan is being modest about his role in coup planning.

On October 27, 1974, the *Times* of London carried a report based on an interview between former Chilean General Carlos Prats and reporter Marlise Simons. Prats had replaced the murdered General Rene Schneider as Commander-in-Chief of the Chilean Army in November, 1970, and been the staunchest military proponent of constitutional rule during President Allende's tenure in office. Ousted from power in August, 1973, exiled from Chile in the aftermath of the coup, Prats found employment as a bookkeeper in Argentina and began work on his memoirs. While writing, he told Simons that the coup had been planned in and coordinated from Valparaiso. "That," the *Times* article reported the former Chilean General as saying, "was where officers in the conspiracy secretly met with a U.S. Marine, and Admiral Toribio Merino (the senior naval officer at Valparaiso) kept touch with the same man—*Lieutenant-Colonel Patrick Ryan.*"

The same month Prats's accusations appeared in print, he was murdered by a bomb blast in Buenos Aires. General Augusto Lutz, the Chilean General who allegedly ordered Charles Horman's execution, was subsequently reported dead by the Junta.

Ryan terms the *Times* article "absolutely false" and "typical of the misinformation and fabricated facts disseminated to the world regarding the coup in Chile." He concedes having contact with Merino on several occasions but explains, "I was a liaison with Admiral Merino about very mundane matters—Can we get spare parts for our destroyers? Can we get Art Creter to come down from Panama to look at the maintenance equipment? We had no more than two or three interviews from the time I arrived until the time of the coup, and they certainly didn't have anything to do with preparation for the coup. Prats," Ryan says, summing up his feelings, "was a bumbling idiot . . . a lackey of Allende."

As for Terry Simon's charges, Ryan says, "We were very frank with Charlie and Terry. We had nothing to hide. We told them what we were doing and how we did it, what our mission was. For example, I've seen something attributed to her about my trip to the States with Admiral Huidobro. She characterizes it as a shopping trip for guns or something. That's not true at all. Charlie probably asked, 'What do you all do down here?' and I said, 'Well, we procure equipment through the military assistance program. For instance, I went to the States last month with Admiral Huidobro to purchase various equipment.'

"The central theme of all my conversations with Charlie and Terry," Ryan continues, "was my concern for their personal problems—their being unavoidably detained in Viña del Mar because of the coup, the transmission of a health-and-welfare report to their parents, and my repeated advice to them to stay put until the situation stabilized . . . . Charlie's stay in Viña was very pleasant, and he should have stayed there. We didn't want him to go, and we strongly advised against it."

As noted earlier, proof that United States military personnel in Viña and Valparaiso were involved in planning the coup would not necessarily mean that they were responsible for the death of Charles Horman. Still, several strange incidents that occurred in Viña require further examination.

The first of these incidents concerns the registration card that Charles filled out when he and Terry checked into the Miramar Hotel. After Charles's death, Frank Manitzas of CBS News visited the hotel and asked for the records of their stay. According to Manitzas, the desk clerk informed him that the card had already been taken by a man who appeared at the hotel with a woman who claimed to be Terry Simon's mother.

"That was quite a shock," Manitzas remembers. "It was obvious to me that someone wanted to cover up the fact that Charles and Terry had been in Viña. When I asked the clerk for the name of the man who had taken the card, he told me that it was an American military officer named Patrick Ryan."

Ryan labels the Manitzas story a half-truth. He admits to asking the desk clerk at the Miramar for the card but says that he never received it. "In a military investigation," the Lieutenant Colonel explains, "you have to come up with physical evidence to support statements of fact. At the direction of Ray Davis, I asked the Miramar to provide me with copies [of the card] to support the statement of fact that Charles had been in Viña. However, the desk clerk on duty at the time [a Friday afternoon] informed me that the hotel accountant controlled the cards and would not be available until Monday. I advised Captain Davis, and he commented, 'It's not important to the investigation of Charlie's death; don't bother pursuing it.' "

As for Manitzas's claim of cloak-and-dagger tactics, Ryan states, "I brought no one to the hotel who purported to be the mother of Terry Simon or anyone else's mother." And he ridicules the theory that he or anyone else would try to cover up Charles's stay in Viña: "It would be impossible to deny that Charlie and Terry were in the Miramar Hotel. Everybody and his brother knows they were there. Everybody in South America knows they were there because we got on the radio from Paul Eppley's house and told the world that they were there."

Ray Davis recalls a slightly different version of events concerning the registration card. His explanation is that during the course of Embassy efforts to locate Charles, someone reported seeing the missing American in Santiago at noon on September 15. Davis knew that this was "manifestly impossible," since he had not driven Charles and Terry to the capital until late in the afternoon that same day. Nonetheless, to make absolutely certain that he had not confused his dates, on his next trip to Viña he visited the Miramar and took the card himself as evidence with a bearing on the case.

Both Ryan and Davis tell credible, albeit slightly differing stories about the hotel registration card. However, the reported appearance of a woman claiming to be Terry Simon's mother adds an air of mystery to the proceedings, and this is compounded by an item uncovered in a study of documents recently released by the Department of State pursuant to the Freedom of Information Act. One of these documents is a file card on Charles Horman maintained by the United States Consulate in Santiago. In relevant part, the card reads:

> Art Creeter—15 ND—
> 2 checked into Miramar Hotel, Rm 315, 2300 on 10 Sept.
> used 425 Paul Harris address
> said "Escritor" left 15 Sept.*

This card is significant because the information on it, which relates to Charles's and Terry's stay at the Miramar, appears to have come from the hotel's registration records. And, more important, it appears to have been transmitted to the Embassy by Arthur Creter. One would not normally expect to find a "naval engineer" leafing through hotel records, and Creter has no explanation for his conduct.

"Do you," he is asked, "recall the circumstances that led you to check out that information?"

"No," he answers, "I'm afraid you've got me at a loss there."

---

* Creter's name is misspelled on the card. "15 ND" refers to the Fifteenth Naval District, United States Navy. "Escritor" is Spanish for "writer."

Lost or not, further examination of Arthur Creter is in order. Officially, he was a United States naval engineer who rose through the ranks and retired to the Panama Canal Zone in early 1973. Unofficially, he may have had a far more interesting job. The Canal Zone serves as headquarters for the United States Southern Command, and a review of Creter's first meeting with Charles and Terry indicates that he might have been quite active in Chile. One day after the coup, it should be remembered, he met the young couple on the patio of the Miramar Hotel and, after announcing that he was with the United States Navy, added proudly, "We came down to do a job and it's done."

Questioned in Panama about his remarks, Creter initially denied any recollection of meeting Charles and Terry. However, his denial could not hold water. On the morning of September 15, Terry had mentioned to him that she might be returning to the United States via Panama, and Creter had suggested that she "let him know" if the eventuality occurred. Then, he had taken her notebook and written his name, address, and telephone number on a blank page. This information, penned in his own handwriting, was partial proof of their meeting. More evidence is in the files of the Department of State. A search of these files shows that on November 21, 1973, the Commander of the United States Naval Mission, Fifteenth Naval District, in the Panama Canal Zone cabled United States Military Group headquarters in Santiago. In remarks headed "Personal for Captain Davis," the cable read:

> Request for information
> Capt. Cummins took action
> Interview with Art Creter reveals following:
> . . . .
> *Creter did meet and did converse with Mr. Horman*
> *Creter did make statements alleged quoted . . . .*

For the record, Department of State personnel now concede that Creter met Charles Horman and Terry Simon in Viña and spoke the words, "We came down to do a job and it's done." The official explanation of this remark is that Creter was in Chile to assist the Chilean Navy with regard to the use and repair of fire extinguishers on board Chilean naval vessels. This, it is claimed, is "why he was in Chile and what job he had done." However, the Department of State explanation fails to explain who came with Creter—the "we" of his remarks; and it also fails to explain why, when Creter spoke with Charles and Terry, he said that the job he had come to perform was "done." When Creter speaks today about his alleged shipboard duties, he concedes that they (as opposed to the coup) had not been completed as of September 12:

Creter: There were about 25 or 30 different items the Chilean Navy was asking me to provide information on. What I had come down there to do, I had just barely got off the ground on it. Then, of course, the coup took place and everything was stopped.

Q: So, in reality, the job you're talking about now hadn't been done at the time of the coup?

Creter: Not at all.

Theories as to just what Creter was doing in Viña at the time of the coup vary. Ed Horman believes that he was in Chile to coordinate communications on behalf of the National Security Agency. Others think he was a CIA agent responsible for funneling supplies to the Chilean military. This suspicion is fueled in part by Creter's own statement that "since I've been here [in Panama], I've picked up quite a bit of information insofar as logistics, and go to various countries in Central and South America as a logistics advisor."

"What type of logistics is that?" he is asked.

"Supply . . . primarily, how to order things; how to set up a supply system; how to figure out what you need based on demand."

Little else is known about Creter's conduct. He admits to visiting Chile several times before the coup, arriving for the last time on September 6. Between the sixth and the eleventh, when the coup occurred, he says he "talked to different officers in the

Chilean Navy" and visited several ports. Based on the "rather unusual" military activity he observed, he suspected that a coup was imminent but disclaims specific foreknowledge. Less than a week after the coup occurred, he was back on Chilean vessels assisting the Navy of the new Chilean government.

The idea that Creter might have been serving in Chile in an undercover role is dismissed by Patrick Ryan as frivolous. "Mr. Art Creter," the Lieutenant-Colonel says, "is a retired Navy Lieutenant who is currently a civilian employee of the Fifteenth Naval District. A more unlikely CIA agent would be difficult to imagine." To this, Ray Davis adds, "Art Creter came down to rewind motors and charge CO_2 bottles. He's a shipboard technician . . . the last guy who's going to organize a revolution."

Still, unanswered questions concerning Creter's conduct remain, and they, in turn, may be linked to Herbert Thompson—an American diplomat who transferred from Panama to Santiago less than two weeks before the coup.

Thompson was born in California and has been a career diplomat for half of his fifty-five years. From 1958 to 1962, he served as Chief of the American Embassy's Political Section in La Paz, Bolivia. Thereafter, he was assigned to the National War College, following which he served as a Political Officer in Argentina. From 1970 through August, 1973, he was Deputy Chief of Mission at the United States Embassy in Panama. On August 29, 1973—thirteen days before the coup—he arrived in Chile to serve as DCM at the American Embassy in Santiago.

The first mention of Thompson's name in connection with Charles Horman occurred in Viña three days after the coup. "It was on September 14," Terry Simon recalls. "Charles and I were quite anxious to get back to Santiago. Pat Ryan advised against our leaving but told us that Ray Davis would be driving to Viña with Herbert Thompson the following day. Then he offered to ask Davis whether there was room in the car for us to return with them when they drove back to Santiago."

Davis, of course, drove Charles and Terry to Santiago alone. Thompson's name was not mentioned to them again, and Ryan subsequently denied saying that Thompson was coming to Viña: "I never told anyone," the Lieutenant-Colonel later declared, "that the DCM was coming to Viña. In fact, I can't think of a more unlikely time for the DCM to absent himself from the Embassy in Santiago."

Ryan is right on at least one point. It is hard to imagine "a more unlikely time" for a Deputy Chief of Mission to absent himself from his post than the week after a coup. Yet, Thompson did just that. Charles and Terry checked out of the Miramar Hotel on the afternoon of September 15. Hotel records reveal that, at 6:00 P.M. the following day, Herbert Thompson (Diplomatic Passport 5909073) and two other persons checked in.

Thompson is extremely reluctant to discuss Charles Horman and seeks to dismiss Arthur Creter as "a silly man who came down from Panama." He is reticent and, at times, hostile when questioned about his stay in Viña. The following colloquy exemplifies his mood:

Q: Do you recall the weekend after the coup taking a trip to Viña del Mar?

Thompson: Yes, I went to Viña.

Q: What was the purpose of that trip?

Thompson: My recollection is that I simply went to see what conditions in Viña were like, never having been there.

Q: Do you recall what they were like when you got there?

Thompson: Roughly, yes. They weren't much different than they were anywhere else.

Q: Why did you choose this time to make the trip?

Thompson: I guess it was the first opportunity I had to travel, but I'm really not disposed to pursue this line of questioning. What I did and why I did it were done for perfectly valid reasons.

Q: Do you recall whether or not you met with Patrick Ryan when you were in Viña?

Thompson: I'm not sure I recall who Patrick Ryan was.

Q: He was second in command to Ray Davis at the Milgroup.

Thompson: Look! I'm just not disposed to answer the questions.

Q: Did you meet with anybody from the U.S. Military Group there?

Thompson: Yes, I presume I did, but I think the point as far as you are concerned is that it's no concern of yours what I was doing in Viña . . . . I went to Viña for official purposes unrelated to the Horman case.

Q: Do you recall what the official purposes were that you went to Viña for?

Thompson: No, I don't but, if I did, I wouldn't be inclined to talk about it.

Q: Did you go with anybody or alone?

Thompson: I don't choose to pursue this line of questioning.

Thompson's answers raise so many new questions that it is hard to know where to begin. One moment, he says he went to Viña "simply to see what conditions were like"; the next, he contends that he was there "for official purposes," the nature of which he does not recall. To say, as he does, that conditions in Viña "weren't much different than they were anywhere else" is ludicrous, given the carnage in Santiago. Similarly, it is hard to believe that Thompson (a Deputy Chief of Mission at the American Embassy) cannot identify Patrick Ryan (the former number two man at the American Naval Mission in Valparaiso).

Yet the most crucial question concerning Thompson's trip to Viña concerns Patrick Ryan's earlier quoted comment—"I never told anyone that the DCM was coming to Viña. In fact, I can't think of a more unlikely time for the DCM to absent himself from the Embassy in Santiago." As previously noted, Thompson checked into the Miramar Hotel at six o'clock on the night of September 16. He and his companions were assigned rooms 305 and 306. Hotel records reveal that, the same evening, an American military man checked into room 318, just down the hall. His name? *Lieutenant-Colonel Patrick Ryan.*

What was going on in Viña? Until that question is answered, the extent of American responsibility for the death of Charles Horman will remain unknown.

Certainly, Ed Horman's belief that the coup was coordinated by American personnel stationed in Viña and Valparaiso is far from frivolous. The Church Committee has declared unequivocally that "the United States sought in 1970 to foment a military coup in Chile. After 1970," the Committee report continues, "it remained in intelligence contact with the Chilean military . . . and received reports on the planning of the group which carried out the successful September 11 coup."

"We're not innocent in the coup," Judd Kessler adds. And, while the jump from coup planning to complicity in the murder of an American citizen is substantial, Ed Horman believes that Charles was executed because he "learned too much" in Viña. He keeps coming back to the statement of Rafael Gonzalez: "Charles Horman was brought from Valparaiso to Santiago. I saw the guys who brought him here."

The man who brought Charles Horman from Valparaiso to Santiago was, of course, Captain Ray Davis.

Ray Davis graduated from the United States Naval Academy in 1942 with classmates Jimmy Carter and Stansfield Turner. He retired from the Navy in July, 1976, and, after a year of relative seclusion in Charlottesville, Virginia, returned to Chile, where he reportedly now lives as a private citizen.

When discussing the coup, the only question apparent in Davis's mind is why the armed forces took so long to act. "If you were in the Chilean military," he says, "and when you walked down the street the women who walked past you called you chicken and threw chicken feed at the doors in your barracks, you'd have another thought."

Of Joyce and Terry, Davis contends, "I'm less than enthusiastic about these kind of people, who make up what I know are stories. Never once has either one of them admitted that anyone did anything to help them in Chile. We tried to find Charles Horman through all the channels we had in the Embassy—that's using our Air Force, Army, and Navy channels—and we didn't get any results, that's all."

Reflecting on Charles as a person, the former Commander of the United States Military Group indicates distaste: "My time spent with Charles Horman was in an automobile on a two-hour ride from Viña to Santiago. For some reason, I don't know why, he chose of his own volition to sit in the back seat and not the front with Terry and myself. Normally, when three people ride in a car, everyone gets in front. I can't drive and talk to someone in back very well."

Of his own role in the investigation into Charles's disappearance, Davis says, "I just went down and offered to help the Ambassador as a member of his staff because I thought it was what I should do at the time. Fred Purdy and his people were up to their necks in other problems. It's the old story. You should never volunteer . . . . I spent a lot of time trying to help them, and all I got out of it was a lot of grief."

As for Charles Horman's fate, Davis observes somewhat unsympathetically, "According to later stories I get, he was doing research on Schneider's death . . . . I don't know what happened to him, but if I came up to New York and started messing around with the Mafia and wound up in the East River and then my wife complained to the New York City Police that they didn't protect me, you'd have an analogy to the Horman case. If I go to New York City, I don't go messing around with the Mafia. You play with fire, you get burned."

Attention has focused on Ray Davis as a suspect in the disappearance of Charles Horman for several reasons. The most significant of these are his connections with the Chilean military. This point is emphasized by Judd Kessler, who states, "My understanding is that, at the point the Embassy believed a coup was inevitable, it called the CIA off of any contact with the [Chilean] military. The guys who still did have contact with the military were guys like [Ray] Davis, who saw them all the time, were well informed, buddy-buddy with them, and were opposed to the Allende government. I'm sure that these guys in their own personal way let them know what they thought."

And then, while not singling Ray Davis out by name, Kessler voices a chilling indictment of American military personnel in Chile: "I was unhappy with the Allende government and thought it posed a danger to democracy in the long term in Chile. But that doesn't mean I wasn't upset with torture and arbitrary imprisonment. It doesn't mean that anyone in our Consulate wouldn't do his job to protect the life of an American after the coup. *It so happens that there were probably some people in our Military Group who, in all honesty, would not think the same way. If some pro-Marxist American got bumped off, so much the worse for him.* I certainly didn't goddamn think that way."

The above words do not come from a radical leftist or a grief-stricken father. They were spoken by the man who was Acting Director of the United States AID Mission to Chile at the time of the coup and still works for the Department of State.

Terry Simon voices accord with Kessler's suspicions, adding, "I can't help but think that, if we hadn't met Ray Davis, Charles would be alive today." Frank Manitzas, the former CBS newsman in Santiago, further fuels the fire. Noting that the United States Military Group had an office on the ninth floor of the Chilean Ministry of Defense, just down the hall from the room where the execution of Charles Horman was ordered, Manitzas says, "That's significant in the extreme. There must have come a time when Charles knew he was labeled for execution. At that point, if not before, he would have told his captors, 'Call Ray Davis. He'll vouch for me.' The Chilean military would never have executed an American citizen under those circumstances—unless, of course, it believed that it already had American consent."

"Ray Davis," Manitzas continues, "is a guy who spouts off on one thing after another and is blindly anti-Communist. Giving him the benefit of the doubt, he could have unwittingly given a kill order. In talking with the Chileans, he might have spoken in such a way that they took something he said as an order with no trouble at all. Just mentioning Charles's name could have been enough to spur those guys into action."

Questioned about Manitzas's statements, Ray Davis admits that he is aware of the charges against him. "There's one concept now," he acknowledges, "that I put the finger on Horman through my Chilean friends. I find that pretty far out." Others

242

are quick to defend the former Military Group head, pointing to the fact that there is no direct evidence linking him to Charles's death. However, their defense is not always complimentary with regard to Davis's character, as is evidenced by one former American military man in Chile who defends his old boss as follows: "If Ray Davis wanted to set Charles Horman up, he would never have brought him back to Santiago. All he had to do was drive around the block in Valparaiso and dump him off with some friends in the Chilean military. They would have taken care of the girl too, and no one would have been the wiser."

Thus, the ultimate question remains. Did anyone in the American military, diplomatic, or intelligence community have foreknowledge of or perhaps order the execution of Charles Horman? Judd Kessler considers it possible that the answer is yes. Others are in accord.

Peter Bell, former head of the Ford Foundation Office in Santiago, was in direct contact with Ambassador Nathaniel Davis on several occasions in the wake of Allende's death. "The reaction in the Embassy in the aftermath of the coup," Bell recalls, "what you felt on the part of the people walking in and out of the Ambassador's anteroom, was one of headiness and rejoicing."

Now serving in Washington as a Special Assistant to the Secretary of Health, Education, and Welfare, Bell declares, "My view is that, if the Embassy had been really diligent in an effort to protect the lives of American citizens within Chile, including Charles Horman, it could have done so. I suspect the attention of the Embassy was elsewhere. Its basic reaction to the coup was one of elation, and it could well be that those officials who would have known of Horman's imprisonment, and I suspect that American officials might have known, may have left him to his fate.

"There could be an even more conspiratorial view," Bell continues, "that his death was ordered by American officials who, for one reason or another, regarded him as having information that could have been harmful to their view of the interest of the American government. That may be true. I just don't know."

Lovell Jarvis, the Ford Foundation Program Advisor who first told Ed Horman that Charles was dead, concurs with Bell and recounts a disturbing incident that occurred several weeks after the coup. "I was with a United States Embassy communications officer at a friend's house," Jarvis recalls. "We were sitting around a table drinking and playing bridge and arguing about the nature of the coup and what was going on. I said something to the effect that a lot more people were being brutally treated and killed than he was willing to recognize and mentioned the fact that several Americans including Horman had been killed. This fellow's reaction was, 'Well, if Horman hadn't been involved in something that he shouldn't have been involved in, he wouldn't have gotten hurt.' That," Jarvis concludes, "is an almost exact quote."

Enrique Sandoval, who first reported Charles Horman's execution to the American Embassy, also suspects United States wrongdoing. "One source in the Chilean military," Sandoval reports, "told me that he had seen an abundant dossier on Horman's activities in the United States. Given the limited scope of our own intelligence-gathering ability at the time, I presume that this dossier came from your CIA or Department of State."

"The United States government let this thing happen," Sandoval continues. "When you Americans are really interested in defending one of your nationals, you do a hell of a lot of things and you have a hell of a lot of power. You could have prevented the death of this man if you had exercised all of your power. The Ambassador could have called Pinochet personally and shown that he was really interested. I was released from the Stadium simply because I mentioned the name of your Ambassador. It's so obvious, really. I didn't see a real interest on their part to locate him or save his life."

The man most directly affected by Sandoval's charges is Nathaniel Davis. The former Ambassador is aware that dissatisfaction with regard to his performance exists in some circles, but he remains unruffled. Now a faculty advisor at the Naval War College in Newport, Rhode Island, Davis maintains that covert American operations in Chile were designed solely "to maintain democratic institutions" and adds, "If anybody lent encouragement to the military to carry out a coup, I am not aware of it."

"Nathaniel Davis," Ed Horman observes, "is a very polished liar."

"Edmund Horman," the Ambassador responds, "has the idea that there was some conspiracy against him. There wasn't. All of the officers in the Embassy whom I had contact with did their level best in that case."

There is, at present, no known evidence linking Nathaniel Davis directly to the death of Charles Horman. However, Senator Jacob Javits, who termed the official Department of State explanation of the Horman case "considerably less than satisfactory," has labeled the Ambassador's closed-door testimony before the Senate Foreign Relations Committee "notably inadequate." And at least one intriguing incident involving Davis has now surfaced.

As earlier noted, prior to the coup the Chilean military compiled lists that served as a guide for detention and execution throughout much of September, 1973. "We know for a fact," John Tipton of the American Embassy explains, "that on the day of the coup and in the days after it, the Chilean military had lists, and they went around and rooted out people. They knew who they were looking for . . . . My guess, like that of most everybody else in the Embassy, is that one of these military patrols found Charlie and, whether he was on the list or not, they picked him up. Those were the days when a lot of people got killed. Charlie was one of them."

According to one American who was in Santiago as the representative of a large multinational corporation, Nathaniel Davis had at least partial access to lists of "suspicious persons" compiled by the government of Chile. This American, who wishes to remain anonymous, recalls, "[Shortly after the coup] the Ambassador asked me to stop by his office and talk with him. He then read me a cable saying that [person A] and I were regarded as suspicious persons by the Chilean government. He didn't advise our leaving the country, although between the lines one could have read his doing that. He said it was up to us."

Both persons named in the cable read by Davis were employed by large corporations. "I wonder," Ed Horman asks, "how Nathaniel Davis got their names and also whether he selectively warned some Americans and not others of the danger they faced. Clearly, this is the sort of question Congress should be looking into. Unfortunately, we're still waiting for a satisfactory answer."

Whether or not that answer will be forthcoming is still unknown. To date, several Congressional committees have touched on the Horman case, but none has undertaken the full-scale investigation that circumstances require. The Church Committee came closest but, as evidenced by remarks from its staff, considerable work was left undone.

"There was a lot of political hardball played on the Committee," one former staff member admits. "The Mondale people wanted to protect the Kennedys and Hubert Humphrey. John Tower and Barry Goldwater wanted to protect someone else. Inevitably, some trade-offs had to be made, and I'm afraid the Horman case might have been one of them."

F.A.O. Schwarz, Jr., and Karl Inderfurth, who served respectively as Chief Counsel and "Chile expert" for the Committee, disclaim any knowledge of such trade-offs. Both men cite "time pressures" as the reason for curtailing the Horman investigation and point to Diane LaVoy (a former Committee staff member) as the person most familiar with the matter. "She was the person who did the actual work on it," Inderfurth says. Schwarz agrees, calling LaVoy, "the person on the Committee staff who had the best feel for the case."

Diane LaVoy now works in Washington, D.C. as a staff member for the United States House of Representatives Permanent Select Committee on Intelligence. Recalling the Senate Committee's investigation of Charles Horman's death, she says, "The

Horman case remained open. We never closed it. It was an area of acute frustration for those of us who worked on it. We proceeded with the story to the point where we felt we could neither confirm nor deny the most upsetting allegation—that the United States was involved in trying to help something happen, either by ordering the death of one of its own citizens or agreeing that the death should occur . . . . Then, we simply didn't pursue it to a head."

Like Ed Horman, Diane LaVoy places special emphasis on United States military activity in Chile. After recounting what is known about the now infamous Tracks I and II, she says, "The major line that I was looking for in the Horman case was a Track III—that is, a line of orders occurring not so much through the CIA, perhaps originating at the White House, being implemented in large measure through military channels. The Horman case would seem to support that kind of a thesis. That's what we were digging for towards the tail end of our investigation when the question of the military track became more and more disturbing to those of us who were working on it. We didn't get beyond a preliminary stage for a combination of reasons that included, at root, timing within the Committee."

And then, the woman "primarily responsible" for the Church Committee's investigation into the death of Charles Horman concurs with what Ed Horman has been saying about that death for over four years: "I believe," Diane LaVoy states, "that there were people within the U.S. government who so completely shared the preconceptions of the military in Chile, perhaps even helped form those preconceptions but, in any case, shared those gut responses about Communists, believed the rhetoric about the need for draconian measures to bring order, and did what they could to bring what they considered to be an undesirable American to justice . . . . *I don't think Charles Horman could have been killed without some rather full cooperation from some Americans.*"

As time passes, the case of Charles Horman becomes more and more difficult to reconstruct. Some witnesses such as Chilean

Generals Prats and Lutz are now dead. Others are scattered around the world. Fred Purdy was reassigned by the State Department to a post in the Philippines, James Anderson to Costa Rica. Dale Shaffer was transferred to the Dominican Republic, John Tipton to Rumania.

Given the inaccessibility of these and other diplomatic personnel, Ed Horman has concentrated in recent years on compiling a documentary record of Charles's death. Relying largely on the Freedom of Information Act, he has made dozens of requests for information and sent hundreds of dollars to government agencies for copies of memoranda, letters, and other documents. As he has learned, the United States has a far-reaching intelligence apparatus, more than one government agency has been connected to the Horman case, and few are willing to divulge the nature of their involvement.

The National Security Agency is an example in point. Established by Presidential directive in October, 1952, the NSA functions as a separate entity within the Department of Defense. Its primary role is the interception, decoding, and analysis of foreign communications. Once this task is complete, the NSA disseminates the material to other agencies within the intelligence community, providing them with information on the military capability and intentions of foreign powers.

The NSA operates without limitation of a statutory charter. Its responsibilities are defined by executive fiat. In testimony before Congress, the Agency's General Counsel has held to the view that "no existing statutes control, limit, or define the signals intelligence activities of NSA, [nor does] the Fourth Amendment apply to NSA's interception of Americans' international communications for foreign intelligence purposes."

On April 20, 1977, the National Security Agency conceded that it had in its possession a file on Charles Horman. However, it refuses to release or comment on any portion thereof on grounds that to do so would endanger "national security."

Department of State officials have been commensurately uncooperative; so much so that their obstinacy has bordered on the absurd. At one point, a Freedom of Information Staff Officer refused to divulge the present business address of Nathaniel Davis on grounds that to do so would "interfere with Mr. Davis's privacy." At the time the request for information was made, Davis was serving as United States Ambassador to Switzerland. His business address was the United States Embassy in Bern.

Far more serious, however, has been the deliberate suppression of documents by the Department of State. In early 1977, Department officials assured Ed Horman that he had received "all relevant material" dealing with Charles's death. Then the dam burst.

On August 1, 1977, a State Department spokesman revealed that the American Embassy in Santiago had "just found" a two-inch-thick folder of documents which "in some ways peripherally relate to the Horman case." Shortly thereafter, the same spokesman conceded that Embassy personnel had conducted and prepared transcripts of four unpublicized interviews with Rafael Gonzalez at the Italian Embassy in Santiago. The contents of the "newly discovered" folder were withheld from the Horman family on grounds that release would be detrimental to "national security." The Gonzalez transcripts were suppressed because, in the words of Kenneth R. Strawberry, a Freedom of Information Act Officer who has been with the Department since 1963, "they have nothing to do with Charles Horman."

"I find that hard to believe," Ed Horman responds. "I don't see how Embassy personnel could meet with Gonzalez on four occasions and not mention my son's name. This is the man who said he was present when the kill order was given. If Department personnel really wanted to get to the bottom of this case, they'd have shown Gonzalez pictures of every American military, diplomatic, and intelligence agent who was in Chile in 1973. That would be one way to find out the name of the American who was in Lutz's office when Charles's execution was ordered."

Yet, rather than actively pursue the Horman case, the Department of State appears intent on stymieing any serious investigation of it. In October, 1977, a Freedom of Information staff officer admitted that, in addition to the "two-inch-thick Santiago folder," some two dozen more documents relating to Charles Horman were being withheld in whole or in part for "national security" reasons. Then, in November, 1977, as the apparent result of a clerical error, the contents of an airgram from the American Embassy in Santiago to the Department of State were released.

Written in March, 1975, by the then Ambassador to Chile David Popper, the airgram contained a stunning revelation. For several years, the scope of Embassy efforts to document the death of Charles Horman had been unknown. Judd Kessler had shed some light on the subject when he told a questioner, "The DCM in Chile, Herbert Thompson, spent the better part of a year on the [Horman and Teruggi] cases in terms of inquiries here and there, going to the Foreign Ministry, and putting together bits of information that came in. He spent a tremendous amout of time on those cases."

Still, few if any documents relating to Thompson's efforts had been produced, and more than one person had begun to wonder why. The Popper airgram suggests an answer. It indicates that the Department of State has not only withheld but also refused to divulge the very existence of certain documents relating to Charles Horman. More specifically, the airgram refers to a large number of "handwritten notes" on file at the American Embassy in Santiago and states that, because they are written rather than typed, "the Embassy believes these are not 'documents' and therefore are not suitable for transmission [to Ed Horman] in response to a request under the Freedom of Information Act." A notation on the bottom of page one indicates that the airgram was drafted by Herbert Thompson and Fred Purdy. Just how many such notes exist is unclear, but Popper states that they are so numerous as to make transcription "impractical."

The content of these Embassy notes, which appear to have been withheld from the Church Committee as well as the Horman family, is subject to speculation. However, Ed Horman has little doubt as to the type of information they contain. "On September

250

24, 1973," he recalls, "Joyce and Terry met with Dale Shaffer at the United States Consulate in Santiago. At that time, they asked for and saw a file card which related to Charles and contained the phrase 'Journalist—working (illegible) extremist.' That card was never produced. I'm sure that this is one of the documents the Department is withholding, and I suspect that other items of a far more incriminating nature exist."

Absent pressure from the media and Congress, the content of these other documents may never be publicly known. However, it now appears that they are overwhelming in number. On April 3, 1978, the Department of State released a statement from Francis J. McNeil, Deputy Assistant Secretary for Inter-American Affairs. In it, McNeil conceded that *sixty-seven* documents relating to the death of Charles Horman were being withheld in their entirety from the Horman family and *forty-six others* were being partially suppressed. The primary excuse offered by McNeil for this state of affairs was "national security." The Deputy Assistant Secretary concedes that at least twenty-seven of the documents withheld are cables and memoranda that relate to Rafael Gonzalez.

"It's all very frustrating," Ed Horman continues. "If the Department of State wants to lie about what's in its files, there's not too much I can do about it. One of the saddest things about our efforts to find out what happened to Charles has been the realization that public officials, who are supposed to serve the American people, very often do no such thing. My family and I have lost trust in the statements, motives, and decency of our government. As an American, I truly regret that loss."

Ed Horman is not alone in his regrets. Many Americans who served in Santiago and carried out United States policy in 1973 are now having second thoughts. Looking back on the coup, Dale Shaffer recalls, "My initial reaction was sympathy for the Junta. I had been in Chile for nine months and seen the confusion that reigned [under Allende]. When the coup came, I felt relief. I thought the military, with its reputation for being apolitical and

251

patriotic, would alleviate the conditions of the Allende regime. My opinion didn't last that long. I found out what was going on in the matter of a week. Let's face it. My sympathies are not with the Junta at this point."

A second Embassy official who was in Santiago at the time of the coup is more direct: "I'm not very proud of what happened. We did some things we shouldn't have, and I'm sorry. But you have to understand, we never dreamed that things would get so bad. The Chilean armed forces had a longstanding tradition of respect for the Constitution. We assumed that they would oust Allende, restore order, and be gone in a year. We thought the Christian Democrats would be back in power by the end of 1974 or early 1975 at the latest."

The line between United States involvement in the coup and responsibility for the death of Charles Horman is difficult to draw. It is now known that our government conspired to assassinate several foreign leaders over the course of a decade. It is also a matter of public record that the CIA took part in a conspiracy that led ultimately to the assassination of Commander-in-Chief of the Chilean Army, General Rene Schneider. Knowing the details of these plots, it is not unreasonable to suggest that our government covertly encouraged or condoned the execution of an American citizen, particularly if the "national interest" was perceived to be at stake.

"The men who run our government," Elizabeth Horman says with more sadness than malice in her voice, "are like early Oriental potentates playing chess with live figures. They sit back and manipulate the pieces without ever realizing the cost in human lives."

Slowly, she rises from her chair and walks past a photograph of Charles as a young boy. "It took me quite a while to realize that Charles would never come home. The day my brother told me he was dead, it seemed very unreal. Nobody rolled drums; nobody fainted; nobody went hysterical. It was as though . . ." her voice trails off in midsentence, than picks up again. "You know, Charles wore a gold wedding band on his left hand. Some-

252

one stole it off his body. I wanted the ring for Joyce, but it wasn't returned . . . . That's the type of recollection I try to avoid now. I won't destroy the memory of a whole beautiful life by dwelling on a few tragic days. Bitterness is an ill-fitting memorial.

"I'm rambling now," she says, looking slightly self-conscious, "but you'll have to bear with me. I learned some very important things from Charles's death, and I have to share them. You see, Chile is not going to be an isolated incident. Italy and France will elect Marxist governments sometime in the future. Other Western countries will follow. We can't be allowed to do to them what we did in Chile. The cost in human suffering is too great. I've learned that the hard way. People who are loved can be killed.

"Charles's death taught me the lesson of political responsibility. I used to think that I could till the soil on my own little plot of land and let the rest of the world care for its own problems. What our country did in Vietnam, what happened to people overseas, was no concern of mine. I was wrong. I know now that each of us is obligated to fight for what is right and take responsibility for what our government does. If we don't, sooner or later it will affect us all."

AUTHOR'S NOTE

The reconstruction of events is frequently difficult. Memories blur, documents are destroyed, and self-dealing by participants oftentimes obscures the truth. Despite these handicaps, I am confident that the preceding work is a fair and accurate reconstruction of events surrounding the death of Charles Horman.

Much of my research has come in the form of extended interviews with my subjects. Other data has derived from public records, historical texts, and documents surrendered by the Department of State pursuant to the Freedom of Information Act. Where conversations are included in quotation marks, they are the result of verbatim transcripts obtained by me or a reconstruction based on the memory of one or more participants to a given conversation. The exception to this rule occurs in Chapter 2, where the campaign speech of Salvador Allende is a composite drawn from several speeches. On those occasions where the memories of participants differ, I have attempted a judgment as to which version is the more credible and noted the dissenting view, if conveyed to me, elsewhere in the text. The only departures from fact of which I am aware occur in Chapters 5 and 13, where the names Manosa, Ogden, and Plank are fictitious and have been used to protect the identities of people still living in Chile. I should also note that, while I did not know Charles Horman well, we did meet on two occasions in July, 1971. There was no contact between us thereafter—a fact I now regret, having come to know him better through the writing of this book.

Like most authors, I am indebted to a wide range of friends and professional associates for their support. Without excluding others, I would like to express particular appreciation to Donald Morris, Elia Racah, Patricia Kiernan, Dee Erwine, Robin Zuckerman, Kim Zeitlin, Nancy Stobie, Debbie Blessing, Ed Goodgold, Thomas Stewart, and Katherine Bak. This list does not include the members of my family, who have been particularly supportive this past year. Additionally, I owe a special debt to Christine DiFrancesco who, more than any other person, was responsible for my leaving the full-time practice of law to write this book.

I am well aware that my manuscript raises serious questions concerning the conduct of certain American military and diplomatic personnel, and would like to caution the reader that a final judgment can rest only upon action by the courts and Congress. I have sought simply to relate as best I can the facts as I found them. If I appear to have emphasized the opinions of Ed and Elizabeth Horman, it is because they are people without a voice in high councils of power and are possessed of a view that I believe merits further investigation. I invite rebuttal by all interested parties.

One final note would also appear to be in order. I grew up with an abiding faith in America. It is, in my estimation, the greatest country in the world—not for its wealth or military might, but because its people have achieved a balance of security, freedom, and human rights unmatched in history. The preceding pages have been written, not to cast doubt on this country or the men and women who serve so well in our military and diplomatic corps, but rather in the belief that only by self-analysis of this kind can we purify our government and make it better.